Derek MINTER

Drawing by
David Boarer.

Derek MINTER

KING OF BRANDS

MICK WALKER

breedon **books**
PUBLISHING

First published in Great Britain in 2008 by
The Breedon Books Publishing Company Limited
Breedon House, 3 The Parker Centre,
Derby, DE21 4SZ.

Dedication

To the memories of the great Norton tuners, Steve
Lancefield and Ray Petty, who played such an important
role in Derek Minter's racing career.

ISBN 978-1-85983-601-9
UPC 8 262051 0014

Printed and bound in China.

Contents

Every so often a unique snapshot of times gone by is discovered in a dusty vault or in shoeboxes in an attic by an enthusiastic amateur photographer. They are living history. Each and every one of us cannot resist the temptation as we marvel at the quality of the images, to let our mind drift back to the good old days and wonder what it was really like.

We at Mortons Motorcycle Media, market-leading publishers of classic and vintage titles, own one of the largest photographic archives of its kind in the world. It is a treasure trove of millions of motorcycle and related images, many of which have never seen the light of day since they were filed away in the dark-room almost 100 years ago.

Perhaps the biggest gem of all is our collection of glass plates – almost two tons of them to be precise! They represent a largely hitherto unseen look into our motorcycling heritage from the turn of the century. Many of the plates are priceless and capture an era long gone when the pace of life was much slower and traffic jams were unheard of.

We are delighted to be associated with well known author Mick Walker in the production of this book and hope you enjoy the images from our archive.

Terry Clark,
Managing Director,
Mortons Media Group Ltd

Preface

This, the sixth in the series intended to cover the world's leading motorcycle sporting superstars, is *Derek Minter – King of Brands*.

And for me this is a very special book indeed: as an enthusiastic teenager Derek Minter, along with Bob McIntyre, was my hero.

Known variously as the 'King of Brands', the 'Mint' and the 'Kentish Flier', Derek was, like Bob, a man who had come up the hard way, with little or no backing at the beginning of his career and certainly no financial support.

Both were also loved and respected by their myriad of fans, who appreciated fighters, individuals who would never give up. Again, both largely shunned the limelight and glamour of the Grand Prix circus, instead grinding out a living week in, week out, with hard-fought winning performances on the British short circuits, plus the annual pilgrimage to the Isle of Man TT races.

Derek Minter – King of Brands is thus something more than simply a biography, but my own personal tribute to a boyhood hero. I was there in person to witness many of Derek's greatest races that appear in this book.

And there was certainly an amazing array of successes, with which came fame, if not fortune. They included a multitude of British Championship titles; record-breaking three-in-a-row 500cc victories; the first over 100mph lap of the TT on a single-cylinder machine; and a controversial TT win on a privately entered Honda in the 1962 250cc event, when he defeated the might of the entire factory team.

Besides Derek and his second wife Jenny, many others contributed to this book with either photographs or information, sometimes both. These include David Lane, Margaret King, Mike Botting, Brenda Scivyer, George Padget, the Summerfield brothers Mike and Jerry, Dick Leather, Bill and Agnes Cadger, David Boarer (who also did the magnificent drawing at the beginning of the book), Adrian R. Sellars, Gerry Brown, Peter Reeve, Rodney Turner, Jasmine Rodger, Ian and Rita Welsh and Derek's first wife, Marian.

Derek Minter – King of Brands is a story I've immensely enjoyed researching and writing. It is a story of guts, determination and a single-minded approach to winning races against the finest riders of the era, including the likes of Duke, Surtees, Hailwood, McIntyre and many, many more.

Mick Walker, Wisbech, Cambridgeshire

Chapter 1

Canterbury Tales

The Canterbury City Council sign, very much promoting a city and country message.

Canterbury as it is today, a mixture of old and new.

Derek's father William and mother Rhoda, together with period sidecar.

D.W. (Derek William) Minter was born in the tiny village of Ickham, some four miles from Canterbury in rural Kent, on 27 April 1932. His father, William George, had married Rhoda Clara Curd in pre-World War One days.

William had begun his working life as a butcher, but following Derek's arrival (he was the couple's only child) he began work at the nearby Snowdown colliery as an ambulance driver. Clara was employed at a fruit farm in Littlebourne (the next village to Ickham), where the family moved to in 1935.

Young Derek began his education at Littlebourne Primary School, and from 1943 onwards he attended a secondary school, Sturry Central. It was here, during 1944 and 1945, that the future 'King of Brands' exhibited vegetables that he had grown on allotments the school used to teach gardening to pupils at its annual Open Pen show, gaining various awards. This experience was to generate an interest in the land which has remained with Derek until the present day.

Thumbs down to school

Except for his gardening classes, Derek freely admits to 'not liking school work' and at the time he 'wasn't interested in any form of sport.'

But there was something that Derek did care about: motorcycles. His father, William, owned a pre-war Ariel Red Hunter three-fifty single. And although

Derek was too young to ride it, he nonetheless became an avid motorcycle fan.

During the school holidays the young Minter worked alongside his mother at the Littlebourne fruit farm, earning pocket money that was later to come in very handy.

Leaving school

Upon leaving school, his first job of work was at the East Kent Bus Company, based in Canterbury, as an apprentice electrician. Derek's mode of transport from there to his home was a pedal cycle. However, as Derek says, 'I soon got tired of this' and with his savings from the fruit farm he purchased his first motorcycle, a brand-new BSA B31 three-fifty from Canterbury dealers Hallets in 1948. It was originally ordered in April, but Derek was not able to take delivery until November due to a lengthy waiting list.

Then 16 years of age, Derek paid for his first machine as he was later to recall 'all in £1 notes'. He continued, 'I saved everything I could from my wages and after work and at weekends continued the routine I had started at school, apple-picking in the lush orchards near my home. I could make £2 a week, with luck, and this went regularly into the motorcycle savings account in the sideboard cupboard. Hallets were the largest motorcycle dealers in the East Kent area and their business was located in St Dunstan's Street, near Canterbury West railway station, and, as Derek says, 'had always held an irresistible attraction for me'.

In his autobiography *Racing All My Life* (published in 1965) Derek enthusiastically recalled: 'The machine gleamed with factory-fresh chrome and paint, and no one in the entire world could have been prouder than I was when Peter Price, the mechanic at Hallets, said I would be OK to ride it.' Derek continued: 'It was the routine then for anyone buying a new motorcycle to be supervised by the mechanic of the shop while riding up and down the road, or round the block. It was an unofficial test of your road worthiness. The "straight" just outside Hallets was quieter in 1948 than it is now, yet inexperienced as I was as a rider, I must have showed myself reasonably responsible on the machine for when I came back Peter smiled and said "OK, you'll do!".'

The young Minter remembered 'clearly' that it 'was a Thursday', and the next day he rode his new purchase to work. Interestingly, at that time he could certainly not be described as a tearaway: 'so thrilled was I, and so scared of damaging it,

Derek's grandparents Fred and Annie Curd.

The young Minter's first motorcycle was a brand new BSA B31, purchased from Hallets in 1948.

that I covered the few miles to Canterbury at a speed only fractionally in excess of my top rate on the old pedal bike.'

He also recalled: 'I could hardly wait until Sunday. I was already a member of the Canterbury Motor Cycle Club, even though until now I hadn't owned a bike of my own, but I used to attend Thursday evening socials and brazenly join in the motorcycle gossip like a veteran.' But on that particular Sunday, there 'was a trial scheduled, through local woods and muddy country lanes; and I was out to show my paces on my new 350.'

A hard lesson

Things did not quite pan out as Derek had imagined. 'I made a good start and had been going well, gaining confidence, when coming up to a right-hand bend I baulked it, lost my balance and fell off. I'd remembered someone at the club advising me to use the front brake.' Although this was good advice for the tarmac, it was not so good for the dirt. And, as Derek was later to recall: 'I'd taken the advice literally, applied the front brake with an alarming lack of finesse and landed up on my back with my legs in the air.' He continued 'we didn't know about crash hats in 1948 or wear proper clothing, and my tousled hair and rather ordinary garb (a slightly too long, too worn overcoat) could only have added to my indignity as I panicked to find my feet again before anyone could see what had happened. I started trying to get up almost before I'd touched the ground, and once on my feet struggled frantically to right the bike.' The event was witnessed by a couple of other competing club members but, as Derek went on to explain, 'I was on my feet without aid. I remounted, shaken and red-faced, and continued the trial.' Although he was 'unhurt' the same could not be said of 'my gleaming 350 BSA on which I had lavished such pride.' This now looked 'slightly less immaculate with a shattered headlamp.' But was nothing to the 'beating my personal pride had taken on this first-ever outing.' At this time it would have been impossible to imagine that the young Minter would one day earn his living racing motorcycles, including a host of Championships and victories over the world's top riders.

Hallets had been started by Marcel Hallet (originally from Belgium), together with his two sons, Bill and Ray. Bill had been a successful grass track racer on an OK Supreme. The younger son, Ray, was more interested in road racing. Armed with a new BSA Gold Star, he entered the Clubman's TT in June 1949 (he also competed later that year on the same machine in the Manx Grand Prix).

Derek Minter's enthusiasm had rubbed off on Ray, and he took the youngster with him to the Island as mechanic/helper. Riding with the number 42, Ray

BSA Gold Star

Many riders began their racing careers aboard the BSA Gold Star, which was produced in 348 and 499cc engine sizes.

The BSA Gold Star was the most versatile of motorcycles, being equally suitable for touring, fast road work, road racing, scrambling, trials, enduro, sand racing, grass track and sprinting. It was also the machine with which Derek Minter began his racing career.

Its origins can be traced back to the success achieved by a specially prepared M23 Empire Star ridden at Brooklands in June 1937 by TT legend Wal Handley, who won one of the coveted Brooklands Gold Stars for lapping the famous Surrey speed bowl at over 100mph. BSA decided to capitalise on this success by introducing the new all-alloy-engined M24 Gold Star for the 1938 season. The engine displaced 496cc (82 x 94mm) running on a compression ratio of 7.75:1 petrol or the optional 12.5:1 for dope; the factory claimed 28 and 36bhp respectively.

Then came the war, and during the immediate aftermath of the conflict no Gold Star models were built at BSA's Small Heath works until 1949. But development had not ceased. First BSA introduced the new 348cc (71 x 88mm) B31 in August 1945, and this became the basis of what was to become known as the pre-unit B range. The newcomer was quickly joined in January 1946 by the 348cc B32 competition model to cater for the Clubman rider of the day.

The three-fifty engine was then bored out to 85mm to become the B34 competition mount later that year. The B32 and B34 employed iron cylinder heads and barrels from the standard roadster range. The machines used telescopic front forks (the pre-war bikes had girders), but the rigid frame was retained. When an alloy top-end conversion became available for the B32 in 1947, many riders specified this fitment in order to lower the overall weight of the trials-orientated machine. This did not go unnoticed among the road racers of the era, and much experimental work was carried out, both by the works and privateers, to gain additional horsepower.

After the inaugural Clubman TT races in 1947, a couple of customers approached Jack Amott at BSA with the idea of building racing machines using trials alloy top-ends, with a view to the following year's Clubman TT. This approach set minds at Small Heath thinking. And so, during late 1947 and much of 1948, secret development was set in motion at the BSA factory, resulting in the surprise announcement of a new plunger-framed, all-alloy B32 Gold Star on the eve of the London Earls Court Show in November 1948.

Coded ZB32, this was essentially a competition bike for the off-road rider, but it could also be quickly converted for tarmac use. The ZB32 Gold Star was capable of 25bhp against 18bhp for the stock B31. A wide range of easily available factory options transformed the Gold Star from its primary role of either trials or roadster into a potent scrambler or fast Clubman's racer. A year later the larger ZB34 arrived, offering even more performance. However, it was the smaller-engined model which was to prove more successful in the early days, because it was not only more competitive in its class, but also more reliable.

The first major change to the Gold Star's specification occurred at the end of 1951, when a redesigned, diecast cylinder head with separate rocker box was introduced. A continuous engine development programme ensured almost yearly changes to specification and performance continued thereafter. For 1953, BSA produced the BB series, essentially using the small fin alloy engine from the B32/34, but mounted in a swinging arm frame.

In the spring of 1954 a new Gold Star made its debut: the CB. The newcomer employed the BB cycle parts but the engine had been considerably altered. The most noticeable external difference was the much more comprehensive finning of the cylinder barrel and head. Besides the updated engine, there were a couple of other important innovations, which the power unit would retain as features of the Gold Star Clubmans until production finally ceased in the early 1960s. These were the now classic swept-back exhaust header pipe and the replacement of the BB's RN carburettor by the new Amal GP instrument. In addition, there were also separate clip-on handlebars for the first time. Coded CB32 and CB34, the newcomers retained their respective bore and stroke dimensions. But even so there were

Gold Star (a DBD34 is shown) engine, showing crankshaft, timing gears, oil pump, piston and valve gear.

numerous changes to the engine, such as a shorter connecting-rod and a correspondingly decreased cylinder barrel height, a new form of tappet adjustment and a slightly altered crank angle, while the 1953 flap-type breathing device had to be dispensed with in favour of a timed rotary breather.

The continual search for superior performance and reliability led the BSA development team to introduce the DB32 and DB34 for the 1955 season. But unlike the previous year, the majority of changes were minor, attention to detail being the key word. 1956 was the final year of the Clubman's TT, and it also saw the final development of the Gold Star, the DBD34, which was actually not that much different from the DB34. The three-fifty was effectively at the end of its development, as no DBD version was ever offered. There was also by now a pukka Gold Star Scrambler, known as the Catalina in the US. This, together with the DBD34, continued to be available until 1962, although a few bikes were built as late as 1964. In fact American dealers were largely responsible for the Gold Star remaining in production after the B31 and B33 roadsters had been axed in 1961 and 1962 respectively.

In the context of this book, the Gold Star had yet another role, that of providing a stepping stone for the up-and-coming road racer Derek Minter, as with a host of others he had his initial successes aboard one of the Small Heath singles on his way to stardom.

Hallet was soon showing his potential. On Friday 10 June he was third fastest in his class with a lap of 31 minutes 16 seconds, a speed of 72.42mph. And his practice form was borne out by his performance in the race itself, coming home fourth in 1 hour 31 minutes 51.6 seconds, averaging 73.97mph for the three-lap, 113.19-mile long race.

When one considers that the fifth-place finisher was a certain C.C. Sandford (Cecil Sandford – later to win two World Championship titles), Ray Hallet's performance becomes all the more impressive.

Joining Hallets

Later in 1949, Derek left his job with the Canterbury Bus Company and joined Hallets as a mechanic.

Then in 1950, upon reaching 18 years of age, Derek was called up for National Service. Joining the Royal Air Force, his initial training was at Padgate, before being posted to Cardington, Bedfordshire (famous as the R101 airship base in pre-war days). Here, in the supply trade, he dished out uniforms to fellow servicemen. It was during his Cardington days that, as he says, 'my interest in motorcycling grew.' And in fact he had his first taste of competition success while stationed there – winning a second-class award in the Services Trial at Bagshot in 1952. The machine he rode was a BSA B32 (essentially the trials version of the Gold Star). On this same machine he travelled home to Kent 'around three times each month.' In fact often his journeys home could be said to have been AWOL (Absent With Out Leave), because he would leave camp illegally on the Friday night – 'over a field to the main road, or out of the back of camp over a railway line', returning the same way between 3 and 4am on Monday morning. Sometimes he would 'simply ride through the main gate when a military policeman I had an arrangement with was on duty.' How was this possible? Well, Derek 'would take the policeman to the Oval (in South London) on the pillion of his B32 and collect him later in the weekend' when the said policemen was not on duty.

As for rank, Derek was an AC2 (Air Craftsman 2nd class).

Demob

Upon his demob later in 1952, Derek took up where he had left off in civilian life, working as a mechanic for Hallets and riding his own B31 machine.

It was at this time that Derek first began to visit the Brands Hatch circuit (some 50 miles from his home) and was 'thrilled by the superb riding of people like the late Les Graham.' His visits to Brands 'became more frequent and seeing folk rushing round the track made me impatient to have a go myself. I remember saying to myself 'I can do that' and even believed that I could race round there perhaps as well as some of those I'd seen.'

Although Derek was 'itching to have a go', to his 'annoyance and frustration, my mother wouldn't let me.' As Derek explained: 'As a responsible mother she was only interested in the safety and welfare of her son.' He continued: 'At the same time all I was interested in was the thrill and glory of motorcycle racing. I was still under 21, and thus a junior; and juniors, before racing at Brands, had to have parents' consent. Dad didn't worry too much, on the basis, I expect, that boys will be boys.' But Derek's mother was adamant. And this led to things boiling over in the spring of 1953.

A cancelled first entry

In fact just prior to his 21st birthday Derek could not accept his mother's restraining hand any longer, and mailed off an entry for the first Brands Hatch meeting of the new season, which was scheduled for Good Friday, 3 April 1953. However, Derek's 21st birthday was not for another three weeks, and when his mother eventually found out she threatened to contact the circuit and tell the organisers that her son was not yet of the required age to enter without her approval. So it was not until several weeks later, on 14 May 1953, that the budding racer actually took part in his first race. So apologising to his mother for pressing ahead against her wishes, Derek remembers saying 'Well Mum, that's it. You can't stop me now.'

His first racing machine

To enable him to go racing, Derek had exchanged his B31 three-fifty for a new BB34 Gold Star, purchased like his previous model from his employers, Hallets.

But at that time the Hallet family could not be persuaded to assist Derek in his racing plans. As he was later to recall in his 1965 autobiography, 'repeatedly I tried to get old man Hallet interested, but he just didn't want to know…I think because of the danger element and in case anything happened to me while riding one of his bicycles. But his sons Bill and Ray were interested and were sympathetic to the idea of getting the firm involved a little more in the racing side of motorcycles.'

Derek gives credit to Ray Hallet (who passed away in March 2007, aged 83), saying 'I suppose Ray was one of my early inspirations and he certainly encouraged me at the very start of my own career. I used to stay on in the workshop at Hallets after normal hours, getting to know all I could about the machine. Ray must have got thoroughly sick with all my questions and my passionate interest, but he didn't complain.'

After his demob from National Service with the RAF Derek resumed work at Hallets as a mechanic, and purchased a new 499cc BSA BB34 Gold Star like the one shown in this 1953 advertisement.

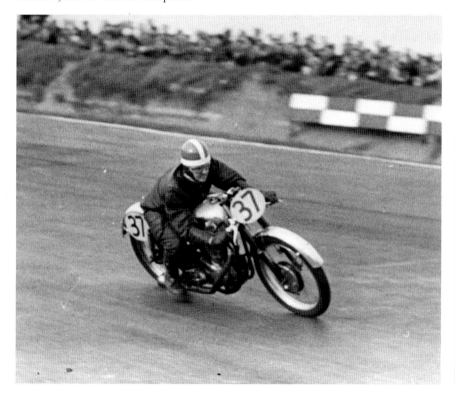

The Gold Star during one of Derek's first race meetings, Brands Hatch 1953.

Michael O'Rourke on Jim (Bill) Oliver's Matchless G45 during the 1953 Senior TT.

As for Ray's own racing activities, these had by now come to an end following a crash at Brands Hatch. Derek commented: 'he retired from racing long before I had hoped he would and thereafter concentrated upon the family business.'

A first outing at Brands

Derek's first outing at Brands Hatch had seen him finish 'midfield' in the non-experts' 1000cc class on his Gold Star. Certainly, as Derek is first to admit, there were no indications at this time of the future potential he would ultimately show. Besides that May date, the name D.W. Minter appeared in the race programme for three other meetings at Brands Hatch that year, on 21 June, 19 July and 27 September.

1954

On 18 April 1954 the first-ever meeting held was over the extended 1.24-mile long Brands Hatch circuit. As *The Motor Cycle* commented: 'The modified course can be seen for almost its entirety by spectators positioned along the starting straight, and from other vantage points lengthy stretches are within view. Most riders settled down to the new curves with complete mastery, and thrilling sport resulted.'

But it was the following weekend, on Sunday 25 April, that the name of Derek Minter first came to the notice of the Brands public, when he finished runner-up in the Clubman's TT Qualifying Race.

Later on the same day Derek came third in the Non-Experts Invitation Scratch Race, behind the winner F.G. (Frank) Perris (later to become a works rider for AMC and Suzuki) riding a Triumph twin and G.A. Matthews with a 7R AJS. 1954 was also notable as Derek rode at Crystal Palace and Silverstone – his first races away from his local circuit.

Probably the most memorable event in Derek's 1954 season was when he overtook the much more experienced Alan Trow at Brands – the only problem being that at the time Derek was on his backside, having just parted company with his machine.

Into 1955

Derek's first victory came at Brands Hatch on Sunday 15 May, when he won Heat 2 of the 500cc race. His speed for the five-lap event was 66.86mph against the winner of Heat 1, John Surtees, the latter having averaged 68.97mph. However, one has to take into account that not only was Surtees riding a factory Norton, but he was also highly experienced. In the 10-lap final Derek came home fourth, behind Surtees, Michael O'Rourke and Alan Trow (both, like Surtees, on Nortons), whereas Derek was, of course, still riding his BSA.

Then, at the Gravesend Eagles' Whit Monday road race meeting at Brands Hatch on 28 May, Derek was looking set for victory in the 10-lap 1000cc final, when on the final circuit the exhaust rocker stuck, holding the valve open. But so great was his advantage over the rest of the field that he was able to push the machine almost half a lap and still finish third!

A highlight that year was Derek's first Isle of Man race, in the Senior Manx Grand Prix, on 8 September. He finished 35th, in a time of 2 hours 55 minutes

Derek seen on his Gold Star during the Senior Manx Grand Prix in September 1955. He finished 35th, averaging 77.62mph for the six-lap, 226.38-mile long race.

Alan Trow, one of Derek's main rivals at Brands Hatch during the mid-1950s.

0.1 seconds, with an average speed of 77.62mph for the six-lap, 226.38-mile long race. His fastest lap, in 27 minutes 48 seconds, came on the third circuit. These figures compared to the winner Geoff Tanner (riding a Manx Norton) with figures of 2 hours 28 minutes 39 seconds, 91.38mph and a fastest lap in 24 minutes 19 seconds. Tanner had also won the Junior (350cc) race a couple of days earlier, so completing a famous Manx double.

But the race which really attracted attention came at Brands Hatch – the final event of the season on Sunday 2 October 1955 – when a record crowd up to that time for the Kentish circuit (said to be well in excess of 60,000) had turned out to watch the action. Against such world class stars as Geoff Duke (Gilera) and John Surtees (Norton), Derek was lying a close fourth behind Duke when the Gold Star's big-end gave out. Although the race was over for the young Minter, the press, organisers and the crowd realised that on that long-ago autumn day here was a potential future star.

On the up

Not only was Derek to receive an offer from Ron Harris to ride MV Agustas in the lightweight classes, but BSA development engineer/rider Roland Pike was now tuning a specially-prepared DB34 engine. The latter came about in the following way. Derek (at that time still employed by Hallets) benefited from the fact that Hallets were the main BSA dealers for the East Kent area, and so had close contacts with the BSA works in Birmingham. After Pike had agreed to oversee the preparation of Minter's engine, it was a relatively simple task for the power unit to be transported to and from the Birmingham factory by regular deliveries of BSA motorcycles and spare parts to the Canterbury dealership.

BSA engineer Roland Pike (seen here with his 350 Pike BSA during the 1952 TT) was responsible for Derek's Gold Star engine preparation during the 1956 season. The motor was transported between Hallets and the BSA Birmingham works by van.

Joining the Harris team

Among that vast crowd at Brands in October 1955 had been Ron Harris (a well-known pre-war Brooklands racer) who, together with Edwin Davis, was on the verge of reaching an agreement with the Italian MV Agusta marque to become their British importers.

Formed as MV Distributors Ltd, with its registered office at 235–241 Regent Street, London W1, the fledgling company began trading in November 1955. Besides the series production 125 and 175cc roadsters, Harris and his partner had also imported MV's 'over-the-counter' customer racing models, the 124cc CS (Competizione Sport) Monalbero and 175cc CSS (Competizione Super Sport). The latter machine was to be more commonly known as the *Disco Volante* (Flying Saucer).

MV Agusta 175 Disco Volante

Although MV Agusta had already become well-known in Grand Prix racing, when news broke at the beginning of December 1955 that the Italian company's series production models were to be imported into Great Britain, little was known of these latter machines at that time in the UK. Among these 'production' models was the 175 CSS Super Sport, more commonly known as the Disco Volante (Flying Saucer). At £434, in December 1955, it was even more expensive than a Manx Norton at that time! As with the standard road bikes, the British importer was the company known as MV Distributors Ltd, run by former Brooklands racer Ron Harris and Edwin Davis. In addition to their registered office in London's exclusive Regent Street, the organisation operated a retail outlet handling MV machines: Breakspear Service Garage in Whetstone High Road, on the site of a Mobil Oil filling station.

As outlined in the main text, to promote the MV name, signed up a trio of racers: Mike O'Rourke, Bob Keeler and Derek Minter. The riders' job, in effect, was not only to race 175 CSS models (and the 125 Sport Competizione), but also to promote the brand. Harris called them 'travelling salesmen.'

As for the 175 CSS Super Sport, this machine had debuted in Italy during the spring of 1955, and had been created expressly for Italian

The Disco Volante (Flying Saucer) with its overhead camshaft single-cylinder engine, duplex frame and Earles-type front forks.

Formula 3 racing. It differed from the existing standard one-seven-five touring and sport models in several ways, most notably in the frame and suspension, the use of an external racing magneto, and a five instead of four-speed gearbox. But it retained the original 172.4cc chain-driven sohc engine dimensions of 59.4 x 62mm. Running on a compression ratio of 9.5:1, the more highly tuned power unit produced 15bhp at 8,800rpm. Carburation was taken care of by a rubber-mounted 25mm Dell'Orto SSI instrument.

The engine's neat power-egg shape had half the offside (right) side of the outer casing axed to enable instant access to the gearbox sprocket (which also saved weight). In addition on this side of the motorcycle was the traditional Italian heel-and-toe gear change lever, now rear-set with a long linkage to the gearbox shaft. The engine itself was mounted in a new duplex frame which, unlike its roadster brothers, was of full duplex layout with loops extending all the way under the engine unit. The rear section of the frame was entirely new and closely followed the 125 racer. Another major departure was the employment of Earles-type front forks; both here and at the rear, the suspension units were fitted with exposed springs.

In the braking department, the CSS used the same diameter hubs as the 125: a 180mm at the front and 150 at the rear. Both wheels featured 19in Borrani welled-type alloy rims and 2.75in section tyres. The first batch of Disco Volantes came with a small cockpit fairing, but by the autumn of that year this had been deleted. Another change was to the silencer, which was exchanged for a design with tail fins. However, in reality most CSS Super Sports were only ever used on the track, so 'street legal' components such as these were usually dumped.

Testing an example of the Disco Volante for *Motor Cycle News* in its 27 June 1956 issue, Alec Menhinick began by saying: 'Only my innate honesty and a couple of veiled threats by telephone have made me give up the finest lightweight racer I have ever had the pleasure of riding. My approach to this road test is that which I would use for a racer, for this is what the Super Sport Agusta really is. It has a few little extras like lamps, hooter, silencer etc. tacked on so that the lucky man who owns one can actually ride it from his home to a racing venue somewhere, or take it out for a ride just for the joy of riding.'

Alec went on to say: 'I had heard a lot of talk of the machine's capacity for revs, its wonderful brakes, its steering and roadholding and so forth, but years of listening to similar rumours from manufacturers makes one realise that enthusiasm can often blind people to a machine's faults...So I started the test with a perfectly open mind.' But, as Alec went on to explain: 'Nothing I was told about the Agusta was overstated. I have never ridden a one-seven-five like it, nor, for that matter a racing two-fifty (other than a works job) which gave such an impression of smoothness, power, speed and controllability. Between about 5,200 and 5,500rpm a vibration period occurred which caused the four gallon aluminium tank to drum, but apart from that, the run through from 2,500 revs to maximum allowed (not by any means the maximum possible) was as smooth as silk.'

Another test in *Motor Cycling* (dated 17 May 1956) had as its headline: 'An Italian Clubman's-type Racing Machine Suitable for Everyday Use.' And that was precisely what the diminutive Disco Volante really was.

The Brands Hatch paddock as it was in 1955. Riders include Michael O'Rourke, Alan Trow, Ginger Payne, John Surtees and John Clarke.

From the end of the month the range was on display at Breakspear Service Station in High Road, Whetstone, North London.

Together with fellow racer Michael O'Rourke, Derek Minter was offered the chance to join the new team as both rider and salesman.

This meant leaving Hallets and moving to the London area (Derek lodged in Bromley). However, the contact with Hallets was retained due to Derek's decision to continue racing his faithful Gold Star into the 1956 season. Actually, more often than not Minter would travel in the MV van, while the Gold Star was transported separately to meetings.

The new season begins

In charge of the preparation of the MV machines was John Hogan, himself a well-known 125 MV rider and tuner of two-stroke engines. Derek's first outings of 1956 came on Good Friday, 30 March, at Brands Hatch, where he finished runner-up in the 1000cc race on the Pike-tuned Gold Star. However, his MV debut ended in a retirement with a faulty plug lead on his 175 'Flying Saucer' in the 200cc event.

Next, on Easter Monday, 2 April, Derek took his machinery to Crystal Palace in South London for the circuit's traditional holiday meeting. Once again his MV was to suffer a retirement, this time due to a broken rocker arm. But it was not an entirely wasted journey, with the Gold Star finishing third in its heat and sixth in the 500cc final.

Programme cover for the Crystal Palace meeting on Easter Monday, 2 April 1956. Derek was third in his heat and sixth in the final; both races were won by John Surtees (MV).

Derek at Brands Hatch with a Pike-tuned DB34 Gold Star engine mounted in Derek's own machine, 1956.

John Hogan (MV) winning the 125cc race at Snetterton on 8 April 1956; Derek was fourth on another of the Italian machines.

First ride on the 125

Derek's first ride on the 125cc MV came at Snetterton in Norfolk, on Sunday 8 April. As the field screamed away from the start, Michael O'Rourke streaked into the lead and remained there until plug trouble forced him to retire on the third lap. This left John Hogan on another of the Italian machines in the lead by a good margin, with J.H. Edlin (MV) second. After a hectic battle E. Pantlin on the LEF finished third, with Derek fourth.

But Derek was unable to start in the star-studded 500cc event (with the likes of Surtees, McIntyre and O'Rourke) as the van carrying his BSA had broken down en route to the circuit.

A very wet Silverstone

The famous annual *Motor Cycling* Saturday international meeting held at Silverstone on 14 April 1956 was a miserable affair due to constant and continuing rain throughout the entire programme. As at Snetterton, Derek was entered in the 125 and 500cc races.

In the former he again finished fourth behind Cecil Sandford (FB Mondial), teammate O'Rourke and Pantlin's LEF. Derek's Gold Star retired in the larger capacity race due to misfiring caused by a faulty spark plug.

Eight days later it was back to the familiar Brands Hatch tarmac. This showed in the results, with a runner-up placing in the 200cc class on the 175 MV (behind O'Rourke). On the 499cc Gold Star, Derek was fifth in the 1000cc event.

Also during 1956 Derek was employed as salesman by the British MV Agusta importers, headed by ex-Brooklands star Ron Harris.

A practice crash in Ireland

Derek's next meeting was the North West 200 in Ulster, but unfortunately it was not to be a happy visit across the Irish Sea as he crashed heavily in practice for the 250cc event on the Ron Harris ex-works dohc 203cc MV Agusta and ended up in hospital, so missing the racing.

If this was not bad enough, he was also destined to be out of action for several weeks. As for his injuries, these consisted of a broken collarbone and cracked skull. This impacted on his entries during this time, which meant he was a non-starter during the same period. Most notably he missed the TT, where D.W. Minter was in the programme for three races: the 125cc Ultra Lightweight (number 20), 250cc Lightweight (number 1) and 500cc Senior (number 59). His MV rides were eventually taken over by Frank Fox.

Getting back in the saddle

In fact it was to be some six weeks before Derek was back in the saddle, at Brands Hatch on Sunday 24 June 1956. Worried about Derek's fitness, Ron Harris would not allow our hero to ride in the 250cc race on the MV. So he could only turn out on his own BSA Gold Star.

The meeting was notable in having an Invitation Team Race between visitors from Cadwell Park and Brands Hatch. The 'home' riders included John Clark, Michael O'Rourke, Ned Minihan and Derek. But Cadwell had sent its own stars, including Peter Ferbrache and Fred Wallis.

By half distance in the 12-lap race the Brands Hatch team held the first seven positions, with Clark on a factory-backed Matchless G45 twin leading the pack. At the flag Derek had brought his Gold Star home into second berth behind the Matchless rider.

Besides the series production road bike MV Concessionaires also entered Derek (and Michael O'Rourke) on 125, 175 and 203cc racing models. A 125 single-overhead cam bike is shown here.

Brands Hatch Invitation Team Race – 12 laps – 14.88 miles
1st   J.R. Clark (Matchless)
2nd   D.W. Minter (BSA)
3rd   M.W. Saluz (Norton)

Then, later in the day, Derek again finished runner-up in the 1000cc final on his BSA, behind Clark. Notably, he finished in front of his MV teammate Michael O'Rourke on a Norton.

1000cc Brands Hatch – 10 laps – 12.4 miles
1st   J.R. Clark (Matchless)
2nd   D.W. Minter (BSA)
3rd   M.P. O'Rourke (Norton)

Castle Combe

Castle Combe in rural Wiltshire was to become a favourite circuit of Derek's in future years, but on Saturday 14 July a wet morning with the promise of more rain later resulted in a somewhat sparse crowd at the circuit for the road race meeting organised by the Wessex Centre of the ACU.

In his three races Derek only crossed the finishing line once, but it was an excellent result, he won the 125cc race on his single overhead camshaft MV Agusta. But the other outings ended in disappointment; in the 250cc event on his larger MV he got no further than practice before a broken rocker arm ended his quest for honours. Then, in a rain-soaked 1000cc race, his BSA was sidelined with water in the electrics.

125cc Castle Combe – 5 laps – 10 miles
1st   D.W. Minter (MV Agusta)
2nd   J. Baugh (MV Agusta)
3rd   D.H. Edlin (MV Agusta)

The Red Rose
More than 180 star riders took part in the international Red Rose meeting over Aintree's 3-mile circuit two weeks later, on Saturday 28 July.

The 250cc and 125cc events were run concurrently, with Geoff Monty (GMS) taking the two-fifty win from Percy Tait (Beasley-Velocette) and Ted Fenwick (Moto Guzzi). Derek was in the 125cc race on his MV, but had to be content with runner-up spot behind Cecil Sandford (FB Mondial) and in front of Bill Webster (MV Agusta).

While well up the field in the Senior (1000cc) race, Derek was well placed when he was forced out due to a bent pushrod/broken rocker. As an example of the top-class entry, the first three finishers in this event were Bob McIntyre, Bob Anderson and Alastair King (all Norton mounted).

Bank Holiday Weekend
The August Bank Holiday weekend saw Derek entered at Snetterton on Sunday 5 August and at the ACU International British Championship meeting at Thruxton on the following day.

The Sunday Observance Act meant that admission was free for the first time at Snetterton since the Norfolk circuit was opened. And spectators were doubly fortunate when, as *The Motor Cycle* report stated: 'with storms swinging black and low all around, not a drop of rain wet the tarmac for the whole of the five hours' programme of racing.' But Derek Minter's fortunes were less rewarding. His best result of the day came in the Ultra Lightweight event when he brought his MV home fourth in the 125s behind the similar machines of O'Rourke, Hogan and Edlin. The 250cc race saw an impressive victory by Bob McIntyre riding the special Joe Potts quarter-litre Manx Norton, with Derek trailing back in eighth position on his 175cc MV, giving away some 75cc. Things did not get any better in the Senior (500cc) event when, after finishing sixth in his heat, the Gold Star stopped after misfiring badly in the final.

Overnight Derek, together with many other competitors, travelled south to take part at Thruxton the following day.

Bob McIntyre scoring an impressive victory on his Potts Norton in the 250cc race at Snetterton, Sunday 5 August 1956.

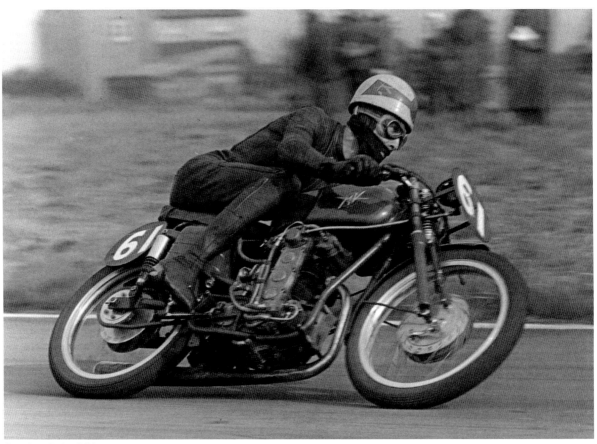

Derek quit the MV Concessionaires team later in 1956. Michael O'Rourke was then joined by Dave Chadwick, seen here at Aintree in 1958 on the 203cc dohc MV single.

Like Snetterton the previous day the weather was kind at the Hampshire circuit on Bank Holiday Monday, with violent storms in the area abating shortly prior to racing getting under way, and rain falling again as soon as the meeting was over. The threat of bad weather had certainly not put spectators off, with the crowds described variously as either 'large' or 'massive'. A true international flavour was evident with the appearance of riders from not only throughout Great Britain and Ireland, but also Belgium, France, Germany, South Africa, Sweden and Switzerland.

After finishing sixth in his 500cc British Championship heat on the BSA, Derek took his place on the starting grid for the first race proper at Thruxton – the 125cc British Championship. This is how the race report in *The Motor Cycle* dated 9 August 1956 described the action: 'A haze of blue smoke from the exhausts of various two-strokes spread across the starting area as 15 one-two-fives got under way. As expected, however, it was the four-strokes which dominated the race – in particular the streamlined MV Agusta's of M.P. O'Rourke and D.W. Minter. The latter rider managed to stay within handshaking distance of O'Rourke for three laps, but the leader then opened up a gap which grew to 50 yards by the finish.'

As far as the 500cc British Championship event was concerned, although Derek qualified by finishing sixth in his heat, in the final he retired with plug trouble.

Following Thruxton, Derek had a three-week interval before he rode his BSA at Brands Hatch on 26 August, finishing sixth in the 1000cc final.

Workwise, things were not good for him at MV Distributors, and in fact he never rode for the company again.

Upon reflection

Derek worked for Ron Harris for several months. He recalls: 'Michael O'Rourke, the well-known grass track rider and one of the up-and-coming boys and myself were employed as salesmen during the week, going round trying to interest dealers in the MVs. But the going was hard. The bicycles really weren't good enough and we finished up after a few months with little to do and, literally, wasting our time. There seemed little future for me in staying with Ron and eventually I returned to Canterbury to live.'

Back home, jobless, Derek exchanged two wheels for four and went taxi driving. As he recalled later 'I wanted desperately to get back to motorcycle sport somehow and wondered what I might do next. In the meantime I spent a lot of my time ferrying inmates from Canterbury jail to other prisons in my taxi. I had to go inside the jail when collecting and delivering prisoners, and never quite got used to the clanging of the doors behind me and the rattling of keys as I went inside.'

Seeing out the season

With the MVs no longer available, Derek saw out the remainder of the 1956 season on his faithful BSA Gold Star, which he once described 'unofficially' as 'the fastest BSA in Kent'.

On 16 September he journeyed up to the Wolds of Lincolnshire for a debut ride at Cadwell Park. Besides all the local specialists such as Peter Davey and Bernard Codd, Derek was ranged against stars such as Bob McIntyre and John Hartle. A 10th in the Senior Championship race was not a bad result considering that most riders were aboard Manx Nortons and were familiar with the twists and turns of Cadwell.

The competition was fiercer still six days later on Saturday 22 September in what *The*

The last meeting of the 1956 season was at Brands Hatch on 7 October and Derek was loaned a 350 AJS and 500 Matchless. He is seen here approaching Druids Hill Hairpin (3) leading a group of riders on the larger model.

A Matchless G45 twin of the type loaned to Derek by dealers/sponsors, the Arter brothers of Barham, near Canterbury...

Motor Cycle headlined 'Total War at Silverstone', the scene being the BMCRC Hutchinson 100 meeting. Here, on what after all was essentially a speed circuit, Derek's BSA was outclassed and after finishing 10th in his 500cc heat, he came home a lowly 23rd in the final.

The following day things got worse still, when in the 1000cc Invitation race at his local Brands Hatch circuit he was forced into retirement when he suffered a broken timing shaft in the Gold Star's engine room. At that time he could little have realised that he had ridden the Gold Star for the final time.

An outing for Arter

The last meeting of the season at Brands Hatch was the big national event on Sunday 7 October. For this Derek was loaned a pair of motorcycles by

...and an AJS 7R single.

Barham (near Canterbury) dealers/race sponsors Arters (owned by the brothers Tom and Egerton), an AJS 7R three-fifty and a Matchless G45 twin cylinder five-hundred. Derek did not disgrace himself, finishing all four of his races: third 350cc heat, fifth 350cc final, second 1000cc heat, third 1000cc final.

1000cc final, Brands Hatch – 10 laps – 12.4 miles

1st	G.A. Murphy (Matchless 498cc)
2nd	W.J. Sawford (Matchless 498cc)
3rd	D.W. Minter (Matchless 498cc)

And so the 1956 racing year ended. At that time Derek Minter's immediate future looked far from bright – a blown up Gold Star engine, little work and no real plans for what might happen to his racing career in 1957.

However, he was about to get his big break – an offer of a new job and the chance to race a pair of gleaming Manx Nortons. And so the closed season of 1956–57 became the turning point in the Derek Minter story. The future King of Brands was about to emerge from the shadows.

Chapter 2

The Wincheap Era

As related in the previous chapter, the 1956 season had ended on a somewhat low note, Derek having left MV Distributors and returned home, and suffered a blow-up on his own BSA Gold Star.

The big break

As Derek described it himself: 'then came the big break I'd been looking for. A local garage was being modernised under new management and I discovered the new outfit – Wincheap Garage (Wincheap being an area of Canterbury) – were keen on motorcycle sport. I was soon round to them and they offered me a job working as a mechanic there. I jumped at the chance.'

Derek pictured with (right) tuner Steve Lancefield; Mr Blundell Senior, the managing director of his 1957 sponsors Wincheap Garage (centre), and the firm's sales manager Eddie Blount (on the left).

The Wincheap organisation actually comprised three car dealerships, in Canterbury, Ashford and Folkestone, with agencies which included Austin and Volkswagen. The controlling company was owned by the Blundell family father and son. But it was the manager, Eddie Blount, who was responsible for Derek becoming involved, as he was 'something of a motorcycle enthusiast'.

Besides his chance to ride Nortons for the first time and thus have more competitive machinery with which to take on his rivals, Derek's job, at the Canterbury branch, was expressly aimed at helping Wincheap to break into the retail motorcycle world, with sales and service.

Practising at Brands

In the 10 April 1957 issue of *Motor Cycle News*, photographer/journalist Ken Jones wrote: 'Anyone casually visiting Brands Hatch last Wednesday afternoon would, by the activity prevailing in the paddock, have been fully justified in thinking that there was at least a Closed-to-Club event in progress.' He continued: 'But it was only last-minute practice and tests although the numbers are an indication of the enthusiasm prevailing in this region for the coming season.'

Ken went on to mention riders present, who included Alan Trow, Bruce Daniels, G.L. (Ginger) Payne – and Derek. Commenting: 'In *"concours d'élegance"* trim was Derek Minter and the 350 Norton which Wincheap Garage in Canterbury are sponsoring this season. Derek will be seen with this machine on both Good Friday and Easter Monday. He told me that the 500 is due any moment to complete the stable.'

An Easter debut

Actually, Derek's Wincheap sponsorship did not get off to the best of starts, as he had plug trouble in both his 350 and 500cc races, and so did not feature in the results. A pity this, because with a star entry which included John Surtees (MV) and Alan Trow (Norton), ideal weather and a good crowd for this Slazenger Trophy meeting – first of the year at Brands – and close on 40,000 enthusiasts jamming every vantage point around the 1.24-mile Kent circuit, the occasion had promised much.

At Crystal Palace on Easter Monday, 22 April, Derek's luck changed and he completed all five of his races (two heats, two finals and a handicap event). Organised by the South Eastern Centre of the ACU, the entire programme was staged in dry, cloudy weather.

His best finish was fourth in his 350cc heat; in the final he was sixth. Then in the 500cc heat he was seventh. But his most promising result came in the

Probably the most famous of all British racing motorcycles, the Featherbed-framed Norton, a 1956 model, is seen here.

Featherbed Manx Norton

Much of Derek Minter's racing career was spent campaigning on a series of Manx Norton machines. And it was with the legendary Norton single that he scored many of his most hard-won victories for over a decade between the mid-1950s and his ultimate retirement at the end of the 1967 season.

Ulsterman Rex Candless had been responsible for the design of the Featherbed frame, and, powered by a works dohc Norton single-cylinder engine, this made its debut in the spring of 1950. Initially ridden only by the works riders, such as Geoff Duke and Artie Bell, the first over-the-counter 'customer' examples arrived the following year. In both cases this signalled the end of the old plunger-framed 'garden gate' models (which in works guise had debuted during the 1936 TT and in production form had been sold from 1946).

The Featherbed (thus named thanks to rider Harold Daniell saying it felt like a 'feather bed' during a test session) created a sensation when it made its winning entrance at the Blandford Camp circuit in April 1950. Geoff Duke was in the saddle that day, as he was when, wearing his innovative one-piece skin-tight leathers, he won the Senior TT a couple of months later. Although Geoff did not win the 1950 World Championship (due to a succession of tyre problems), the same rider/machine combination took the 350/500cc World Championships double in 1951, retaining the 350cc crown for Norton in 1952. For 1951 the production Manx models were given the Featherbed chassis for the first time, together with several other improvements pioneered on the 1950 work's models. It is also worth pointing out that the production machines were constructed in a different area of the Bracebridge Street, Birmingham factory and were the responsibility of Edgar Franks (later design chief at the Ambassador works) rather than Joe Craig.

The pukka works specials were raced until the end of 1954. Then, with Joe Craig in charge, works development versions of the standard production version were entered in selected meetings by the trio of

Surtees, Hartle and Brett. The over-the-counter customer Manx 40M (350cc) and 30M (500cc) continued with yearly updates until production finally came to an end in 1962. During the 1950s 'customer' meant someone who was approved by the company. This approval meant the rider had to use his new machine in an international event, such as the TT, Ulster Grand Prix or a Continental European Grand Prix.

The first (1951) production Manx models displaced 499cc (79.62 x 100mm) and 348cc (71 x 88mm). Then, for the 1954 season there was a major engine redesign, with shorter-stroke dimensions: 86 x 85.62mm for the larger unit and 76 x 76.85mm on the three-fifty. There were also detail changes in most years: Amal GP carburettors (1952); rotating-magnet magneto (1956); redesigned vertical drive shaft (1959); Amal GP2 carb (1961); dual 7in front brakes (1962).

The classic double-overhead camshaft Norton engine with exposed hairpin valve springs, Lucas magneto and Amal GP carb of the type used by Derek for much of his career.

During much of the 1950s Norton engines were widely used in Formula 3 (500cc) racing cars. But Norton would not supply separate engines and transmissions, instead customers had to purchase a complete bike and dispose of the cycle components themselves. This meant that redundant Norton Featherbed frame assemblies were used to house a variety of other engines; notably 500 and 650cc Triumph twins. And thus the now-famous Triton special was born.

1000cc final, when he brought his brand new five-hundred Manx Norton home in a very respectable fifth – his first meeting on the machine (if we discount the non-event at Brands four days previously).

Derek also finished ninth in the solo handicap race.

1000cc Crystal Palace – 10 laps – 13.9 miles

1st   R. Anderson (Norton)
2nd   P. Ferbrache (Norton)
3rd   N. Minihan (Norton)
4th   G. Tanner (Norton)
5th   D.W. Minter (Norton)

Dicing at the Combe

Five days after Crystal Palace Derek was in action at Castle Combe on Saturday 27 April 1957.

As *Motor Cycle News* reported, 'in spite of a cold wind and overcast skies – not to mention petrol rationing [this was of course only a few months after the Suez Crisis] – a record crowd of enthusiasts turned out to support the stout efforts of the Wessex Centre, who went ahead with the organisation in spite of a heavy financial loss last year and the withdrawal of car racing from the circuit. Officials estimated the crowd at around the 12,000 mark and this will go a long way to ensuring that racing continues at this popular – if bumpy – 1.84-mile circuit.'

Derek was in action with his two Nortons. The two heats of the 350cc event saw victories for Geoff Tanner, riding a streamlined Norton, and Bob Anderson, on another of the Bracebridge Street machines.

350cc final, Castle Combe – 10 laps – 18.4 miles

1st   R. Anderson (Norton)
2nd   G.B. Tanner (Norton)
3rd   B.D. Codd (Norton)
4th   G.C.A. Murphy (AJS)

5th   D.W. Minter (Norton)

6th   N. Minihan (Norton)

The 500cc race brought to the line all the men from the 350cc final, plus John Clark on a 1956 works single-cylinder Moto Guzzi. From the start, Clark assumed the lead – and from the back of the grid. But by the end of the first lap Bob Anderson (Norton) came through a few lengths ahead of the Guzzi with Geoff Tanner (Norton), Derek and George Murphy (Matchless) in a tight bunch only lengths behind. Both Tanner and Derek got past Clark – the latter finding the Guzzi suspension set for Monza useless on the bumps of Castle Combe – while Murphy was only a length astern of the Guzzi rider in sixth. Tanner and Derek then duelled for second place, the result going, eventually, to Tanner.

500cc final, Castle Combe – 12 laps – 22.08 miles

1st   R. Anderson (Norton)

2nd   G.B. Tanner (Norton)

3rd   D.W. Minter (Norton)

4th   G.C.A. Murphy (Matchless)

5th   J.J. Clark (Moto Guzzi)

6th   F.A. Rutherford (Duke BSA)

'Minter's Day at Brands'

So said the *Motor Cycle News* headline for the report of the Brands Hatch meeting in the newspaper's 15 May 1957 issue. The report began: 'Rain or fine made no difference to Derek Minter (Nortons) at Brands Hatch on Sunday. On dry and wet roads he beat the established Brands stars and won all four big races – a feat unequalled since John Surtees joined the Italian MV team.' Certainly it was a day for all Derek's friends and family to marvel and enjoy.

Dry conditions gave way to a heavy rain shower as the 350cc finalists lined up on the grid. From the fall of the flag, Derek took the lead and, although L.S. Rutherford (AJS) challenged for four laps, the Wincheap-sponsored rider pulled away towards the end to win comfortably.

The second of Derek's four victories that day came in the 350cc Invitation Race. From the start Peter Murphy (AJS) took the lead with the pack close behind. Derek battled his way into second spot after four laps and set off after the New Zealander. On lap six Derek went ahead and, although Murphy drew level several times in the remaining nine laps, he could never get ahead and Derek won by what one journalist described as a 'wheels' length.

The 500cc final brought together Derek and Alan Trow (Norton), the latter fresh from his sensational and highly publicised victory over John Surtees (MV four) at the Easter Brands meeting. Ned Minihan (Norton) made a lightning start and stayed ahead for two laps before Trow took over the lead. At half distance the pattern of the race looked set, with Alan Trow leading Minihan by 100 yards with Derek a further 100 yards back in third place. But in a truly sensational storming finish Minter first caught and passed Minihan, and on the seventh lap he took the lead to score a wonderful victory.

Due to a cloudburst the last race of the day, the 1000cc Invitation event, was cut from 15 to 10 laps. From the start, Minihan was once again first away but Derek was well away too, and completed the first lap only a machine's length behind. On the second lap he swept ahead, and although George Murphy (Matchless) challenged strongly he held on to score his fourth win of the day.

350cc final, Brands Hatch – 10 laps – 12.4 miles
1st   D.W. Minter (Norton)
2nd   L.S. Rutherford (AJS)
3rd   R. Mayhew (Norton)
4th   F.A. Rutherford (Duke BSA)
5th   P. Murphy (AJS)
6th   G.C.A. Murphy (AJS)

1000cc final, Brands Hatch – 10 laps – 12.4 miles
1st   D.W. Minter (Norton)
2nd   A. Trow (Norton)
3rd   G.C.A. Murphy (Matchless)
4th   J.L. Payne (Norton)
5th   E.J. Washer (Norton)
6th   R.E. Rowe (BSA)

Non-appearance at the Palace
The 22 May 1957 edition of *Motor Cycle News* carried a story headlined 'Ferbrache Substitutes and Stars.' It continued: 'Thanks to the non-appearance of Derek Minter – due it was said to tuner Steve Lancefield wanting to take no risks with the two Nortons he will be using in the Isle of Man – Peter Ferbrache got into the programme for last Saturday's meeting at Crystal Palace as a substitute rider; and became the solo star of the day.'

Lancefield had in fact been recommended to Derek by Bryan Johnson, a personal friend who at that time was a mechanic to Stirling Moss in the 500cc car world. Looking back now, it will no doubt seem strange, but Derek's first reaction was to say 'Steve who?' It was to prove a pivotal moment in Derek's racing career and the Minter/Lancefield partnership was to blossom into a historic period for both men over the next five years or so.

The Isle of Man TT

Entered by the Wincheap Garage, Derek's riding numbers in the 1957 Golden Jubilee TT were 67 Junior and 40 Senior.

In fact, as was usual at the time, the Junior (350cc) race opened the programme and, again as usual, was run over seven laps of the 37.73-mile long Mountain circuit, a total of 264.13 miles.

In contrast to the previous year when he was unable to take part due to injury, Derek was destined to finish both races that he had been entered in. In the Junior he came home 14th, completing the distance in 3 hours 1 minute 40 seconds, an average speed of 87.23mph. The winner, Bob McIntyre (Gilera), achieved 2 hours 46 minutes 50.2 seconds (94.99mph).

In the Senior race Derek came home 16th in 3 hours 23 minutes 2.8 seconds, averaging 89.19mph, this being almost 10mph slower than the winner, Bob McIntyre (Gilera), who not only completed a famous Junior/Senior double, but also became the first man to lap the TT course at over 100mph. Another notable statistic was that this was the only eight-lap TT, a race distance of 301.84 miles.

Derek's 1957 TT performances were very much the right approach: consistency and reliability rather than risking a slightly better result by trying too hard for his limited experience of this, the most gruelling of all races.

Doing it again at Brands

As *MCN* said in its race report dated 12 June 1957, 'Minter does it again at Brands Hatch.'

The Ken Jones-written story went on: 'In brilliant style, Derek Minter and his brace of Nortons topped the opposition for the second successive meeting with four decisive (five, if you count the heats) victories at Brands Hatch on Whit Sunday.'

This time the main opposition came from the New Zealand stars John Hempleman, Noel McCutcheon and J.D. Anderson, making their Brands debut.

Intermittent heavy rain kept speeds fluctuating during the afternoon.

Derek's opening victory came in the 251–350cc event. Taking the lead on lap two, he then led to the finish.

That the New Zealanders were getting the hang of the circuit became apparent as the meeting unfolded, but none could hold the 'flying Minter' (*MCN*) who led comfortably in both the 1000cc races. He also won the 350cc Invitation event.

Foreign debut

Derek's first foray into continental Europe was the Dutch TT on Saturday 29 June 1957. A massive crowd of over 125,000 packed every vantage point of the sun-drenched 4.75-mile Van Drenthe circuit near Assen in the north of the country to watch the third round of that year's World Championship series.

In both races Derek competed in, the 350 and 500cc events, there was a magnitude of star riders and fierce battles right down the field. Australian Keith Campbell (Moto Guzzi) won the 350cc from Bob McIntyre and Libero Liberati (Gileras), while John Surtees (MV) was victorious in the 500cc, but this was after Bob McIntyre (Gilera) had crashed out when striving to make up lost ground following a pit stop to change spark plugs.

In the 350cc class there were many works entries, not only from MV and Gilera, but also from Moto Guzzi and Norton, while BMW could be added to this list for the larger capacity event.

Like the TT, in Holland Derek rode consistently to finish both races in respectable positions: seventh in the 350cc and ninth in the 500cc.

350cc Dutch TT – 20 laps – 95.74 miles

1st	K.R. Campbell (Moto Guzzi)
2nd	R. McIntyre (Gilera)
3rd	L. Liberati (Gilera)
4th	J. Brett (Norton)
5th	K. Bryen (Norton)
6th	J. Hartle (Norton)
7th	D.W. Minter (Norton)

A magnificent third in Belgium

If the Dutch TT results were good, eight days later in the Belgian Grand Prix Derek's performance was outstanding. Although his smaller Norton was down on power and he could only finish a lowly 16th in the 350cc, the 500cc Grand Prix saw Derek gain a first rostrum finish in an event counting towards World Championship points – with a third place.

Actually, the race result was subject to controversy, as the Italian Gilera works rider Libero Liberati, who had crossed the finishing line first, was downgraded in favour of Englishman Jack Brett riding a works development

Michael O'Rourke leading
Derek during the 500cc
Belgian Grand Prix in July
1957 aboard the larger
Wincheap Norton. He
eventually finished a
magnificent third.

Norton machine. This was because Liberati had started the race on fellow Gilera teamster Bob McIntyre's machine – without advising the organisers of this change.

500cc Belgian GP – 15 laps – 131.34 miles

1st   J. Brett (Norton)
2nd   K. Bryen (Norton)
3rd   D.W. Minter (Norton)
4th   M.P. O'Rourke (Norton)
5th   H. Jager (BMW)

Back Home

Then it was back home to England, with meetings at Castle Combe and Snetterton on Saturday and Sunday 13 and 14 July respectively.

At the Combe, Derek's first race was the 350cc heat, in which he finished fourth, then in the final, there was a four-way battle between

Geoff Tanner, Alastair King, Bernard Codd and Derek, which Alastair won, with Derek runner-up after Codd had been forced to retire with mechanical trouble.

But as *Motor Cycle News* reported, 'It wasn't until the second heat of the Senior [500cc] event that the crowd had some inkling of what was to follow later in the day. That heat brought Derek Minter and Alastair King together in a fight for the lead that went on for the full five laps. Always in doubt, the issue was not decided until the last few yards of the final lap. Minter, hard on the heels of King, came alongside as they swept towards the chequered flag and won.'

Then in the final, the early stages saw these two, plus Bernard Codd, Geoff Tanner and Jimmy Buchan (who had travelled down from Scotland with King) fight out a tremendous five-way battle during the early stages. Then, coming into Camp Corner, the long, fast curve which leads into the home straight, the five riders were still in close company and set to begin their fourth lap. Then catastrophe! Suddenly King was off the road and onto the grass, a brief excursion that cost him the lead and left him in fourth position behind Tanner, Codd and Derek. In spite of the cracking pace, King fought his way grimly back and on the sixth lap he was hard on the heels of the leader, Tanner. For the remainder of the 12 laps it was wheel to wheel tussle between the pair, with Derek close behind. The victory ultimately went to Tanner 'by the smallest of margins as the chequered flag fell to end a thrill packed race' (*MCN*), in which Alastair King had pushed the outright motorcycle lap record up to 85.79mph. Derek finished third, beating a host of far more experienced riders. But even this early in his Norton career he had shown that he could mix it with the finest boys, clearly displaying great potential for the future.

A crash when leading

At Snetterton the following day, after finishing runner-up in his heat, Derek was leading the 350cc final when he crashed. He recovered to take fourth in the 500cc final – behind Bernard Codd, Jimmy Buchan and Peter Ferbrache.

However, when Derek returned to Brands Hatch exactly seven days after Snetterton, on Sunday 21 July, it was back to winning ways. In the 350cc race he finished some nine seconds ahead of second man Tom Thorp. In the 1000cc Derek had a much harder time – even though he still emerged victorious – with serious challenges from Bob Rowe, Ned Minihan and 'Ginger' Payne.

The British Championships

August Bank Holiday Monday, 5 August, saw the 1957 British Championships take place over the 2.75-mile Thruxton airfield circuit, staged by the Southampton and District MCC on behalf of the ACU.

Two of the previous year's title holders – Bob McIntyre (250 and 500cc) and Bill Lomas (350cc) – were unable to defend the Championships due to injuries sustained in the Dutch TT, while the 125cc title holder – Michael O'Rourke – was to suffer a broken collarbone when he tumbled in the 250cc race. But with 1956 World Champion John Surtees mounted on a four-cylinder MV Agusta in the 500cc race (and a quick Norton in the 350cc event) the opposition, including Derek, would always be at a disadvantage.

The day was blessed with ideal weather conditions and this was no doubt largely responsible for a record crowd at the Hampshire course.

The meeting got under way with two 350cc heats, won by Surtees and Alan Trow (Norton). In the 18-lap final Surtees got off to one of his lightning starts and simply streaked away from the rest of the field. Derek eventually finished sixth (the same position as in his heat).

In the 500c Championship race, although he made a poor start (not unusual throughout Derek's career), he climbed through the field to finish an excellent fourth, with only Surtees, King and John Clark (Norton) in front after the 18 laps.

500cc British Championship, Thruxton – 18 laps – 49.5 miles

1st J. Surtees (MV Agusta)
2nd A. King (Norton)
3rd J.R. Clark (Norton)
4th D.W. Minter (Norton)
5th F.G. Perris (Norton)
6th R. Fay (Norton)

Improving all the time

It was evident to anyone who had been watching Derek's progress since gaining the Wincheap sponsorship that he was improving in leaps and bounds. This was never more evident than at Crystal Palace at the star-studded BMCRC meeting on Saturday 17 August 1957, when he finished runner-up to John Surtees in the main race of the day, the 1000cc Championship event. This is how one commentator of the period described the action: 'Surtees started the 1000 final in the expected manner, flashing into the lead at the fall of the flag. After the opening lap Alastair King (Norton) held second place, with John Clark (Norton), Peter Murphy (Matchless) and Derek Minter (Norton) in a bunch behind him. After five of the 15 laps Minter, riding superbly, had shaken off Clark and Murphy and was well after King. On the tenth lap he caught the Glasgow rider and from then on pulled steadily ahead to finish second behind Surtees, with King third. Derek was also fourth (behind Surtees, Murphy and King) in the 350cc final.'

John Surtees (MV Agusta four-cylinder) winning the Isle of Man Senior TT in June 1960.

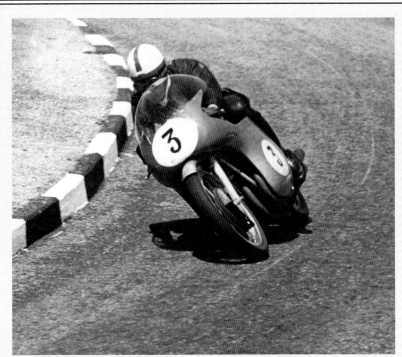

John Surtees

Born in the pretty village of Tatsfield on the Kent-Surrey border, a couple of miles south of Biggin Hill Airfield, on 11 February 1934, John Surtees succeeded Geoff Duke as 500cc World Champion. John's first motorcycle race came as a 14-year-old when his father Jack recruited his services as a passenger. The pairing actually won the event but were subsequently disqualified because of John's age. His first solo victory came at 17, at the tree-lined Aberdare Park circuit in South Wales. He was riding a 499cc Vincent Grey Flash single, which the young Surtees had constructed while serving his apprenticeship at the company's Stevenage works.

Except for a 1953 TT practice accident while riding an EMC 125, John would have been a Norton teamster that year. As it was Norton retired from fielding full Grand Prix 'Specials' at the end of 1954. However, John (together with John Hartle and Jack Brett) was signed to race works development Manx models for the 1955 season. He responded by having an excellent season, the highlight of which was winning the British Championship title.

Then he signed for the Italian MV Agusta concern to race its four-cylinder models during the 1956 season. In doing this John was following in the footsteps of Geoff Duke (although Duke had gone from Norton to Gilera). John made his MV debut at Crystal Palace near his south London home during April 1956 in winning style. Then he went on to win the 500cc World Championship title – even though he suffered a fall in Germany at the Solitude circuit. Although he had broken his right arm, which effectively kept him out of racing until the following year, John had already amassed enough points to carry off the title.

Although John could only finish third behind the Gilera pairing of Libero Liberati and Bob McIntyre in the 1957 500cc title race, he had the honour of giving MV its first-ever victory with the smaller 350 four at the Belgian Grand Prix in July 1956. Then came the golden trio of double 350cc and 500cc World Championship title years, when John won just about everything in 1958, 1959 and 1960. Having nothing else to prove in the two-wheel world, Surtees moved to four wheels, first as a driver for Ken Tyrrell, then as a member of the Lotus F1 team. In 1962 came a switch to a Lola, plus drives in a Ferrari 250 GTO in sports car events.

Next came a move into the full Ferrari team, competing in the 1963 and 1964 Formula1 series. In the latter year he won the world title and thus became the only man ever to achieve the feat of taking the premier Championship crowns on both two and four wheels.

After Ferrari came a spell with Honda, whom he joined for the 1967 season, and finally BRM in 1969. He then founded his own team, drivers for which included Mike Hailwood. Team Surtees was disbanded towards the end of the 1970s, its F1 'position' being acquired by Frank Williams.

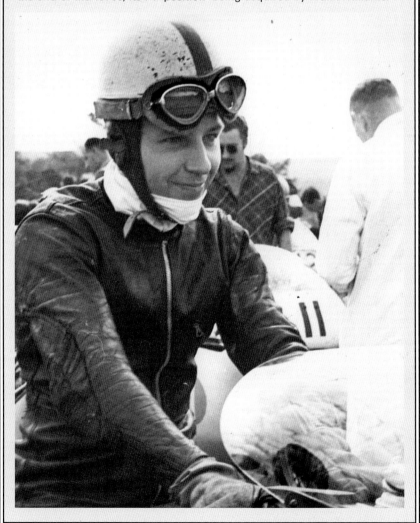

John Surtees, seen here prior to the start of the 1959 Ulster 500cc GP.

1000cc Crystal Palace – 15 laps – 20.85 miles

1st   J. Surtees (Norton)
2nd   D.W. Minter (Norton)
3rd   A. King (Norton)
4th   P. Ferbrache (Norton)
5th   J.R. Clark (Norton)
6th   G.C.A. Murphy (Matchless)

More victories at Brands Hatch

Next Derek scored five more victories at Brands Hatch on Sunday 8 September (350cc heat and final; 500cc heat and final; 500cc Invitation). His performances at the Kent circuit were by now becoming something of a legend. He would actually have scored six victories had his debut ride on Bob Geeson's home-built dohc REG twin not come to an abrupt end when an oil leak soaked the rear tyre in lubricant. The actual 250cc race result ended with a victory by Dick Harding (GMS) over Mike Hailwood (MV) and Alan Pavey (NSU).

After sunny dry conditions at Brands, 14 days later, on 22 September, for the national road races at Snetterton, heavy storms made conditions treacherous – with flooding in some parts of the Norfolk circuit.

This is how *Motor Cycle News* described the situation: 'Rain and drizzle fell continuously during the first half of the meeting, organised by the Snetterton combine, and after a final heavy storm, racing had to be held up for about 20 minutes while pumps were put to work in the flooded Esses and water was brushed from the back straight and hairpin.'

After finishing runner-up in his 350cc heat, Derek was forced to retire after his rear tyre went flat in the final when he was lying third.

The 350cc race winner, Alastair King, was expected to make it a double in the 500cc final. For the first three laps he had a comfortable lead, but Derek was battling with the Scot neck-and-neck as they crossed the line at the end of lap four. The last lap saw Derek with a comfortable lead, which King was unable to shorten. Derek also made the fastest lap of the day at 80.6mph. His time for the race was 16 minutes 49.4 seconds, a race speed of 72.01mph.

A shock for the racing world

At the end of September 1957, the racing world was shocked by the announcement that Gilera, Moto Guzzi and FB Mondial were to quit racing. Obviously, at this stage in his career it did not affect Derek directly, but indirectly it was to have implications for the future chances of up-and-coming riders getting factory contracts.

A first international victory

'Rain Ruins Aintree Meeting' shouted the headline in the 2 October 1957 issue of *Motor Cycle News*. The meeting itself took place on Saturday 28 September. *MCN* went on to say: 'while most of England basked in Indian Summer sunshine, non-stop rain ruined the last international road race of the British season held at the three mile road circuit built round the famous horse racing steeplechase course at Aintree and organised by the North Western Centre of the ACU.'

This meeting was also to see Derek score his first international victory. Not only this, but it was his first victory over the 1956 500cc World Champion John Surtees.

This historic event came about in the following manner. In pouring rain and with the few spectators scattered in the vast grandstand, the first race of the day – the 350cc event – got away soon after 10 o'clock. From the start Surtees, on his light blue, fully streamlined (dustbin-faired) Norton took the lead and, sweeping into sight to complete the first lap in a plume of spray, held a clear lead over Ken Patrick, John Hartle and Derek (the latter two, like Surtees, Norton-mounted).

Weather conditions were truly awful and many riders were in trouble with goggles and water-affected machines. But Surtees swept on, while Derek was seen to be 'clearly closing the gap' (*MCN*) in second place on the fifth lap after a tussle with Brian Purslow who lay third, with Alastair King (Norton) fourth and Ken Patrick fifth. On the seventh lap Derek went ahead and Surtees seemed content to stay with him. The two circulated together, never more than a few yards apart, well ahead of the rest of the field led by Purslow and King. On the final lap everyone expected a burst from Surtees, but nothing happened and he crossed the line behind Derek. There is no doubt that this result was a great boost for Derek, who went on to a famous victory, even though, subsequently, John Surtees was disqualified.

Later the same day, Derek was to finish an equally impressive runner-up to Surtees (now MV mounted) in the Aintree Senior 500cc race, and achieve third in the Aintree Century Class Solo Handicap. The results of both these events are listed below.

Aintree Senior 500cc – 20 laps – 60 miles

1st	J. Surtees (MV Agusta)	
2nd	D.W. Minter (Norton)	
3rd	J. Hartle (Norton)	
4th	R. Anderson (Norton)	
5th	K.H. Patrick (Norton)	
6th	R. Fay (Norton)	

The Aintree Century Class Solo Handicap – 34 laps – 102 miles

1st   T. Robb (247cc NSU)
2nd   J. Surtees (500cc MV Agusta)
3rd   D.W. Minter (348cc Norton)
4th   A. King (348cc Norton)
5th   D. Christian (498cc Matchless)
6th   W.H. Dixon (499cc BSA)

Derek's view of Aintree? 'A funny circuit; particularly riding across the railway lines – in the wet it was a bit slippery!'

Minter versus Surtees

The front page of the 16 October 1957 issue of *Motor Cycle News* was dominated by the headline 'Minter does "a Surtees" – on Surtees.' It went on to explain: 'Saturday's national road race meeting at the 1.24-mile Brands Hatch circuit near Farningham in Kent made a wonderful finale to the season in the South. A huge crowd saw some of the most exciting solo scrapping ever; with ex-World Champion John Surtees being beaten fair and square in the 350cc race by local boy Derek Minter.' Not only this, but both Surtees and Derek were mounted on what could be truthfully described as production model Manx Nortons, which proved more than a match for the official Norton factory entries of John Hartle, Jack Brett and Alan Trow. And if anyone needs convincing that these were official Norton entries, their three machines arrived in the Norton factory van and were accompanied by factory mechanics!

The first round of the contest that everyone had come to see was the 350cc race. Hartle was first away and after him came Surtees, Trow and then Derek. That order was maintained for the first lap, but as the leaders tore along the back straight for the second time it became evident that Hartle was slowing (it later transpired that his rear brake was binding) and he toured in to retire. That left Surtees in the lead, followed by Derek. And the latter was catching up fast. By the fourth lap the pair were side-by-side and by the fifth lap Derek led – and not only did he lead, but he seemed to be drawing away. As *MCN* reported: 'the crowd were electrified – all eyes were on Surtees and Minter and for all the interest they created the remainder of the field might well not have existed.'

By the seventh lap Minter led by three-fifths of a second, by the eighth by a whole second (about 50 yards) and by the ninth lap by even more. The entire length of the straight separated Surtees from Trow, still third, while Jack Brett was fourth, with privateer Laurence Flury (AJS) fifth and Bob Anderson (Norton) sixth.

Already the tailenders were beginning to be lapped, but still Derek maintained his lead. He was riding with grim determination against a much more experienced rider and former World Champion. By the three-quarter race distance (it was a 15-lap event) a few baulks by slower riders allowed Surtees to close a little and for a time it seemed possible that he could well catch Derek. Spectators wondered if perhaps Surtees had not been trying too hard and was only now getting going? But no. Both leaders were now lapping the midfield men and it was Surtees's turn to be held up. During the final lap Derek drew ahead to such purpose that he won by more than 100 yards and, with a circuit at 74mph, broke the all-time Brands lap record.

Derek proudly displays the Brands Hatch Shield after winning it for the first time in 1957.

Another Brands Shield shot in October 1957 showing, among others, left to right: Alan Trow, John Hartle, Eddie Blount (Wincheap Garage), Derek and Jack Brett (in dark suit).

350cc Brands Hatch – 15 laps – 18.6 miles

1st	D.W. Minter (Norton)
2nd	J. Surtees (Norton)
3rd	J. Brett (Norton)

In the first of two experts' 1000cc races, the 20-lap Slazenger Trophy, Derek and John again put on a tremendous show, completely eclipsing the remainder of the entry, but this time Surtees emerged on top with Derek close behind. Alan Trow was a distant third.

It had been hoped that the 15-lap Deventh Trophy Invitation race would provide a third round of the Surtees/Minter duel, but it was not to be. Surtees got away 'like greased lightning' (*MCN*), but Derek could not free his clutch and was almost last away. Then, having worked his way up to sixth place at the halfway stage, Derek came off (without serious injury) on the top bend of the hairpin (the front wheel slid away from him, he said later in an interview) and that was that. Earlier in the day Derek had finished fourth in the 250cc race on the REG.

Derek misses Oulton

Derek had entries for the final meeting of the year at Oulton Park. But although he was there spectating, Derek's arm was 'very stiff' following his tumble a week earlier at Brands. But it was not so stiff as to prevent him driving his new Volkswagen Beetle. Derek says that he received the car in lieu of monies owed to him by Wincheap – 'I was worried that otherwise I might lose out' – and drove it on the round trip of over 400 miles to the Cheshire circuit.

Around the same time *Motor Cycle News* published an article entitled 'The Canterbury Flier', written by Ken Jones. Ken said 'If there's one reason for visiting Canterbury in Kent there's a

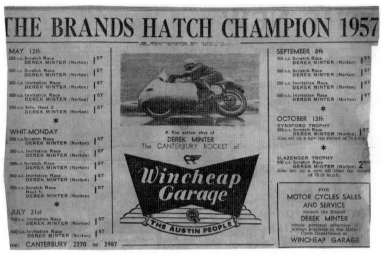

Wincheap Garage advertisement, late 1957, listing the successes of 'Derek Minter, The Canterbury Rocket'.

hundred. But 1957 has, in the motorcycle world at least, produced yet one more – "The Canterbury Rocket" or, as the programmes call him, D. Minter, 350 and 500 Nortons.' Outlining his rise from novice to Brands master, Ken ended with a look into the future: 'with a career that is obviously in its infancy, one cannot fairly sum up, but it can, I think, be assessed from the foregoing that "The Rocket" from Canterbury has by no means reached its peak.'

How correct Ken Jones's words were to be only became evident as the 1950s unfolded into the 1960s, when 'The Rocket' became 'The King'!

The 13 November issue of *Motor Cycle News* commented: 'the Nortons which carried him [Derek] to fabulous success this year are up for sale, as is the big green transporter.' This was in reference to the disposal of these items by the Wincheap organisation.

Derek's next career move was to become a full time professional road racer, this coming a few months later in early 1958.

And although he was leaving the Wincheap organisation, Gordon Cornelous, whom he had met and befriended during the 1957 season, was to continue assisting Derek with various aspects of his racing in future years, including getting the machines to and from meetings.

An interesting footnote was that while at Wincheap Garage Derek pioneered the use of small, lightweight glass fibre fuel tanks on his pair of Nortons – a fashion which was to take hold for short circuit use over the next few years. But Derek Minter was the first!

Chapter 3

Going Professional

1958 was a landmark year in Derek Minter's racing career – he made the bold decision to go professional. This decision was made after what he described in his 1965 autobiography *Racing All My Life* as 'a disagreement with Wincheaps', but he never actually said what this was, other than it 'upset me at the time.' But today, half a century after the event, the author can reveal that this disagreement centred around Wincheap Garage's demand that Derek should give the company half the prize monies he received from racing.

Going it alone

So in early 1958 Derek decided to leave the Wincheap organisation and go it alone – in other words as a full-time professional road racer. In his 1965 book he commented: 'If it hadn't happened I wonder if I would today be earning my living by racing motorcycles?' It is an interesting thought, and just maybe Derek's subsequent racing career might well have turned out quite differently.

It was a big decision and there is no doubt that had Derek not been confident of making it a success, he would not have quit a safe job with the use of two Manx Nortons paid for and maintained at Wincheap's expense. This was also the first clear sign that Derek Minter was, as Murray Walker so accurately described him, 'essentially an individualist, frank, outspoken and a fighter every inch of the way. He is, too, always far happier as a freelance rider than a team member, and does not happily submit to being told what to do.'

Derek himself recalls: 'Although financially I was skating on very thin ice indeed, I just didn't mind. I wasn't married, though by now I was 26, and the thrill of being a professional racing motorcyclist made up for all the shortcomings of such a hazardous existence as I would now have to lead as a pro trying to establish myself. Many riders had more experience. Many riders had been in the game much longer. Yet here was young Minter, really without

In 1958 Derek became a full-time professional rider for the first time. Here he is seen on his larger Norton. Note the massive fabricated aluminium air scoop for the Manx Norton front brake.

a big race win to his name, an out-and-out professional. How cheeky can you get? But I was now determined to make motorcycle racing my career, and I just had to be successful. Being a professional meant, if nothing else, that I could concentrate on the job more.'

The Norman Trials Bike

In January 1958 it was reported that Derek had taken delivery of a one-off Norman 225cc trials machine. This was very much a local tie-up, as the Norman factory was at nearby Ashford, only a few miles from Derek's home. It was also a relationship which was to continue for several years, with Derek also later having the use of a B4 Sports Twin roadster, besides the dirt bike. Interestingly, both machines had the same registration number plate...

When Mick Woollett published his weekly *Paddock Gossip* column in the 26 February 1958 issue of *Motor Cycle News*, Derek had not completely quit the Wincheap organisation, as the following story reveals: 'Talking of Derek Minter reminds me that I met him down at Brands the other Sunday running in his new 500 Norton. He is also having a new 350. The 350 which he rode last year is for sale. It is the actual machine that holds the Brands record and has been maintained by Steve Lancefield. Anyone interested in buying it can contact Derek at Wincheap Garage during the day, phone Canterbury 2270.' The story continued: 'This year Derek will be a freelance with his two Nortons and he also plans to ride one of Bob Geeson's REG twins whenever possible. After a preliminary look at the Continent last year Derek hopes to do quite a few meetings over there this season including the Dutch, Belgian and German Grand Prix.'

Duke buys the 350

So who actually bought Derek's 1957 350 Norton? The answer is none other than multi-World Champion Geoff Duke, who was returning to the ranks of privateer after several years with the Italian Gilera factory and prior to that as a works Norton rider between 1949 and 1952 (see the companion volume in this series, *Geoff Duke: The Stylish Champion*, Breedon Publishing).

The season opener

The new racing season, at least as far as Derek was concerned, began at Brands Hatch on Good Friday, 4 April 1958. Not only were there near-record crowds, fine weather and what *MCN* described as 'hard fought races', but, after a day of 'tremendous dicing', Derek also emerged the victor, but had to fight all the way against three rivals.

Derek (11) pictured stalking Alan Trow at Brands Hatch in spring 1958, before going ahead to win the main 1000cc event.

The last rider to race Bob Geeson's home-brewed REG dohc twin was Fred Hardy, seen here in action during 1962 TT practice.

REG 250 Twin

The story of the most famous of all British specials began back in 1948 when, 12 years after the last victory by a British machine in the Lightweight (250cc) TT, a letter appeared in the BMCRC (British Motor Cycle Racing Club) club magazine, Bemsee. It suggested a consortium of interested and qualified parties to enable Britain to get back into top line racing in the class again.

In Croydon, south London, Bob Geeson, a long-time Bemsee member and pre-war competitor at Brooklands, Donington and the Manx Grand Prix, read the letter with interest. This brought him into contact with toolmaker Gordon Allen, who was, as it happened, already well advanced with the building of a prototype two-fifty parallel twin. But up to that time Allen's efforts had been directed towards the bottom end of the engine, let alone the top end – and certainly not the chassis. The result was that Allen and Geeson decided to pool their talents and in the very short space of 31 months the pair conceived a racing two-fifty called the Allen-REG.

The frame and cycle components were all the work of Geeson, many coming from the REG Rudge single, which its creator had ridden during 1948, including the Hutchinson 100 and Manx Grand Prix. The engine, with its 54 x 54mm (249cc) bore and stroke, all-alloy construction, gear-driven, double overhead camshafts, roller big-ends and three bearing crankshaft, was as the name implied, part Allen and part Geeson.

If the results obtained during 1949 by the Allen-REG – three starts and three retirements with seized big-ends – were anything to go by, Bob Geeson should have called it a day there and then. But of course he did not. During the winter of 1949–50 Geeson took over sole responsibility for the project, now renamed REG. The main differences of the subsequent engine

Fred Hardy working with REG, *c.*1962. Derek had earlier raced the REG during 1958 and 1959.

redesign were at the bottom end: Allen's built-up crank was thrown out to be replaced by a one-piece Nitralloy assembly, machined from solid and supported on lipped roller bearings at each end of a plain centre bearing; the seizure-prone roller big-ends were axed too, with Hiduminium con-rods running direct on the crankpins. The valve gear and its drive train, having displayed weakness during 1949, were likewise modified.

Like later versions, the first pure REG which arrived in 1950 was mostly, but not exclusively, the work of Bob Geeson. However, not one to hog the limelight, he also acknowledged the assistance from Edgar Buckingham and Roger Ajax, all three at that time working for the Metal Box Company – Bob Geeson as a senior engineer designing and developing highly-complex production machinery. Unfortunately, Ajax was to meet his death in a road accident during 1952.

Other technical details of the REG design included camshaft drive by six spur gears, each supported on both sides by ball bearings, thus reducing friction to the minimum. The oil pump was driven from the timing chain and lubricant for the dry sump system was fed under pressure to both camboxes. Oil was pumped through the hollow crankshafts to a point midway between the big-ends. Both bearings were thus assured of an equal supply of lubricant. Con-rods were RR56 forgings and ran directly to the crankshaft. The small-ends were unbushed. An outside flywheel was employed. The crankcase and timing case were of magnesium, the ignition by magneto.

Although the initial REG engine design was completed in January 1950, the complete machine was not ready until the later stages of TT practice that June. As a result of various problems with the cycle parts, only three practice laps were completed, but in the race itself Geeson finished 12th after losing 16 minutes as a result of a broken oil pipe.

The remainder of that season and the following year brought their quota of teething problems, but reasonable reliability seemed to be established and several promising results were achieved, including seventh place in the Ulster Grand Prix and a fine second place behind Maurice Cann's Moto Guzzi at Boreham. A redesigned valve gear promised even better in 1952, but persistent magneto gremlins did not help; even a temporary change to coil ignition did not effect a cure.

With the ignition problems finally behind them, the REG was entered for the 1953 Lightweight TT, the result being a creditable 10th at an average speed of 71.74mph. From then on things began to look up. John Surtees's services were acquired, Bob Geeson having decided to let someone else do the riding, as until then he had not only been the designer/mechanic, but also the rider. At Blandford in August John rode the REG to third place in the 250cc final behind the Guzzis of Fergus Anderson and Cann. Subsequently, further valve gear modifications added an additional 5mph to the maximum speed, and later in the season Surtees took the REG to a sensational victory in the 250cc race at the important end-of-season Brands Hatch Championship meeting in October 1953. Not only this, but the future World Champion demonstrated the potential of the home-built twin by establishing lap and race records for the class.

The glory days for Bob Geeson's special came in 1954. With Surtees aboard, the REG scored 15 victories (plus an extra one with Bob himself riding). In addition, no fewer than seven times, the Surtees/REG pairing set new race and lap records. At the end of the season the original bike was sold to Australian Jack Walters. The next year, 1955, was devoted entirely to manufacturing sets of components for two more complete machines, one of which Geeson assembled as soon as these were ready, which was in the following summer, when it made its debut with Jim Baughn at the controls.

But it was not to be for almost another three years that circumstances permitted the simultaneous operation of both REGs. Experimentally, during 1958, a switch was made to coil ignition, then, after a season back with magnetos, Geeson adopted twin-plug ignition. But this dual ignition experiment was not a success and, in combination with certain other factors, led to a spate of stripped timing gears.

It was around this time that Derek Minter rode the REG to a number of victories, notably at Brands Hatch. Other riders included Arthur Wheeler (1956), John Hartle and Jack Brett (1957), Bob Anderson (1959), 'Ginger' Payne (1959–61), Norman Surtees (1960), Syd Mizen (1961), Ray Fay (1961) and finally Fred Hardy (1961–62).

Firstly, the young Mike Hailwood, who had just returned from a successful winter's racing in South Africa. Mike had won the day's opening race, the 200cc event on an MV. In the 250cc race Mike challenged Derek on the REG all the way – riding the ex-John Surtees NSU Sportmax. Then, in the 350 and 1000cc races, it was Laurence Flury, riding Tom Arter's AJS and Matchless machines, who diced throughout the entire race distances with Derek and only lost by lengths in both events. Completing the troublesome trio was the

A youthful-looking Derek during the 1958 season.

Rhodesian newcomer Jim Redman, who put up what *MCN* called 'a remarkable performance' to finish second to the Canterbury ace in the final 1000cc Invitation race.

250cc Brands Hatch – 15 laps – 18.6 miles

1st	D.W. Minter (REG)
2nd	S.M.B. Hailwood (NSU)
3rd	D.F Shorey (Norvel)
4th	J.D. Hamilton (NSU)
5th	A. Pavey (NSU)
6th	T. Thorp (TTS)

350cc Brands Hatch – 20 laps – 24.8 miles

1st	D.W. Minter (Norton)
2nd	L. Flury (AJS)
3rd	T. Thorp (Norton)
4th	J. Redman (Norton)
5th	P. Driver (Norton)
6th	J. Lewis (Norton)

1000cc Invitation – 20 laps – 24.8 miles

1st	D.W. Minter (Norton)
2nd	J. Redman (Norton)
3rd	R.E. Rowe (Norton)
4th	B. Daniels (Norton)
5th	J.R. Holder (Norton)
6th	L. Flury (AJS)

Two days later, on Easter Sunday, 6 April, Derek suffered mixed fortunes at Snetterton's 2.71-mile circuit between Thetford and Norwich, next to the A11 trunk road. Firstly, having won his 350cc heat from Peter Ferbrache, he was forced into retirement in the final when, making excellent progress from a poor start, his machine developed gearbox troubles. Then in the 250cc event he could do no better than fourth.

In fact Derek's only victory came in the 500cc final, when he beat Mike Hailwood.

Easter Monday at the Palace

Some 20,000 spectators braved what can be best described as arctic-like conditions at the south London Crystal Palace circuit the next day, Easter Monday. With his five-hundred Norton sorted out overnight, Derek scored superb double 350/1000cc victories and also set the fastest lap in the 350cc final, at 73.81mph.

Mike Hailwood won both the 200 and 250cc races, with Derek having to retire his REG in the latter.

The 350cc heats were dominated by Tom Thorp, Laurence Flury and Derek, but in the final it was the Canterbury man all the way.

There was some fine racing in the 1000cc heats. Peter Ferbrache won the first, then Bruce Daniels held off a terrific last-minute challenge from Derek to take the second, while Ned Minihan got the better of Ernie Washer in the third.

This is how *Motor Cycle News* described the final: 'What a great race it was, with Ferbrache quickly into the lead and well clear for the first four laps. Minter soon displaced Daniels from second position and then, by some magnificent riding, proceeded to reduce the gap between himself and Ferbrache. It was not until the eighth lap (of the 10-lap race distance) that he was within striking distance, he forced his way to the front on the next, finally winning an excellent race by a matter of seconds.'

Warm and sunny Silverstone

In stark contrast to the wintry conditions experienced over the Easter weekend, close on 30,000 people who lined the 2.9-mile Silverstone airfield circuit for *Motor Cycling's* annual Saturday meeting on 19 April 1958 were treated to a pleasantly warm and sunny day.

Derek's boyhood hero, Geoff Duke, stole the headlines by winning the 350cc race and setting the fastest lap. Derek finished sixth. And in the 500cc race our hero came home fifth behind race winner Terry Shepherd, followed by Bob McIntyre, Bob Anderson and John Holder.

Only in the 250cc race did Derek regain something, finishing runner-up on the REG to the Australian Harry Hinton Jnr (NSU).

250cc Silverstone – 15 laps – 43.5 miles

1st	H. Hinton Jnr (NSU)
2nd	D.W. Minter (REG)
3rd	R.N. Brown (NSU)
4th	P.H. Tait (Beasley Velocette)
5th	T. Thorp (TTS)
6th	J. Murgatroyd (Beasley Velocette)

A hard-fought double

At Castle Combe, on Saturday 26 April 1958, Derek battled his way to victory in both the 350 and 500cc races after two race-long battles with Bob

Anderson (Nortons). As *Motor Cycle News* reported: 'these had the spectators' pulses leaping with excitement.' With riders of the calibre of Mike Hailwood, Phil Read, Tony Godfrey and the like, competition was hot to say the least. Earlier Hailwood had put his ex-Surtees NSU in front of Derek (REG) to win the 250cc event.

De-tuned

At Brands Hatch on Sunday 4 May, in his heat for the 250cc race, Derek, riding the REG, equalled his own class lap record at 69.32mph and his race speed of 65.32mph was the same as Mike Hailwood's in the other heat. However, the expected battle in the final did not develop as Minter slid off on the first lap and was narrowly missed by J.D. Hamilton (NSU).

There is no doubt that this incident had a de-tuning effect on Derek and in the subsequent races he was not his usual self. For example, in the 350cc Invitation event Mike Hailwood got away to a flying start and stayed out in front all the way to record his first-ever 350cc race win. Derek finished behind him as runner-up.

In the last race, the 1000cc final, Hailwood crashed on Druids Hill Bend and, with oil from previous incidents, that corner became a handicap to all the riders. The race was won by Bob Anderson, with Derek again finishing runner-up.

A horribly wet Aintree

In the words of 'brilliant' triple winner Alastair King, 'it was good racing, but a pretty horrible day' when in soaking leathers the Scot collected the Red Rose Trophy on Saturday 10 May. The other solo winner was Fron Purslow (124cc Ducati and 247cc NSU). As for Derek, his best placings that rain-soaked day were a third in the 250cc race on the REG and a fourth in the 350cc final on his smaller Norton. In the 500cc final he was forced into retirement with a waterlogged magneto. All in all it was not a day which Derek has fond memories of.

The TT

The Aintree meeting was the last one for Derek before leaving for the TT in the Isle of Man. He had three entries in the 1958 series: 250cc (number 10), 350cc (number 4) and 500cc (number 16).

Actually, the REG proved a problem throughout the practice week and was still in trouble and misfiring badly during the final practice session for that class – in spite of a switch to coil ignition earlier in the week.

The Junior (350cc) race came first on Monday 2 June. *Motor Cycle News* said: 'Derek Minter is well ahead of the field at Keppel Gate and before long

Geoff Tanner, seen here pushing the 350cc Norton with which he took third place in the 1958 Junior TT. Meanwhile, Derek was ninth in the Junior and fourth in the Senior events.

he flashes through to complete his first lap.' And of the first lap leaders he was seventh, behind the front man John Surtees (MV) followed by the Nortons of Bob McIntyre, Alastair King, Bob Anderson, Geoff Tanner and Keith Campbell. *Motor Cycle News* again (second lap): 'Still leading on the roads and demonstrating that he is as good a long circuit racer as he is on the short tracks. Derek Minter completes his second circuit.' Even on the final (seventh) lap Derek was leading on the roads, with *MCN* commenting: 'Minter's dark green machine is sighted safely through Sulby; he reaches Ramsey and sets off on the last long grind up towards the bungalow and the crest of the mountain climb. At Keppel Gate, only four miles from home, he is still out in front. Minter is signalled approaching the last slow hairpin turn at Governor's Bridge and he comes in to pass the chequered flag.'

Derek's final position was ninth, in a time of 2 hours 55 minutes 4 seconds, a speed of 90.52mph, some 6.4 minutes slower than the winner John Surtees (MV Agusta); he had gained a silver replica.

Problems with the REG continued into the Lightweight race (held on the much shorter 10.79-mile Clypse circuit) and was run on Wednesday 4 June. And unlike the larger capacity classes, the 250s got under way in a mass (short circuit-style) start. On the first lap Derek got as far as the Nursery Hotel, between Onchan and Signpost Corner, before he was forced to stop due to serious misfiring, and he dismounted to change plugs. Then, at the end of the lap, he limped into his pit and made another plug change, but got no further than Willaston before retiring.

On Friday 6 June came the climax of the 51st Isle of Man Tourist Trophy races, with the Senior (500cc) event. But although visibility all round the course was perfect, the weather appeared to be on the turn, with grey sky instead of the brilliant blue that riders and spectators alike had enjoyed for the earlier race days. The entry included a pair of MV fours ridden by John Surtees and John Hartle, plus Geoff Duke's BMW. However, although Surtees was to win the race, thus scoring a Junior/Senior double, Hartle's machine caught fire and burned out, while Duke retired with brake and handling problems on his German machine. But Derek put in a tremendous performance – not even in the first 12 at the end of Lap 1, he was to finish a magnificent fourth, after working his way up through the field.

Senior TT – 7 laps – 264.11 miles
1st   J. Surtees (MV Agusta)
2nd   R. Anderson (Norton)
3rd   R.N. Brown (Norton)
4th   D.W. Minter (Norton)
5th   D.V. Chadwick (Norton)
6th   J.D. Anderson (Norton)
7th   G.A. Catlin (Norton)
8th   E. McG Haldane (Norton)
9th   P.R. Dawson (Norton)
10th   R.H. Dale (BMW)

Nine days after his Senior TT success, on Sunday 15 June, Derek was back in action, this time at Snetterton, where, after winning his heat and setting a new class lap record, he finished runner-up to Mike Hailwood (Norton) in the 350cc final. Then, in the 500cc final, he beat Hailwood to victory, and both Derek and Mike went round quicker than John Surtees's MV lap record for the Norfolk circuit, set two years earlier.

Going Dutch

Then it was a case of crossing the Channel to race in the Dutch TT at Assen. Even though there was heavy rain on the previous day, Saturday 28 June was just about perfect for racing: slightly overcast and with only a light wind blowing.

Always well supported, the Dutch TT was to become Derek's favourite foreign circuit. This is how *Motor Cycle News* described the setting for the 1958 event: 'Long before the riders come to the line for the first race, the wonderful 4.79-mile Van Drenthe circuit – a real riders' course – is crammed with spectators who must number nearly two hundred thousand; not an inch of the huge grandstand or the earth banks round the course remain free.'

Derek had only entered on his two Nortons, worried perhaps that the REG would play up as it had a few weeks before at the TT.

The 350cc race

With a star-studded entry of riders from all over Europe, Derek could well have been overawed. But as events were to prove, in fact this was just the reverse, and with his Lancefield-tuned Norton going extremely well, he was the danger man in both his races to the more established runners, which included the likes of Surtees, Hartle, Duke and many more.

Easily the fastest in practice, Surtees was on the front row alongside his teammate Hartle and Bob Anderson. On the second row were Duke, Terry Shepherd and the Australian Eric Hinton.

By lap 2, Surtees enjoyed a commanding lead, with Hartle in second spot pursued by Bob Anderson, who had passed fast-starting Jim Redman, but Shepherd was already in trouble and coasted into the pits to retire with a Norton engine lacking vital revs.

At the quarter stage – the fifth lap – Surtees was still at the front, with Hartle some way behind. Third man Anderson was closely followed by Hinton only a few yards behind. The first real battle though was for fifth place, with Switzerland's Luigi Taveri just ahead of Keith Campbell and Derek.

Then, on the sixth lap, both Anderson and Hinton slowed and by the seventh lap the order was: Surtees, Hartle, Campbell, Anderson, Derek, Hailwood, Hinton, Taveri, Driver, Brown, Chadwick, Hempleman, Dawson and then Geoff Duke, whose Dearden Norton was seemingly down on power.

The eighth lap saw Anderson drop another place to Derek, while Geoff Tanner cruised in to retire.

At the halfway stage Surtees led by an impressive 57 seconds from Hartle, who was second ahead of Campbell, with Derek fourth in front of Hailwood. And that was how they stayed to the finish. An interesting fact is that Derek rode so hard to catch up in the early part of the race that he ripped away the side of the sole and upper from his right boot and part of his toe when cranking his Norton over to the very limit! And when one considers the only men to beat him were the two MV riders and the 1957 350cc World Champion, Derek could be proud of his achievement indeed.

350cc Dutch TT – 20 laps – 85.69 miles
1st   J. Surtees (MV Agusta)
2nd   J. Hartle (MV Agusta)

Steve Lancefield

As detailed elsewhere, in June 1960 Derek Minter became the first man to lap the Isle of Man TT Mountain circuit at over 100mph on a single-cylinder machine. The bike? A 499cc Manx Norton prepared by Steve Lancefield.

A Londoner, born on 4 November 1903, S.S. (Steven Silvester) Lancefield never liked the word 'tuner', a point he stressed when the author carried out a day-long interview with him in May 1989, only a few months before his death. Instead, he preferred the term 'engineer'.

Lancefield began his motorcycling career aboard a borrowed Triumph two-stroke in the 1920s, thereafter owning an ABC flat-twin and a Model 18 TT Replica Norton. In 1929 he completed 28 laps of Brooklands in the MCC (Motor Cycle Club) High Speed Trials on the Model 18, averaging 80.13mph on petrol. His first Brooklands victory came the following year. Soon he made the decision that he was better suited to working on motorcycles than riding them. A trip to Donington Park with Harold Daniel in the early 1930s proved that a Lancefield-prepared Norton was quicker than a Daniel one, with the result that he joined Harold in the latter's motorcycle business at Forest Hill. So a hobby became a profession. He also found time to marry Harold's sister, Clare.

World War Two caused a break in racing activities, but Lancefield's engineering skills were put to good use, first with Rolls-Royce and later with the British Aircraft Company. Lancefield and Daniel resumed their business after the cessation of hostilities and continued together right up until 1949, when Steve was invited to join the Norton works team, Daniel already having been a works rider for the Birmingham company for several years. Team boss Joe Craig had noticed his skills, which had included a couple of seconds for Lancefield-prepared bikes (both Nortons) at Daytona the previous year, with Billy Mathews losing the all-important 200-miler by a mere 18 seconds following an extended pit stop. Earlier, in 1947, for the first time ever, one rider

Steve Lancefield (with glasses and tie) and Jim Russell, after the latter had won the *Daily Telegraph* International Trophy at Brands Hatch on 2 August 1954, driving a Lancefield-tuned, Norton-engined Cooper car.

had won three Isle of Man races in one year. Lancefield Nortons carried Eric Briggs to victories in the Senior Clubman's in June, and the Junior and Senior Manx Grand Prix that September. The two Manx winning bikes were completely stock, just 'carefully assembled', as Mr Lancefield told me himself during my 1989 interview, while the Clubman's mount was a borrowed roadster.

For most of the 1950s Steve Lancefield was deeply involved with Formula 3 (500cc) racing cars, in which the top drivers, including the likes of Stirling Moss and Jim Russell, used Lancefield-tuned Norton engines. But by the end of that decade, with the death of Formula 3, Lancefield was back to his original love, motorcycles. This culminated in the honour of preparing the first 500cc single-cylinder machine to lap the Isle of Man at over 100mph, with Minter aboard.

Never one to seek publicity, believing results were what was really

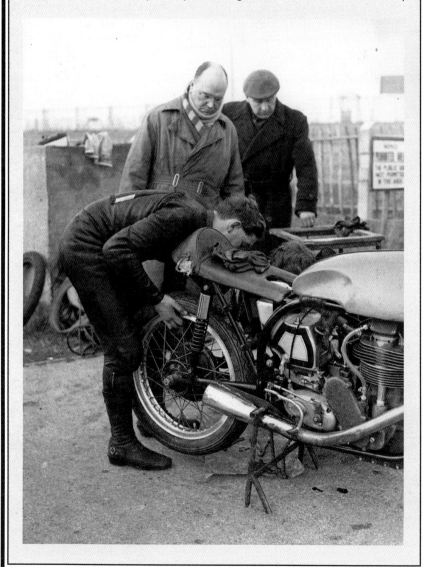

Steve Lancefield watches as Derek Minter changes a wheel while tyre testing at Brands Hatch on 6 January 1960.

important, Steve Lancefield continued working on Manx Norton engines until the early 1970s, when he assisted Tom Dickie, but he told the author that Steve Spencer's 100mph lap in the latter's first TT, in 1967, was the highlight of the latter-day Lancefield-Norton era. Spencer eventually finished third behind Mike Hailwood (Honda) and Peter Williams (Arter Matchless).

Without a doubt Steve Lancefield was completely dedicated to the job of making Norton singles both fast and reliable. He once put things like this: 'Some people say I take racing too seriously; to me it's a religion and science and nothing is too good to ensure success. In this respect often I express my considered opinion and it is not liked.' But in my dealings with Lancefield I found him forthright, but genuinely wanting to do a good job. And one must remember that racing at the top level is a serious business and requires 100 per cent commitment and expertise; in this respect S.S. Lancefield could not be faulted.

In Derek Minter's case, he found Ray Petty much easier to get on with, but both he and Lancefield were at the very top in the preparation stakes. One of the latter's customers referred to Lancefield's workshop as having 'the clinical cleanliness of a surgeon's operating room.'

3rd	K.R. Campbell (Norton)
4th	D.W. Minter (Norton)
5th	S.M.B. Hailwood (Norton)
6th	L. Taveri (Norton)
7th	R.H.F. Anderson (Norton)
8th	P. Driver (Norton)
9th	R.N. Brown (Norton)
10th	J. Hempleman (Norton)

Note: ninth onwards only completed 19 laps.

The 500cc race

Again the front row of the grid held both MV riders, Surtees and Hartle, plus the German Champion Ernst Hiller riding a BMW with a works short-stroke engine. The second row comprised Terry Shepherd, Noel McCutcheon and Derek. As with the 350s, the 500cc starting grid was determined by practice times.

When the traffic light starting system changed from red to green, Surtees made his characteristically quick getaway, followed by Hartle and Hiller. Following the three factory entries came two riders from Africa, Gary Hocking and Paddy Driver, followed by a bunch of Nortons with a BMW and Matchless mixed in with them – Hempleman, Campbell, Shepherd, Derek and Alan Trow – plus the works development Matchless G50 ridden by Australian Jack Ahearn.

By the seventh lap, Surtees was a mile ahead of Hartle, who was almost the same distance ahead of Hiller. But Derek had fought his way through the field (after another poor start) and was right on the BMW rider's tail, with Bob

Anderson fifth. Then came Hocking, Shepherd, Driver and the BMWs of Dale and Duke.

Next lap Derek moved his private Norton ahead of Hiller to make the order MV, MV, Norton, BMW – a brilliant performance.

With a third of the race gone the order was Surtees, Hartle, Minter, Hiller, Anderson, Hocking, Shepherd, Duke (also on a works BMW), Dale, Driver, Hempleman and McCutcheon.

Duke went out (brake trouble), and the race settled down for the closing laps with Anderson and Hiller still fighting it out behind the leading three.

With storm clouds gathering, darkening the sky, Surtees began his last lap, overtaking fifth man Hocking in front of the grandstand opposite the pits. Unlucky Bob Anderson ran out of fuel to be denied a finish.

500cc Dutch TT – 27 laps – 129.18 miles

1st	J. Surtees (MV Agusta)
2nd	J. Hartle (MV Agusta)
3rd	D.W. Minter (Norton)
4th	E. Hiller (BMW)
5th	R.H. Dale (BMW)
6th	G. Hocking (Norton)
7th	N. McCutcheon (Norton)
8th	J. Hempleman (Norton)
9th	T. Phillis (Norton)
10th	R.N. Brown (Norton)

Note: fifth onwards only completed 26 laps.

The Belgian Grand Prix

The Belgian Grand Prix, staged over the 8.77-mile Spa Francorchamps circuit in the heavily wooded eastern part of the country near the German border known as the Ardennes, has always had what is best described as its own weather systems. And this was certainly the case for the 1958 races, with one newspaper commenting 'the traditional torrential rain showers during practising for the Belgian Grand Prix here have once again seriously interfered with training and have made it extremely difficult for riders to check carburation and gearing and to learn the circuit.'

But as the riders came out for the 11-lap 350cc race on Sunday 6 July, the heavy cloud had given way to sunshine and conditions were described as 'ideal for racing' (*MCN*).

Fastest in training had, as was to be expected, been the two MV riders Hartle and Surtees, then Geoff Duke, Dave Chadwick (both Nortons), plus

Franta Stastny, on a works Jawa twin, to complete the front row. The second row comprised Campbell, Derek, Gustav Havel (on the second Jawa), Brett and Dale.

From the start Surtees led, closely followed by Stastny. But at Stavelot (about halfway round) the order was Surtees, Hartle, Duke and Brett.

Coming past the pits to complete the first lap Surtees was well in the lead, but second man Hartle had the 1957 350cc World Champion Keith Campbell right on his heels, and Keith was tailed by Duke, Brett, Chadwick, Hempleman, Derek and Taveri (all besides Hartle on Nortons).

By the completion of the fourth lap Campbell was still behind the two MVs, but Derek had moved ahead of the other riders. And by the eighth lap Derek led Campbell, Duke and Chadwick, but the four Norton riders were all close together.

And it was Derek who still had his nose in front as the quartet of Norton riders began their last lap. *Motor Cycle News* described the finish thus: 'Here they come round the hairpin and it's Keith Campbell first across the line [the two MVs having also crossed it] to repeat his Dutch TT third place. Minter is on his tail fourth with Duke and Chadwick feet apart fifth and sixth – what a dice!'

Later that day Derek lined up on the front row of the 500cc race – having been fourth-fastest in practice behind the two MVs and Geoff Duke's factory BMW. But unfortunately Derek was an early retirement in the race, thus dashing hopes of another high finish.

350cc Belgian GP – 11 laps – 96.32 miles

1st	J. Surtees (MV Agusta)
2nd	J. Hartle (MV Agusta)
3rd	K.R. Campbell (Norton)
4th	D.W. Minter (Norton)
5th	G.E. Duke (Norton)
6th	D.V. Chadwick (Norton)
7th	L. Taveri (Norton)
8th	J. Brett (Norton)
9th	J. Hempleman (Norton)
10th	R.H. Dale (Norton)

Back to the short circuits
Then it was back to the British short circuit scene, with two meetings in two days at Castle Combe on Saturday 12 July and Brands Hatch the following day.

At the Combe, Mike Hailwood had entered all four solo classes (125cc Ducati, 250cc NSU, 350 and 500cc Nortons). He was out to clean up. But there was one man who could be relied upon to challenge for honours, even if he was only entered in the larger classes: Derek Minter. And so it turned out. After relatively easy victories in the Lightweight classes, Mike faced much sterner opposition in the 350 and 500cc events.

After both men had won their respective heats, the first clash between the two came in the 350cc final. Although Mike came out on top, it was a close thing, with only a machine's length separating the pair. But it was Derek who had the last say in the 500cc final. *Motor Cycle News* takes up what happened: 'dismay had come when Hailwood was left at the start and pulled the Norton across the grass – an oiled plug was the suspected fault. To Mike was left the dubious pleasure of watching Derek Minter score a runaway victory with the Norton well ahead of a second place scrap between Tony Godfrey and John Holder (Nortons).'

Next day at Brands Hatch Derek would surely have won all three classes he was entered in (250, 350 and 500cc), but after winning his heat on the REG a mechanical fault left him stranded on the line in the final. But in the 350cc Invitation Derek got his revenge from the day before by coming through from a slow start to overtake Hailwood well before the finish. In the 1000cc Invitation race Derek had an easy victory with Mike a non-starter.

British Champion – twice

Next came the British Championship meeting at the newly revised 2.275-mile Thruxton circuit, sponsored by the *Daily Herald* newspaper on August Bank Holiday Monday, with a record crowd for the Hampshire venue of over 40,000 enthusiastic spectators. And as the headline on the front page of *Motor Cycle News* boldly shouted: 'Minter Bags 2 Titles.'

Actually, had his REG not fired on only one cylinder for the first lap, Derek could have been a triple British Champion! But as it was he had to be content with fourth in the 250cc Championship race, behind Fron Purslow (NSU), Geoff Monty (GMS) and J. Hamilton (NSU).

The Swiss star Luigi Taveri was badly left at the start of the 350cc Championship race, and it was Ginger Payne who led on the first lap, closely followed by Derek, Tom Thorp, Derek Powell and Fron Purslow (all Norton mounted). Derek took over on the second lap. At the halfway stage the order was Derek, well ahead, from Thorp, Purslow, Payne, Monty and Taveri. On the 13th lap Monty's machine expired with a broken valve and was passed by Payne and Taveri, while Powell just beat Lewis and James after a race-long duel.

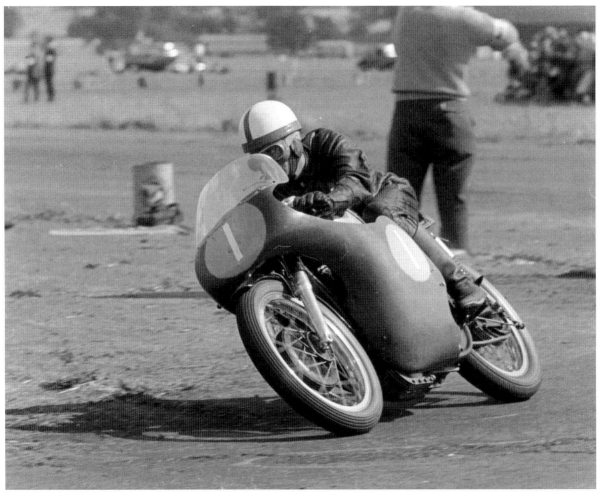

A wonderful action shot of Derek on his way to victory in the 350cc British Championship race at Thruxton on August Bank Holiday Monday 1958, on his Norton.

350cc British Championship, Thruxton – 18 laps – 40.95 miles

1st	D.W. Minter (Norton)
2nd	T. Thorp (Norton)
3rd	G. Payne (Norton)
4th	L. Taveri (Norton)
5th	F. Purslow (Norton)
6th	D. Powell (Norton)

It took Derek two laps to assume the lead in the 500cc Championship race, but once there he was never challenged, and German Champion Ernst Hiller, with a works-supported BMW, was an equally comfortable second. John Lewis came home third after finally shaking off Tony Godfrey, who had challenged him for the first 10 laps.

Derek not only set up three lap records, but also won the *Daily Herald* award for the best aggregate performance of the meeting.

After winning the 350cc British title, Derek made it a double at Thruxton when he won the 500cc Championship.

500cc British Championship, Thruxton – 18 laps – 40.95 miles

1st   D.W. Minter (Norton)
2nd   E. Hiller (BMW)
3rd   J. Lewis (Norton)
4th   A.M. Godfrey (Norton)
5th   F.A. Rutherford (Duke Norton)
6th   D. Powell (Norton)

Over to Ulster

Cyril Quantrill, writing in *Motor Cycle News* dated 13 August 1958, described the weather conditions that prevailed at the previous Saturday's Ulster GP in the following terms: 'Rain before seven, dry by eleven – indeed! Well before seven rain was splashing from an overflowing gutter outside my hotel bedroom in Belfast, but although a local weather prophet had just quoted the old adage, there is not the slightest sign of the rain relenting as an announcement is made that the start of the meeting, scheduled for 10 am, will be postponed half-an-hour. Grey, wringing wet cloud hangs low over the hill country through which the 7.49-mile Dundrod circuit runs. The green fields squelch and turn brown with mud under the tread of enthusiasts who laugh aside a soaking in order to line the banks to watch the 30th Ulster Grand Prix; and the occupants of the grandstand glance apprehensively upward at the sagging green tarpaulin "roof". Bad visibility, where the cloud level is down to road level (some 1000 feet above sea level) between Tornagrough and the hairpin is delaying the racing.'

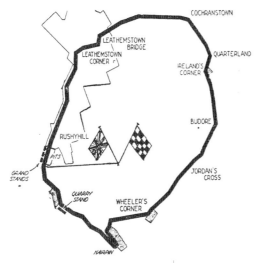

Ulster GP, Dundrod circuit.

It was certainly not a day for the faint hearted! And it was Derek Minter's initiation to the Ulster.

The 1958 Ulster Grand Prix consisted of a four-race programme – all solos (125, 250, 350 and 500cc) and thus no sidecars.

Fine drenching rain was still falling when the 500cc race, the second of the day, came to the line. There were 51 starters for the 20-lap event, including the two works MVs of Surtees and Hartle. Practice performance had put Bob McIntyre (Norton) second to Surtees and Terry Shepherd, a late entry also on a Norton, was on the front row of the grid with them. But it was the young Mike Hailwood who made the best start of the non-MV men.

At the end of the first lap the race order was Surtees and Hartle, Shepherd, Duke, McIntyre, Bob Brown, Hailwood, Ralph Rensen, Chadwick, Taveri and then Derek (11th).

At quarter-race distance Surtees and Hartle were wheel to wheel as they sped past the pits, some 40 seconds ahead of Shepherd and a full minute in front of McIntyre, who was closely followed by Duke. Taveri had taken sixth place from Hailwood, who was being chased by Brown, Derek (now ninth), Rensen, Chadwick and Hempleman. Then on the 10th lap Derek took eighth place from Hailwood.

Towards the end of the race, with the rain at last over and the roads beginning to dry, Derek went ahead of Taveri to take sixth place.

350cc Ulster GP – 20 laps – 148.32 miles

1st	J. Surtees (MV Agusta)
2nd	J. Hartle (MV Agusta)
3rd	T.S. Shepherd (Norton)
4th	G.E. Duke (Norton)
5th	R.G. McIntyre (Norton)
6th	D.W. Minter (Norton)

Save for the presence of Ernst Hiller and Dickie Dale (BMWs) and the absence of Dave Chadwick, the line-up for the 500cc race (the last of the day), again 51 riders, was similar to that of the 350cc class. Geoff Duke had the use of one of the special 93mm bore engines for his Norton, while Jack Ahearn and Jackie Wood both had single-cylinder ohc Matchless machines.

Conditions were considerably improved over what had been experienced earlier in the day, with very little rain and misty conditions only prevailing in the section approaching the hairpin.

After a tangle on the start line with three riders, the rest of the entry eventually got under way with Surtees, Hartle and McIntyre at the head of the pack. At the end of the lap these three were still in front with Shepherd and Brown battling it out for fourth, and Derek, Dale, Hiller, Jackie Wood and Rensen all in the running.

By lap 3 more clouds had rolled in, bringing yet more rain, but as the *MCN* race report revealed: 'the pace, considering the conditions, is fantastic.' By lap seven, in places around the circuit, 'visibility is down to no more than 30 yards' (*MCN*). Even so, Derek had climbed to fifth.

As the race came to a close, Derek, now minus his megaphone but riding a 'magnificent, steady race' (*MCN*) was fourth, one place in front of his boyhood hero, Geoff Duke. And even though he had not competed in all the rounds, Derek was lying fifth in the 500cc World Championships.

500cc Ulster GP – 20 laps – 148.32 miles

1st	J. Surtees (MV Agusta)
2nd	R.G. McIntyre (Norton)
3rd	J. Hartle (MV Agusta)
4th	D.W. Minter (Norton)
5th	G.E. Duke (Norton)
6th	R.H. Dale (BMW)

Note: sixth finisher onwards only completed 19 laps.

Derek still tops at Brands

Derek proved he was still tops at his local circuit when he gave a 'convincing display' (*MCN*) to win both the 350 and 1000cc Invitation races at Brands Hatch on Sunday 24 August 1958. But he was not so fortunate in the 250cc race. His REG once again gave trouble and Mike Hailwood (NSU) romped home, creating new class lap and race records into the bargain.

The weather, which had been damp and dismal earlier, had cleared by the time racing started. Mike Hailwood 'shot off the grid' (*MCN*) at the start of the 350cc race. At the end of the first lap the order was Hailwood, Laurence Flury and Derek. Slowly Derek cut down Hailwood's lead until after seven laps he was only feet behind Mike's machine. On the next lap Derek got past as they went into Paddock bend and from then on he drew slowly away to win.

350cc Experts Invitation – 15 laps – 18.6 miles

1st	D.W. Minter (Norton)
2nd	S.M.B. Hailwood (Norton)
3rd	L. Flury (AJS)
4th	B.J. Daniels (Norton)

5th   D. Craig (Norton)
6th   D.F. Shorey (Norton)

Bruce Daniels led for the first lap of the 1000cc Invitation event, but then Derek took over and in spite of rain, which was beginning to sweep across the track at this stage, he kept piling up his lead and all interest centred around the battle for second spot between Flury (Matchless) and Daniels (Norton). First Flury dropped back after taking to the grass, but he then came back and held second place until the last lap, when Daniels came through to pass him on the line. John Hartle (Norton) came fourth, but interestingly, as *MCN* described: 'P [Paul] Dunstall put in a very fine effort to bring a Norton Dominator 99 home fifth.'

The Hutchinson 100
Compared with his lowly position of 12 months before, Derek's showing in the Hutchinson 100 meeting at Silverstone on Saturday 13 September 1958 proved what incredible progress he had made between the two meetings. In the 350 and 500cc Championship races the 'Mint' put in what can only be described as incredible performances to finish runner-up in both to Bob McIntyre. This is what was said at the beginning of a front-page story in *Motor Cycle News* dated 17 September 1958: 'After one of the most thrilling and closely fought duels ever seen at Silverstone, Bob McIntyre (Norton) beat Derek Minter (Norton) by a length to win the Senior Championship race, and both share a new motorcycle lap record of 97.18mph. The old record was set up in similar circumstances when Surtees (Norton) beat Duke (Gilera) way back in 1955 and both shared the old record of 96.45mph.'

An early morning fine weather haze that later turned into perfect weather blessed the 2.9-mile Silverstone circuit on the borders of Northamptonshire and Buckinghamshire.

Besides their wheel-to-wheel battle in the 500cc class, Bob and Derek also came out top in the 350cc race, but this time the Scot was mounted on a recently acquired AJS 7R. At first Mike Hailwood was the main challenger to McIntyre, but this ended when Mike hit ignition glitches, leaving Derek a secure second, although some 100 yards astern of Bob at the end.

Again McIntyre got a flyer of a start in the 500cc event, but this time he could not get away from Derek – even though the latter had made a 'shocking' (*MCN*) start from the back row of the grid. This was how *Motor Cycle News* reported the action: 'Lap three and Minter was second and now the heat was on! Riding absolutely on the limit with both wheels sliding across the tarmac

Silverstone.

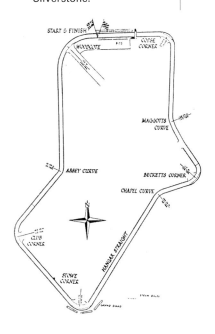

Dan Shorey

Dan Shorey probably rode in as many races with Derek Minter as any other rider. And Dan, like Derek, rode a considerable variety of machinery, both British and foreign.

Born in Banbury, Oxfordshire, on 22 April 1938, Dan left school in July 1954 to work with his father Bert at North Bar Garage, Banbury, where the family had agencies for Triumph, AJS, James and Reliant three-wheelers. As Dan himself explained: 'We opened seven days a week until 10pm serving petrol and repairing bikes, cars and commercial vehicles.'

Dan's father was a pre and post-war road racer and grass tracker, who won the famous Red Marley hill climb in 1938 on a 250 Rudge. Dan was interested 'in bikes from an early age because my father was a mechanic and racer.' His first competitive riding came during 1954, when he took in local scrambles and grass track events. The bikes were a 197cc Villiers-powered Norman and the 250cc Rudge his father had used to win Red Marley. When Dan became a successful road racer he continued to ride in trials during the winter months, either solo or sidecar, the latter on a 500cc Ariel outfit, until the late 1960s.

His first race was a one-hour MCC High Speed Trial at Silverstone in 1955 on a Triumph Tiger Cub, where he finished first in the 200cc class. His first pukka road race came at Mallory Park the following year, on a 250cc Pike Rudge, where he came home in a respectable midfield position. During the close season of 1956–57, Dan purchased a 250cc Norvel during petrol rationing caused by the Suez Crisis.

During 1957 Dan scored second, third and fourth position, but no victories, on the Norvel. His first Manx Norton, a 1955 three-fifty, was purchased from Kings of Oxford in 1958. The same year Dan scored the first victory of his career on the Norvel at Alton Towers. Other results in

Dan Shorey racing his three-fifty Manx Norton at Snetterton, summer 1966.

1958 included winning the 'Reg Cross' race at Cadwell Park on his three-fifty Norton, the first prize being a new pair of leathers (manufactured by Reg Cross in Louth).

Between 1957 and 1958 Dan worked at the Triumph factory at Meriden, near Coventry. In June 1958 he won the Thruxton 500-mile race on a Triumph Tiger 110, partnered by Mike Hailwood (Mike and Dan were working together at Triumph at the time). In 1958 he also purchased an ex-Hailwood 125cc MV Agusta. And for the 1959 season he acquired a brand new three-fifty Manx and an ex-Jack Brett, ex-Slazenger five-hundred Manx. Then in August 1959 he purchased an ex-Hailwood 125cc Ducati Grand Prix.

Dan was presented with the Pinard Prize (for the best all-round rider under 21 years of age). He received the award at the Banbury Norbac MCC annual dinner in mid-January 1960. The official reason given was that: 'the trophy is awarded to a rider up to 21 years of age, who is deemed by the trustees to have made the year's most meritorious achievement in the field of motorcycle sport.' Dan had raced at no fewer than 32 meetings during 1959 and had finished no lower than fifth in 72 individual races and was also runner-up in the 1959 ACU Road Racing Star series.

Hailing from Banbury, Oxfordshire, Dan Shorey had many great battles with Derek Minter over the years and they remain good friends today.

During his career Dan held lap records at many circuits, including Scarborough, Cadwell Park, Biggin Hill and no less than four lap records in a single day at Aberdare Park (125cc Bultaco, 250cc NSU, 350cc Norton, 500cc Norton) in 1961. Earlier in 1961 he had become a works rider for the Spanish Bultaco concern and in 1962 scored several top-six finishes in the 250cc World Championship series on a 196cc air-cooled machine. He also won the 125cc ACU Star in 1961, and the 125 and 250cc titles in 1962.

During 1962 and 1963 Dan was sponsored by the leading AMC entrants, Arter Brothers of Barham, Kent, riding 350cc AJS and 500cc Matchless machines. But it was back to his own Manx Nortons for 1964, with some engines prepared by Ray Petty from September that year. For the remainder of the time Dan used Manx Nortons (which was to be to the end of 1968).

Two notable highlights (among many) while riding Petty-tuned Nortons were winning the 500cc Austrian Grand Prix (1965) and finishing runner-up (to Giacomo Agostini) in the 500cc West German Grand Prix at the Nürburgring.

In 1969, in his final season, Dan purchased a three-fifty Drixton Aermacchi and a five hundred Seeley Matchless. The last meeting of a long and successful career came at Oulton Park later in 1969, when he practised but was unable to race due to a trapped nerve in his shoulder. Then in 1987 Dan rode his own Ray Petty-prepared five hundred Manx in the classic race at the Dutch TT at Assen – but unfortunately the big-end went during the race. He also took part in various parades from the mid-1980s onwards, using either of his own 350 and 500cc Norton machines, and is still a regular visitor to CRMC events today.

the British Champion relentlessly closed the gap. On the fourth lap Mac led by 100 yards, fifth 70, sixth 50, seventh 30, eighth 20, ninth 10 and after 10 laps Minter was right up with Mac. This was racing at its best, with both men using every ounce of power and every inch of road. On the 12th lap Minter got past but Mac was back in front on the 13th. On the last lap Minter made his final effort, but McIntyre's years of experience told and he crossed the line a length ahead.' What a race!

Senior Championship, Silverstone – 17 laps – 49.64 miles

1st	R. McIntyre (Norton)
2nd	D.W. Minter (Norton)
3rd	A. Trow (Norton)
4th	A.M. Godfrey (Norton)
5th	E.J. Washer (Norton)
6th	J.H.L. Lewis (Norton)
7th	B.J. Daniels (Norton)
8th	J.R. Holder (Norton)
9th	R. Fay (Norton)
10th	F.G. Perris (Norton)

Tony Godfrey, the 1958 500cc ACU Star winner.

Four races, four wins

Among a galaxy of stars from both hemispheres it was Derek, with four wins in four rides, who shone the brightest at Brands Hatch on Sunday 21 September. In the 250cc race Derek was back riding the REG. And for eight laps Dave Chadwick, on the Ron Harris ex-works 203 dohc MV single, made the running, but Derek on the Bob Geeson bike (which, although sounding healthy for a change, was emitting more smoke than was desirable), slip-streamed him until on lap nine he passed for what *Motor Cycle News* described as a 'neat' victory.

With the 350cc Invitation event came the first of three Minter versus Trow battles. From a good start Alan Trow (Norton) led from Harry Hinton Jnr (AJS), with Derek further back after his by now customary poor start. But in two laps Derek had taken Hinton and by lap six was in front of Trow.

Again it was Trow who led the 1000cc Invitation event, with Derek fifth behind Hinton at the end of lap one. Hinton was giving the new G50 Matchless production racer its Brands debut. Hinton fell off, breaking his collarbone, on the fifth lap, while Derek had closed with the leaders and by lap eight passed Trow at Paddock Hill, but it was a fighting Trow who led from Druids. Two laps from the end and Derek passed Trow again, this time making the move permanent.

The final race of the day, for the giant Mockford Trophy, brought a repetition of the two previous duels with Alan Trow. Again the latter stormed into an early lead, but after what *MCN* described as a 'dead heat finish of the eighth lap', Derek went through as they descended Paddock Hill, going on to score his fourth victory of the day.

Aintree

With practice on Friday 25 September and racing the following day, north-west race-goers were treated to two days of excellent sport and an entry to grace any continental GP. For a start John Surtees and John Hartle brought their works four-cylinder MVs to the start line for both the 350 and 500cc races. And with riders such as Bob McIntyre, Alastair King, Mike Hailwood, Gary Hocking and the like it seemed Derek would have to be at his very best to get a top-six finish. Actually, he gained two superb thirds. In the 15-lap 350cc race Surtees and McIntyre were the ones who beat him – but in the 500cc class it was only the two MVs. And

Aintree.

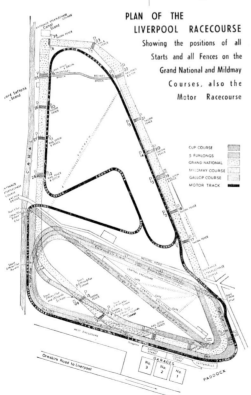

PLAN OF THE
LIVERPOOL RACECOURSE
Showing the positions of all
Starts and all Fences on the
Grand National and Mildmay
Courses, also the
Motor Racecourse

On Saturday 25 September 1958 all the top stars were at Aintree near Liverpool. Derek is shown on his three-fifty Norton during the 102-mile Aintree Century solo handicap race.

in usual Minter fashion he had to come through the field to do it, with *Motor Cycle News* taking up the story: 'On the last lap Minter, who had been gaining ground, put in a great effort to catch McIntyre and, taking the Scot unawares, snatched third place on the line.'

The 102-mile Aintree Century solo class handicap was a far less interesting affair, which soon settled down into a 'rather difficult to follow' (*MCN*) battle between class leaders Alastair King (250cc NSU), Derek (350cc Norton) and John Surtees (500cc MV). The previous year's winner Tommy Robb (NSU) went out with a seized engine.

500cc Aintree – 15 laps – 45 miles
1st   J. Surtees (MV Agusta)
2nd   J. Hartle (MV Agusta)
3rd   D.W. Minter (Norton)
4th   R.G. McIntyre (Norton)

5th	A. Trow (Norton)
6th	S.M.B. Hailwood (Norton)
7th	G. Hocking (Norton)
8th	P. Driver (Norton)
9th	R.H.F. Anderson (Norton)
10th	W.A. Holmes (Norton)

The following day at Mallory Park (not one of Derek's favourite circuits), Derek was out of tune and had a miserable day at the Race of the Year meeting watched by some 35,000 spectators. The main 40-lap, 54-mile Mallory Park Challenge Trophy race went, as expected, to the 1958 500cc World Champion John Surtees on his works four-cylinder MV. Derek pointed out to the author that he never liked Mallory and considered the Devil's Elbow section to be 'dangerous'.

Minter beats Surtees

Then came Derek's final meeting of the 1958 season, and with it his biggest victory to date. *Motor Cycle News* dated 15 October carried the story on its front page: 'In a momentous 1958 racing finale at Brands Hatch on Sunday, Norton rider Derek Minter became the first [and only] man this season to beat World Champion John Surtees on the howling Italian four cylinder MV.'

Besides winning both 1000cc races, Derek also stormed from 16th position at the end of the first lap to finish second behind Surtees in the 20-lap 350cc event, after a spectacular first-corner spill involving Frank Perris, Alan Trow, Mike Hailwood, George Catlin and Derek himself. Fortunately, none of the riders involved was seriously injured.

Once again, Derek's REG was a non-starter in the 250cc race – lying silent in the paddock after blowing up during practice. But his Norton performances more than made up for this single glitch.

Although the day had begun with blue skies and morning sunshine – which had encouraged vast crowds to attend – plus of course the chance to see the MVs, rain had moistened the circuit during the 350cc event. It fell more heavily later in the programme.

Although Derek's first 1000cc victory over Surtees benefitted from problems with the latter's MV, in which he lost a lap due to a plug change, the second – what *MCN* referred to as 'the last epic race' – the MV World Champion was 'decisively defeated by Derek Minter on his Lancefield Norton' (*MCN*).

In fact, the only rider not lapped by Surtees and Derek was John Holder (Norton). At the end, everyone agreed that the crowd had had its money's worth, and Minter's win could not have been more popular.

1000cc Brands Hatch – 20 laps – 24.8 miles

1st	D.W. Minter (Norton)
2nd	J. Surtees (MV Agusta)
3rd	J.R. Holder (Norton)
4th	J.L. Payne (Norton)
5th	L. Flury (Norton)
6th	P. Dunstall (Norton)

Note: riders from fourth onwards only completed 19 laps.

A fantastic season

And so came to an end a fantastically successful season, which had begun with victory on the REG in the 250cc race at Brands Hatch on Good Friday, 4 April, and ended some 6½ months later with the famous win over the 500cc World Champion at Brands as detailed above. In all, Derek scored 24 victories, won the 350 and 500cc British Championships, finished fifth in the 500cc World Championships and eighth in the 350cc class. No doubt he would have won the 350 and 500cc ACU Road Racing Star titles if he had competed in more rounds. As it was, in the latter series he was exceedingly unlucky, missing the 500cc star by one point, the 350cc by two.

In the very first *Motor Cycle News* 'Man of the Year' poll, Derek came fourth behind the winner John Surtees, Mike Hailwood and Bob McIntyre, but in front of Geoff Duke who was fifth.

The following is an important extract from Derek's autobiography *Racing All My Life*, published in 1965, and shows how he viewed the 1958 season in retrospect:

When I entered the TT in 1958 I had less than £100 left in my Post Office savings account. Perhaps you may think £100 a lot of money, but it isn't really, and wasn't then either. For now I was riding Nortons of my own, and Norton spares are expensive. To realise just how close to the wind I was sailing, financially, you need only to consider that I required only one blow-up and the bulk of that £100 would have gone in an instant. It would take all of that to get the bicycle up to competition standard again.

He continued:

It was 1958, the same year and my first as a professional, that I became the uncrowned 'King of Brands'. In some ways a spectacular rise, but as always, with people who allegedly 'arrive' overnight, a much more dogged step-by-step climb than many fans realised. But certainly, 1958 was a good year. I came fourth in the Junior TT and collected good money to boost my savings. I raced as often as I could throughout the season and increased my financial status to a much healthier level. At Thruxton I clinched the British Championship and won the 350 and 500cc races that day at record speeds, establishing lap records too. With these successes under my belt, and a few more £'s in the bank, I finished the 1958 season feeling well pleased with my performances and beginning to enjoy the feeling of being one of the few professional riders in Britain. But more than all this perhaps, I was now really enjoying racing as only a professional can…knowing that what he enjoys doing most of all in life is earning him his living.

It is also worth pointing out that 1958 was the year when the 'King of Brands' tag came about. This was thanks to commentator Murray Walker, who broadcast the title over the Brands public address system. But as Derek was to recall later:

> while I loved him for it at the time, I have since, on more occasions than I would want to count, cursed him for it also. Make a man a king and there are plenty of people itching to take away his crown. It's only natural that competitors try to beat me, with a keener sense of competition and 'occasion' at Brands than at other tracks, and however relaxed I look I'm always more tense there than at Snetterton, for instance. It's a tough job staying a King in the hotly contested world of motorcycle racing.

1959 arrives

With the arrival of 1959 came not only a new year, but a new set of challenges.

Derek pictured at Silverstone on his 350cc Lancefield-tuned Norton in 1959.

After a winter's rest – and trials riding on his Norman – Derek was 'keen for the new season to begin.' As he recalls, he was 'still flushed by my successes of 1958.'

The new season started 'disappointingly', as Derek was to describe it later, at Brands Hatch in his first meeting. At first everything appeared fine – except the weather that is.

Derek's main opposition in the initial outing was Bob McIntyre in the 20-lap 350cc race, which 'began in vile drizzle and finished in blinding rain' (*The Motor Cycle*). For the first two laps McIntyre led by a length or two, before Derek exploited his own superior track knowledge and took over. The next 12 laps saw no change and it seemed just a matter of the laps unwinding before the 'Mint' was home. However, by then the track surface was really treacherous and riders began to tumble 'like ninepins' (*The Motor Cycle*). Among the leaders Derek was first off – at Clearways – then McIntyre lost his front end on Druids Hill Bend, with the race victory eventually going to Alastair King.

Although Derek did win the first 1000cc race, it was to be his only victory of the day. He finished runner-up to McIntyre in the second 1000cc event and third in the 250cc on the REG.

Things did not improve much at Oulton Park three days later on Easter Monday, or at Silverstone almost three weeks later on Saturday 18 April. At the latter his best result was another third on the REG, but a crash on the smaller Norton and a sixth in the 500cc event.

The following day it was back to Brands Hatch, where Derek scored a double victory in the two 1000cc races he contested, beating John Lewis in the first and Ginger Payne in the second. He also finished runner-up on the REG in the 250cc class to Dave Chadwick (203cc MV). His 350cc Norton was still out of action due to the previous day's crash damage. Also noteworthy was his first-ever outing on Joe Ehrlich's EMC 125 two-stroke single (in the 200cc race, in which he was third behind Chadwick and Ken Whorlow – both on MV175s).

Aqua Sport!

'Aqua Sport!' said *The Motor Cycle*'s race report headline for the Castle Combe road races of Saturday 25 April 1959. This was in response to what was referred to as 'probably one of the wettest race meetings on record.'

After finishing runner-up to Mike Hailwood in the 125cc event on the EMC, Derek beat Mike in both the 350 and 500cc races – and also set the fastest laps in both, with speeds of 72.46 and 71.83mph respectively.

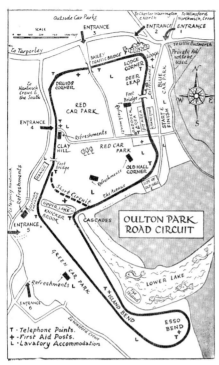

Oulton Park.

Glorious weather at Oulton

In sharp contrast to the rain-sodden Castle Combe meeting, Derek's next outing three weeks later at Oulton Park was held in glorious weather. The main event of the day was the Les Graham Trophy Race over 19 laps (52.5 miles), and for the first time the event was for a specially invited field of 350cc riders from an entry of 280 competitors.

By the start of the second lap the Scottish pairing of Bob McIntyre (AJS) and Alastair King (Norton) led the field, followed by the Nortons of Ray Fay, Bill Smith, Gordon Bell and Derek, while Alan Shepherd's factory AJS was holding off Geoff Duke (Norton).

By lap 10, King and McIntyre were over 10 seconds ahead and it seemed highly unlikely that anyone would challenge them. To their rear Derek had by now moved up to third.

The £100 first prize seemed to swing 'like a pendulum' (*The Motor Cycle*) between the two Scotsmen. But as the laps unfolded, Derek was seen to be eroding their lead. *The Motor Cycle* report takes over: 'Minter was gaining ground. And how! The 1958 double British Champion slammed in a searing record lap of 85.69mph to send King's old record of 84.09mph reeling.'

With two laps to go Derek was right on McIntyre's rear wheel. But then Bob's AJS began to slow with engine trouble. This left Derek and Alastair a minute up on the rest of the pack. *The Motor Cycle* again: 'Taking almost impossible lines on the bends to get past slower men, King and Minter thundered on. As the chequered flag flashed down King was still in front, but it was a near thing: Minter was only half a second behind.' And the big question was left unanswered. If Derek had made his effort earlier could he, not Alastair, have won the race?

Earlier, after crashing out of the 350cc race on the REG, Derek had finished third (behind King and Alan Shepherd) in the 350cc event.

Mixed fortunes at Blandford

McIntyre, King and Derek clashed again two days later on Whit Monday, 18 May, at Blandford, Dorset, the scene of the Blackmore Vale Club's international road race meeting.

Undoubtedly the finest race of the programme was the 500cc final. Although Derek had set the fastest laps in his four previous races (including heats), he had managed only one victory. On each occasion Derek had made a poor start and at the end of the first lap of the 500cc final he was placed no higher than eighth. But after what was described by *The Motor Cycle* as 'a fantastic second lap' he came round almost sitting on the tails of the first and

second men, Alastair King and Bob McIntyre. On the fifth lap all three were nose-to-tail, Bob in front; next time it was Derek. And although Bob tried 'very hard he could not hold the flying Minter.' Derek also set the fastest lap – a new outright course lap record of 92.21mph.

In the 250cc event Derek, riding the REG, chased Tommy Robb (GMS) so hard that he not only put up the fastest lap, but also broke Fergus Anderson's six-year-old class record. However, fate then took a hand and Derek coasted over the line into second place when the magneto packed up on the last lap.

Hard luck in the Isle of Man

After his excellent results in the 1958 TT series Derek was hoping for even better in 1959; but he was to be bitterly disappointed, with his only finish in three races an eighth in the Junior. His official numbers for the TT in this year were: 250cc, 19; 350cc, 12; 500cc, 11.

In his other two events the REG retired with a mechanical problem early in its race, while Derek, in describing his retirement in the 500cc class, said 'there was so much rain that I just couldn't see where I was going, and I packed it in before it was too late.'

The first works ride

Then came the Dutch TT at Assen, and Derek's first full works rides – on an MZ in the 125cc and a Moto Morini in the 250cc. These and other early rides for foreign factories are described in chapter four. It was perhaps fortunate that these

After his excellent 1958 TT results Derek was hoping for even better in 1959, but he was to be bitterly disappointed with his only finish in three races being an eighth in the Junior.

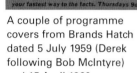

A couple of programme covers from Brands Hatch dated 5 July 1959 (Derek following Bob McIntyre) and 15 April 1960.

rides came along as they did because Derek's only decent finishes in both the Dutch TT and the Belgian GP, which followed eight days later, came in the smaller classes: Dutch TT: fifth 125cc MZ; third 250cc Morini, Belgian GP: fourth 125cc MZ.

As for his Norton results, these make dismal reading – certainly when compared with 12 months earlier. Dutch TT: no start in 350cc; retired 500cc, Belgian GP: 10th in both 350 and 500cc races.

Then it was back to Derek's 'bread-and-butter' – the British short circuits, with Castle Combe on 11 July and Snetterton on 19 July. His best results were a win in the 350cc race at the Combe (and fastest lap), while at Snetterton he won both the 350 and 500cc races and set the fastest lap in each.

A set-back at Oulton

Derek suffered a major set-back in his plans to defend the British Championship titles won the previous year, when early in the programme at Oulton Park (replacing Thruxton as the venue) he was involved in an unfortunate accident in the 250cc race that opened the day's racing. It happened like this: Derek sustained concussion when thrown from the REG twin after colliding with Ken Martin's NSU, which had seized and tossed its pilot. Ken suffered a broken ankle.

Back in action

Both Derek and the REG were back in action just under three weeks later at the BMCRC Hutchinson 100 Silverstone meeting.

As *The Motor Cycle* reported, 'Minter, riding one of Bob Geeson's two REG twins, was once more making up ground lost at the start but he had not got the speed to get higher than sixth.'

Derek's best performance at Silverstone came in the BMCRC 1000cc Championship event, held over 15 laps. After his usual less-than-perfect start, Derek finally caught up the second and third-place men, Alastair King and Mike Hailwood. King accepted the challenge and swapped places 'furiously' (*MCN*), with Minter, while Hailwood, trying to stay with them, got into a monumental slide at Copse Corner and thereafter eased the pace for the final two laps. Not so Alastair and Derek, who fought it out to the finish, with the latter getting the better of it by a length or two to finish runner-up behind the winner Bob McIntyre. Derek also set the fastest lap with a speed of 97.35mph.

Minter the Master at Brands

The Motor Cycle dated 27 August 1959 carried the headline: 'Minter the Master at Brands. Famous Kent Idol Supreme in Main Races.' The report continued: 'Convincing wins rarely provide the most exciting racing and the

Bob McIntyre

Robert Macgregor (Bob) McIntyre was born on 28 November 1928 in Scotstoun, a suburb of Glasgow. His father had worked as a riveter, building ships on the shores of the River Clyde. Bob's first job was in a large motor garage near his home and his first motorcycle was a 16H Norton of 1931 vintage. After completing his national service, the young McIntyre returned home and purchased an Ariel Red Hunter, and it was upon this bike that he began his competitive career at a scramble event at Auchterarder, near Perth. After competing in off-road events for some months and getting hooked on motorcycles, Bob found a job with Glasgow dealers Valenti Brothers. His work involved servicing and repairing touring bikes – the firm having little connection with the sport at that time. After watching his first road race at Beveridge Park, Kirkcaldy, Bob borrowed a friend's 350 BSA Gold Star and entered his first race at Ballado. Riding pillion to the airfield circuit on the bike, they then removed the silencer and lights. His rivals were mounted on pukka racing bikes, including KTT Velocettes, AJS 7Rs and Manx Nortons, but the track was covered in loose gravel and Bob's scrambling experience came to the fore. The result was three wins in four races – and the only reason Bob did not win the fourth race as well was because he fell off.

At that time, 1950–51, there was very little trade support for racing in Scotland. However, in 1952 Bob was asked to ride for Troon, Ayrshire, dealers Cooper Brothers in the Junior Clubman's TT in the Isle of Man on a ZB32 Gold Star. As Bob was later to recall, 'that race made me'. He finished runner-up behind the winner Eric Houseley and set the fastest lap (a new class record) at 80.09mph. Not only this, but a couple of days later he finished second in the Senior Clubman's on the same bike. That September he returned to the island, this time to ride an AJS 7R in the Junior Manx Grand Prix. Bob not only won but, again riding the same

Bob McIntyre at Oulton
Park in 1960; his mechanic
'Pim' Fleming is in the
white overalls.

machine, finished runner-up in the Senior! From then on he mixed it with
the big boys and, after a spell working for London-based AMC (Associated
Motor Cycles – the makers of AJS and Matchless), began a highly
successful spell with tuner Joe Potts in Bellshill, Glasgow. Besides a
famous 250cc Manx, Bob also rode 350 and 500cc Manx models for the
Potts stable, as did his close friend Alastair King.

By the end of 1956, the McIntyre reputation had become international.
The result was that when Geoff Duke was injured at the beginning of 1957,
Bob effectively replaced him as Gilera's team leader. The Scot proved his
worth by scoring a famous double TT victory in the Jubilee races that year.
He also broke the one-hour speed record (on a 350cc Gilera) at Monza later
that year, after Gilera quit GP racing. In fact, when Mike Hailwood finally
bettered Bob's hour record at Daytona in February 1964 it caused
considerable controversy – even Mike saying that Bob's achievement in
setting up his record on the bumpy Monza speed bowl in the autumn of
1957 had been 'an incredible feat of endurance and guts'.

Later Bob rode works bikes for the likes of Bianchi and Honda, but it
was on the British short circuits that he continued to make his mark. And
it was during this period of the late 1950s and early 1960s that he was to
duel with Derek Minter on many occasions, and in the process they
became good friends.

Then came that fateful day at Oulton Park in August 1962, when, riding
his Joe Potts-tuned 499cc Norton, Bob crashed heavily in torrential rain,
receiving serious injuries from which he was to die nine days later. *The
Motor Cycle* dated 23 August 1962 carried the following tribute: 'though
we mourn, we can be proud that the sport he graced and those who were
privileged to enjoy his friendship are richer for his impact.' It continued: 'a
life of adventure was as compulsive to Bob as flying is to a bird. Challenge
and conquest were food and drink to his spirit.'

meeting at Brands Hatch on Sunday was no exception. Under a cloudless sky and burning sun Derek Minter (Nortons) stole the show in both the main races of the day, well meriting his title of uncrowned King of Brands Hatch.' Not that there was a lack of rivals, including the likes of Alan Trow, Ginger Payne, Dan Shorey and Bruce Daniels to name but four.

At first it seemed as though Trow (Norton) would be a close contender, for in the 350cc race he roared away well ahead of the pack. But his glory was short-lived, and the third lap saw Derek streak to the front and on the seventh circuit Trow's engine went sick and he coasted in to retire. For the remaining 13 laps Derek continued to increase his lead with Shorey, Michael O'Rourke and Payne (the latter AJS-mounted) widely spread out behind him.

A similar pattern emerged in the 1000cc race. Here, once again, Trow took the initiative, but Derek was in the lead by the third lap 'going like lightning' (*The Motor Cycle*). Behind him both Trow and Dan Shorey were relegated to the sidelines with engine trouble, leaving Ginger Payne (out on a newly acquired Matchless G50), G.C. Young and Bruce Daniels to fight it out for the runner-up berth. Meanwhile Derek was moving ever further ahead. By the time he had completed the 20-lap race distance, Derek had lapped all save Payne and Daniels.

After his Brands triumphs, Derek's next port of call was Monza in Italy, the scene of the Italian Grand Prix. Here he rode a works single-cylinder Moto Morini 250 and works MZ 125. Suffice to say he finished fourth in both races, as the full story of his efforts are contained in the next chapter.

Back to Brands

After his Italian trip, it was back to Brands for more action on his local circuit. The following is how the 24 September 1959 issue of The *Motor Cycle* began its report: 'Battle of Britain Sunday commemorated the RAF's epic struggle for supremacy 19 years ago. This year, as though to awaken memories of that "finest hour", the roar of warring machinery again echoed over Kent's sunlight fields. The noise came from Brands Hatch where a galaxy of road racing stars gave a large crowd a thrilling afternoon.'

Derek's first outing was in the 350cc Experts event. And the competition was hot to say the least, as ranged against Derek was a star-studded field which included Bob Anderson, Jim Redman, Paddy Driver and Ginger Payne (Norton), Gary Hocking on a Dearden-prepared Norton and Dickie Dale (AJS).

In typical Minter fashion he was well down the field at the start, but had deprived Ginger Payne of fourth spot as they began their second lap. *The Motor Cycle* takes up the story: 'Minter went on. His knowledge of the course took him into the lead at the end of the third lap and once in front he couldn't be caught.'

Then Derek was forced to sit out the 250cc race when his REG would not start on the line.

However, he soon had the opportunity of proving he was back to his very best. After starting badly in the main race of the day, the 1000cc Experts, Derek lay a lowly 15th at the end of the first lap. And as *The Motor Cycle* pointed out: 'there followed an unequalled display of riding. Bruce Daniels (Norton) led for two laps – until Payne (Norton) levered his way past. Then Anderson shot into the lead, but by that time Minter was within striking distance and the seventh lap saw him draw ahead. Anderson and Payne were bitterly engaged and throughout the field positions changed every few yards, but to no avail: Minter again won.'

Frustration at Aintree

Derek was up in the north west of England, at Aintree, on Saturday 26 September 1959. After finishing runner-up to Bob McIntyre in both the 350 and 500cc events, he suffered frustration when it came to the main race of the day, the Aintree Century. On this occasion it was an Invitation race for the fastest 20 riders from the 350 and 500cc classes and for the best 10 two-fifties. It was run over 34 laps (102 miles) of the 3-mile circuit and all riders set off together. There was no handicap: instead there were class awards and prizes of 100, 50 and 40 guineas respectively for the first three men home.

Controversially, Derek, together with Jim Redman, came to the start, but was not able to compete. An official stated that they had been invited to ride on their 500cc machines, but they had both come from the paddock with their three-fifties. In the author's view this was officialdom for officialdom's sake. Certainly neither the spectators nor the two riders received justice.

Biggin Hill – a famous World War Two RAF fighter base – was the setting for a road race meeting on Sunday 4 October 1959. Derek only rode Joe Ehrlich's 125cc EMC, finishing ninth in the 200cc class and 16th in the 250cc on the same machine.

The reason why he did not ride his Nortons, in Derek's own words, was 'I was told by Steve Lancefield that if I damaged the engines at Biggin Hill, he could not get them done for the final meeting at Brands Hatch.'

More Brands successes

A week later came the season's finale at Brands Hatch on 11 October. This had attracted a superb entry including Bob McIntyre, Bob Anderson, Mike Hailwood, Dickie Dale, Paddy Driver and Jim Redman, plus many of the Brands regulars including Derek.

After finishing runner-up to Dan Shorey (Ducati) in the 200cc races on the EMC, Derek's next race was the 350cc event over 15 laps. This was described as 'a wonderful clash' (*The Motor Cycle*). To start with Hailwood led, then McIntyre. But soon Derek was leading and 'going like a jet' (*The Motor Cycle*). At the front these three riders 'sliced' their way through slower riders whom they were already lapping (by lap 6). But first McIntyre retired to the paddock (nursing an aching right wrist, a memento of a fall at Scarborough three weeks earlier) and, in spite of some 'ferocious efforts' by Hailwood, Derek went on to victory. He also set the fastest lap at 74.15mph.

Hailwood got his revenge in the 500cc event, when Derek stepped off at Clearways on the second lap.

As riders came to the line for the Invitation Race, a fine drizzle began to fall and eventually it gave way to heavy rain. The following is an extract from *The Motor Cycle* race report of what followed: 'Whatever hope anyone may have entertained of catching Minter on a dry track was certainly dispelled on a treacherously wet surface. Riding with incredible élan, Minter built up a tremendous lead and won as he pleased, in the process gaining sufficient points to enable him to tie with Bill Boddice (Sidecar) for the Brands Hatch Aggregate Shield, awarded on points over the season's meetings.'

Dixon's Pen Portrait

What *The Motor Cycle* journalist David Dixon described as a 'Pen Portrait' of Derek was published in the magazine's 3 December 1959 issue. An interesting snippet of information to emerge from Dixon's piece was that 'although he enjoys riding lightweights, except around the Clypse circuit [the 10.79-mile course in the Isle of Man, which at the time was used for 125, 250 and sidecar TTs], which he dislikes, he derives more satisfaction from bigger models.'

Certainly when asked what his future plans were, Derek did not reveal very much, simply saying 'they are not unconnected with Nortons, Lancefield and Hallets of Canterbury – my present sponsors.'

But what the David Dixon article did prove was that by now Derek had become firmly established as a fixture in the racing establishment and thus worthy of interest by the press.

1960

And so into 1960 and the start of not only a new year, but also a new decade. What would this bring for Mr Minter? Certainly motorcycling in Great Britain had never been more popular, with sales of new motorcycles, scooters and mopeds reaching record levels, with around 350,000 finding customers during 1959.

When the 1960 racing calendar was published it was noticed that the Dutch TT and Thruxton 500-mile race were on the same date. Derek had

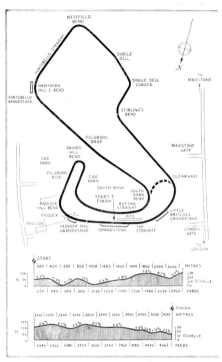

Brands Hatch 2.7-mile circuit.

anticipated doing both, but had to forgo Thruxton in favour of the Dutch (a favourite of his). He voiced concern about having his machines ready for Holland only eight days after the Senior TT. Derek also pointed out to Charlie Rous of *Motor Cycle News* that the international event at Blandford on Whit Monday occurred during the TT practice period.

Changes to the Brands circuit

Another talking point at the beginning of 1960 was that approval had been granted by the Kent County Council for an extension to the Brands Hatch road racing circuit. The extension, on which work was to start immediately, was one that John Hall, managing director of Brands Hatch Stadium Ltd, had been ready to put into action for some six years. Utilising the wooded ground through which the existing scrambles circuit ran, it would produce an international course measuring some 2.7 miles in length, while leaving the present circuit intact for alternative use. The first motorcycle meeting on the newly extended long course was scheduled for mid-July that year.

Tyre testing with Dunlop

Like other top riders, Derek was often to be seen testing, mainly at Brands Hatch, so in early January 1960 he was engaged on tyre testing with Dunlop. *Motor Cycle News* commented: 'the day was far from perfect, so was the course, there being damp patches all the way round the circuit, but this did not prevent Derek from putting in consistent laps of 63 seconds on this 1958 Norton – minus streamlining.'

Derek had also just taken delivery of a new Bedford van to which he had had various extras fitted, the most significant being an overdrive.

Less than a month after his Brands tyre testing session for Dunlop, Derek was at Silverstone testing Avons. Recalling his last ride on the circuit back in September 1959 and the fact that he became 'unseated' at Becketts Corner, Derek negotiated this point quite slowly on his first exploratory lap. He commented: 'Just as well too, because the corner now is entirely different – the apex of the turn has been altered so that it now closely follows that used for car racing.'

A setback in Italy

Derek flew out to Italy in mid-March and signed to ride the newly developed twin-cylinder Bianchi on Friday 18 March. However, as covered fully in chapter four, Derek later crashed the same day (after an engine seizure) at

Monza while testing and suffered a broken collarbone. Even so, after being treated in a Milan hospital he was able to fly home over the weekend – and was pictured on the front page of the 30 March 1960 issue of *Motor Cycle News* shaking hands with AMC dirt bike star Gordon Jackson at the Invitation Scramble on Easter Monday at Lydden, near Canterbury, not far from his home.

Derek was missing from his first scheduled meeting of the year – Silverstone on Saturday 9 April. But it was not for the want of trying. He had been at Brands Hatch two days previously riding the 500cc Lancefield-tuned Norton and was 'circulating in grand style' (*MCN*), but decided that his shoulder was still too painful to risk it. But he was 'confident' that he would be fit for Easter, and Derek planned to be at Brands, Snetterton and Oulton Park over the holiday weekend.

Fit again

Any doubts about Derek's fitness after his unfortunate Bianchi test session accident in Italy were dispelled at the first meeting of the 1960 Brands Hatch season on Good Friday, 15 April. Derek, Mike Hailwood and Bill Ivy (in the 500cc) were responsible for smashing all solo race and lap records!

Mike broke the 200cc and 250cc speeds, while Derek topped the bigger class honours.

From the start of the Experts 350cc, Hailwood tore off the line, leading Phil Read, Bob Anderson and Derek by 50 yards at the end of lap one. But Derek proceeded to 'relentlessly cut down' (*Motor Cycle News*) Mike's lead and slipped ahead at Paddock Hill bend after four laps. Then for the next 11 laps they swapped places. But with 15 laps completed – five to go – Derek took the lead, but only inches separated the two as they lapped many slower men.

As *Motor Cycle News* said: 'Time and time again Minter cracked the record. Then, as the end drew near, he pulled out all the stops, and riding absolutely on the limit, beat Hailwood by 30 yards.'

The new class lap record was set at 75.41mph; the old record (also held by Derek) had stood at 74.40mph.

350cc Experts, Brands Hatch – 20 laps – 24.8 miles

1st	D.W. Minter (Norton)
2nd	S.M.B. Hailwood (AJS)
3rd	P.W. Read (Norton)
4th	R.E. Rowe (Norton)
5th	J.H.L. Lewis (Norton)
6th	T. Thorp (AJS)

The anticipated Minter-Hailwood struggle renewed itself on the first lap of the Experts 500cc race with Mike leading and both riders well clear of the field. But then Derek assumed the lead, until half distance when our hero suddenly gained a 50-yard advantage. Then with five laps to go, Derek showed why he was still the master of Brands with a new class lap record, beating Hailwood by over 20 seconds; Ron Langston (Matchless G50) came home third.

The last of a record-breaking day's performances came in the All-Star Invitation race for up to 1000cc machines. Hailwood made another 'fantastic start' (*MCN*), but Derek had caught him by the end of the first lap, thereafter proceeding to improve his existing race record; he also equalled his outright lap record of 76.97mph for the Kent circuit – and won by the best part of half a lap!

1000cc Invitation, Brands Hatch – 20 laps – 24.8 miles

1st   D.W. Minter (Norton)
2nd   S.M.B. Hailwood (Norton)
3rd   T. Thorp (Norton)
4th   R.J. Langston (Matchless)
5th   R.E. Rowe (Norton)
6th   D.F. Shorey (Norton)

A double at Snetterton

After his record-breaking victories at Brands, it was more of the same two days later at Snetterton on Easter Sunday, 17 April.

Thirty-six riders came to the line at the Norfolk circuit for the 350cc final – 12 from each of the three heats – won by John Lewis, Bruce Daniels and Derek. The latter had also set a new class lap record of 88.69mph. But it was Phil Read who made the early running from the start of the final, and held it for the first six of 10 laps. But as the *Motor Cycle News* race report reveals:

> the eventual winner, Derek Minter, made a slow start and was well down the field during the early stages but it was obvious that he was making a terrific effort when he came from fifth on the second lap to second place at the end of the fourth. The question was – could he challenge Read? It seemed doubtful. But he did and was in the lead from the seventh lap onwards and in drawing away from the rest of the field he set another new lap record of 89.83mph.

An interesting feature of Derek's three-fifty Norton was its Italian Oldani front brake (similar to that fitted to Hailwood's 250cc Ducati and 350cc AJS machines). And what of Mike Hailwood himself? Well, he had crashed earlier in the day while lapping a slower rider in the 250cc race on his new Ducati Desmo twin, and put himself out of action.

350cc final, Snetterton – 10 laps – 27 miles
1st   D.W. Minter (Norton)
2nd   P.W. Read (Norton)
3rd   R.J. Langston (AJS)

Once again in the 500cc final (having won his heat) Derek had trouble getting his bike going and was well down the field as the pack took the first bend, but in his typical tigerish fighting spirit had fought his way through to second place as Tom Thorp came through in the lead at the end of lap 1. Derek took command on the third lap and drew well clear of the battle that had emerged between Thorp and Phil Read. Later Tommy Robb (riding Geoff Monty's G50 Matchless) caught and passed Thorp to take third. As for Derek, he had been circulating 'comfortably' (*MCN*), but still managed to set a new outright lap record for the 2.7-mile Norfolk circuit.

500cc final, Snetterton – 10 laps – 27 miles
1st   D.W. Minter (Norton)
2nd   P.W. Read (Norton)
3rd   T. Robb (Matchless)

The Big Battle
The really Big Battle of the holiday weekend took place at Oulton Park on Easter Monday, featuring Derek and Bob McIntyre. The *Motor Cycle News* front page story in its 20 April 1960 issue read: 'Fantastic dices in the 350 and 500cc classes highlighted the international meeting at Oulton Park on Monday.' It continued:

> In both events Derek Minter (Norton) and Bob McIntyre (AJS and Norton Special) battled away for the full race distance and honours were shared, for Minter took the bigger class and raised the lap record to 88.75mph, while Bob Mac won the 350cc race. In the smaller class the two of them shared the new lap record of 86.43mph.

500cc Oulton Park – 19 laps – 52.45 miles
1st   D.W. Minter (Norton)
2nd   R.G. McIntyre (Norton)
3rd   R.H.F. Anderson (Norton)
4th   R.J. Langston (Matchless)
5th   P.W. Read (Norton)
6th   D.F. Shorey (Norton)

A last lap shock

At Castle Combe road races near Chippenham, Wiltshire, on Saturday 23 April, Mike Hailwood (AJS) produced a last corner, last lap shock for Derek in the final race of the day. Derek was leading the 350cc final, when Hailwood cut through inside him on the right-hander leading to the finishing line and reached the chequered flag a split second ahead. In doing so, Mike put up a new 350cc class lap record for the 1.84-mile circuit at 85.79mph. However, Derek had already well beaten Mike and the rest of the field in the 500cc final on his Lancefield-tuned Norton, and in the process raised the outright motorcycle lap record to 88.31mph.

500cc final, Castle Combe – 10 laps – 18.4 miles

1st	D.W. Minter (Norton)
2nd	P.W. Read (Norton)
3rd	S.M.B. Hailwood (Norton)
4th	D.F. Shorey (Norton)
5th	A.M. Godfrey (Norton)
6th	D. Williams (Norton)

Mick Woollett's lead story for his *Paddock Gossip* column in *Motor Cycle News* dated 27 April 1960 concerned what he called the 'scintillating display of high speed dicing' put on by Bob McIntyre and Derek at Oulton Park on Easter Monday. He went on to say: 'I'm sure those of us who were lucky enough to be there will remember the 350 and 500cc races for many a long day.'

It was also revealed that Derek would 'probably' ride his new 350 Norton, which he had 'picked up from the factory over the Easter weekend (on the Sunday)' and had been 'down at Brands Hatch on the Wednesday after Easter running it in'. Derek had mentioned to journalist Charlie Rous, who was there, that it 'seemed very "stiff"' but it was expected that tuner Steve Lancefield would be hard at work solving the problem. It should be pointed out that the bikes used by Derek over the Easter weekend were both basically 1958 models.

The Lancefield connection

The start of the 1960 season for Derek had been tremendous. Twelve starts, a tally of 10 wins and two seconds, with new records from every one of them. That is how the team of Hallet, Minter and Lancefield had begun its operations. Derek, the rider, and Ray Hallet, the entrant, had been good friends for more than 10 years. As far as Steve Lancefield was concerned, their connection was far more recent, 1957 in fact. And it must be said that from their first meeting they developed a good (although not given to the warmth of Derek's later relationship with Ray Petty) connection. But Derek's early dealings were very much as one of Steve Lancefield's customers rather than anything more. The term 'customer' was still valuable as in the Lancefield book it meant that customer's engines 'were prepared and assembled with all the necessary attention demanded by standard production engines.'

But Lancefield's own engines were special. He made no attempt to suggest they were standard or contained stock parts. He explained when interviewed by the author in May 1989, before his death in early 1990, 'The only similarity my engines had to a standard unit was that they looked alike on the outside.' It's likely then that Bill Boddice had this in mind when he approached Lancefield in 1958 and intimated that it would be an idea if Derek and Steve teamed up, enabling Derek to receive the full benefit of Lancefield's knowledge and the opportunity to ride what Boddice described as 'a pukka Lancefield motor.'

'I thought about this' said Steve Lancefield 'and at the time I just sat on the idea, but it never left my mind.'

Boddice brought the subject up again after Derek's engine failed during the 1959 500cc Dutch TT, commenting: 'You should fix Minter up with one of your own engines.' But things were already on the move and a 350 motor was in the course of preparation but was still incomplete. An idea occurred to Boddice then that as the 1959 season was already drawing to a close and Lancefield's personal 500cc Formula III car engine was finished, he should offer it to Derek for the final meeting at Brands Hatch. That the offer was accepted was perhaps obvious.

'What a day that was!' recalled Steve Lancefield. 'Derek fell off in the 500cc event but won the Unlimited (1000cc). It was a bad day really because the weather was damp and not the best for trying out such an engine as that…it was very pokey! But we learned a great deal and I had an idea for the future because that meeting showed me that something could be done with this Formula III type of motor.'

And so to 1960 and the formation of the Hallet, Minter, Lancefield 'official' trio.

The foregoing helps explain just why Derek had begun the new season in such blistering form. In truth, in the author's opinion, he was, in those early days of 1960, a match for anyone in the world, if they were riding similar (single-cylinder) machinery.

Victory at the North West 200

Although forced to retire in the 350cc event when holding a comfortable second place when his engine failed after only two laps, Derek scored a magnificent victory in the 500cc race at the North West 200 in Ulster.

The meeting – no longer a true 200-mile race – was again organised by the North of Ireland Motor Club, but a worthwhile innovation had been the introduction of separate 350 and 500cc races, which had formerly been combined, thus giving most riders two races instead of one.

Heavy showers, before and during the closing of the improved 11-mile 110 yard Port Stewart – Coleraine – Portrush road circuit, put a positive dampener on new record speeds, but in the 500cc race both Derek and Tommy Robb (Matchless) lapped at 102.3mph, just one second short of Bob McIntyre's record.

Derek also won the Newcomers Award. At first there was some doubt as to his eligibility, as he had entered for the 1956 races, but it was discovered that he had not completed a practice lap on that occasion.

500cc North West 200 – 9 laps – 100 miles

1st	D.W. Minter	(Norton)
2nd	T.H. Robb	(Matchless)
3rd	A. Shepherd	(Matchless)
4th	R.J. Langston	(Matchless)
5th	R.E. Rowe	(Norton)
6th	E. Crooks	(Norton)
7th	R. Ingram	(Norton)
8th	T.S. Shepherd	(Norton)
9th	A.M. Godfrey	(Norton)

More successes at Brands

Although without a three-fifty following his machine trouble in Northern Ireland, Derek still managed to dominate the two 500cc races at Brands Hatch on Sunday 15 May. *Motor Cycle News* stated: 'Derek Minter's superiority in the two major 20-lap 500cc events was such that on each ride he shattered his own records for the course. He led both races from the start and just could not be challenged. Mike Hailwood finished second, some way behind, on both occasions.'

In fact, Derek, and the other riders who rode in the North West 200 and then hurried back overnight to race the following day at Brands certainly set themselves a task. Derek, in fact, only just made it, for there was a delay in unloading his van at Heysham, and then, when travelling down the M1 between Birmingham and London, ignition trouble struck on his van. They rectified the trouble and arrived at Brands shortly before racing got under way!

Silverstone

Silverstone on Saturday 27 May 1960 saw Derek (and John Hartle) both shatter the existing 350cc lap record for the Northamptonshire circuit – with

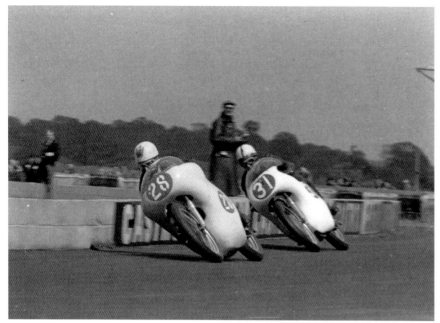

At Silverstone on Saturday 27 May 1960 Derek (31) and John Hartle (28) had a fantastic battle in the 350cc race on their Nortons. Derek eventually crossed the line first, the race lasting 17 laps (49.759 miles).

Derek not only taking the victory, but also setting the class benchmark at 98.48mph – faster than the old 500cc record! Behind the bare facts was another storming performance which had seen Derek make his customary poor start. Hartle had, from the drop of the flag, piled on the pressure to pull clear of his pursuers. And by the 10th lap Hartle had an advantage of 10 seconds over Derek, who had climbed up to second – forcing his way through and in the process overtaking men such as Bob McIntyre, Phil Read, Tom Thorp and Mike Hailwood. Then on lap 17 (the last circuit) Derek closed right up on Hartle and at Stowe Derek zoomed past to score a brilliant victory, which had the huge crowd on its feet with excitement.

350cc Silverstone – 17 laps – 49.759 miles

1st	D.W. Minter (Norton)
2nd	J. Hartle (Norton)
3rd	P.W. Read (Norton)
4th	J.H.L. Lewis (Norton)
5th	F.A. Rutherford (Norton)
6th	W. Siddles (Norton)

The favourite for the 500cc race was Derek, his 350cc victory coupled with the fact that during practice he had lapped at 100.93mph, the first over the 'ton' lap by a motorcyclist at Silverstone.

But by the end of the first lap it was Mike Hailwood who thundered through with a lead of over 100 yards, and by the time Derek emerged into

Derek became the first rider to lap the 37.73-mile TT Mountain Circuit at over 100mph in the 1960 Senior TT. He is seen here at Ramsey Hairpin.

Derek seen here during his historic lap, when he took his Norton round at 101.05mph.

second spot by the fifth lap he could not make up the lost ground to Mike-the-Bike. He thus had to settle for the runner-up spot, which he duly achieved.

High and lows of the TT

In 1960 Derek was to experience the high and lows of the Isle of Man TT. The lows were retirements in both the Lightweight 250cc (Bianchi) and Senior (Norton) races. The highs were a fourth place in the Junior and the first-ever 100mph TT lap by either a British motorcycle or a single-cylinder machine. The experiences with the Bianchi are fully covered in chapter four.

Derek's starting numbers that year were 250cc: 15; 350cc: 7; 500cc: 5. And by now Derek's name was being put forward as a possible winner in both the Junior and Senior races.

For the Junior event, on Wednesday 15 June, the Isle of Man woke to glorious sunshine, conditions which were to continue throughout the day. And Derek experienced a consistent ride on his Lancefield Norton, being fourth throughout the entire race, which in itself was extremely unusual for the six-lap, 226.38 mile-long event. His fastest lap was 23m 47.4s, compared to the race winner John Surtees (MV) with 22m 49.4s. As he finished *Motor*

Cycle News commented: 'Minter's home for a sure fourth place after riding a steady and beautifully judged race, proving that he can star in the Isle of Man as well as at Brands Hatch.'

And an even higher finish looked on the cards after Derek held third place in the Senior TT a couple of days later on Friday 17 June for the first two laps, before being forced into retirement due to a split oil tank. But before that Derek had attained a lap of over 100mph on his Norton – a first in TT history – when he took his machine round at 101.05mph. Even though Mike Hailwood also beat the ton figure later in the same race his speed was less – 100.37mph.

Junior TT Isle of Man – 6 laps – 226.38 miles

1st	J. Hartle (MV Agusta)
2nd	J. Surtees (MV Agusta)
3rd	R. McIntyre (AJS)
4th	D.W. Minter (Norton)
5th	R.B. Rensen (Norton)
6th	R.H.F. Anderson (Norton)

An unhappy debut

The new, extended 2.65-mile Brands Hatch circuit welcomed motorcycle racing for the first time on Sunday 10 July 1960. But this debut day was marred by heavy showers. At the start of the 350cc race the heavens opened and rain bucketed down. Mike Hailwood (AJS) took the lead, but Derek passed him to head the field for two laps before disaster struck and he crashed heavily at Paddock Hill bend. With a badly gashed ankle, Derek was unable to take part in the remainder of the meeting. So that man Hailwood rather than Derek made the headlines that day.

Actually Derek had been rather more seriously injured than at first thought. From Brands Hatch he was taken to Dartford Hospital, where he had six stitches in his right ankle. His long-term friend Bryan Johnson took him home, but that night Derek was to suffer from an acute pain in his neck. The following morning he went to Canterbury Hospital, where an X-ray revealed a chipped vertebra at the top of his spine. That in itself was not serious, but he came as close as that to a broken neck. He stayed in the Kent and Canterbury Hospital for four days. As his ankle was also giving trouble, it was expected that he would be on the sidelines for at least a month.

Derek was spectating at Oulton Park at the end of July, but he was still 'not fit' to race and in fact his injured ankle needed a skin graft. But he said he hoped to be fit for Brands Hatch on 21 August.

Programme cover for the one-off Brands 50 international meeting held on Saturday 9 July 1960, the first ever to be staged over the new 2.65-mile GP circuit.

South African Paddy Driver was a regular on British circuits in 1960. He is seen here at Thruxton in August that year.

Spine-Tingling

'Spine-Tingling' was the front page headline in the 24 August 1960 issue of *Motor Cycle News*. Held over the old short circuit at Brands Hatch, MCN went on to explain: 'The meeting had everything – thrilling race-long dices; record laps; high speed crashes with the victim remounting to finish well up; a Japanese works machine; a standard Steib sidecar among the racing chairs; the debut of Norman Surtees at the "Hatch"; and the return of Derek Minter to racing after a six weeks lay-off to recover from that nasty ankle injury he received at the Brands Hatch International.'

And it was a triumphant return for Derek. He won the 500cc race on his Lancefield-tuned Norton, pushing the lap record up to 78.59mph – a record he shared with Mike Hailwood – Hailwood crashing his Norton at around 70mph on Clearways when challenging Derek. Mike remounted to finish third.

Derek also went on to win the 1000cc race, with Hailwood in his shadow all the way. The lap record, set up only an hour earlier, was repeatedly shattered by both riders and by the end Derek had raised it from 78.59 to 79.15mph – the old record of 77.77mph set up on 15 May that year was well and truly beaten!

Although Mike had earlier beaten Derek in the 350cc race another headline claimed that Derek was 'Still Boss at Brands'. All in all it was a day to remember – a brilliant return to racing, huge crowds and, as *MCN* described in its race report, 'delightful summer sunshine.'

1000cc Brands Hatch – 20 laps – 24.8 miles

1st	D.W. Minter (Norton)
2nd	S.M.B. Hailwood (Norton)
3rd	T. Thorp (Matchless)
4th	B. Daniels (Norton)
5th	T. Phillis (Norton)
6th	L. Young (Norton)

Snetterton

Besides Brands Hatch, Snetterton was a much-visited circuit by the Minter team. And once again it was very much a case of Derek versus Mike. And again the Canterbury rider came out on top, winning both his races.

There were three heats for 350cc machines. The first was won by Michael O'Rourke, after several riders (including Hailwood) had crashed out. The next heat went to Tony Godfrey, with Derek taking the third. And Derek easily won the final after the early leader Tony Godfrey retired with plug trouble.

Hailwood made no mistake in the first heat of the 500cc race, with Derek taking the second heat. In the final, for once, Derek made a good start, as did Mike, but Tony Godfrey proved the main challenger. The result was Minter, Godfrey, Hailwood at the line.

350cc final, Snetterton – 10 laps – 27.9 miles

1st	D.W. Minter (Norton)
2nd	T. Thorp (AJS)
3rd	B. Setchell (Norton)
4th	T. Pound (Norton)
5th	V. Cottle (Norton)
6th	D. Degens (AJS)

500cc final, Snetterton – 10 laps – 27.9 miles

1st	D.W. Minter (Norton)
2nd	A.M. Godfrey (Norton)
3rd	S.M.B. Hailwood (Norton)
4th	T. Thorp (Matchless)
5th	B. Daniels (Norton)
6th	T. Charnley (Norton)

Another set-back

After Snetterton, Derek flew out to Italy to race the Bianchis in the 250 and 350cc Italian Grand Prix at Monza. But, as detailed in chapter four, Derek's

The up-and-coming Fred
Neville (Matchless G50) at
Brands Hatch, summer
1960.

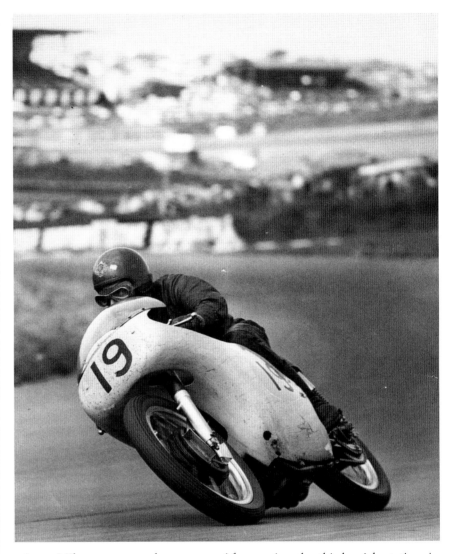

trip to Milan was not a happy one. After setting the third-quickest time in
350cc practice, he crashed on the 250cc model when it seized and pitched him
off at high speed. Although it looked a serious accident, he escaped serious
injury, suffering a broken nose, badly cut forehead and extensive bruising that
kept him in hospital for several days.

This set-back also meant that he missed some five weeks of racing and was
not fit enough until the final meeting of the year at Brands Hatch on Sunday
9 October.

Actually Derek had been entered for the Oulton Park meeting on Saturday
8 October, but was a 'non-arrival'. And certainly at Brands the following day
he was not his usual self, finishing fifth in the 350cc race and fourth in the
1000cc event. *Motor Cycle News* referred to Derek's performances that day
as 'gradually settling down.'

And so ended a season which had begun in such a tremendous way, with a string of victories plus race and lap records wherever Derek went, but ended with very much of an anti-climax. In between there had been a number of high and low moments of equal balance. And, in retrospect, his Bianchi association had been a disaster.

In the final analysis Derek Minter had shown that with the correct machinery he was equal to anyone: the record-breaking victories and lap records had proved that. And of course there was that lasting testament to his ability with the first-ever lap by a single-cylinder machine at over 100mph in the Senior TT.

In early December 1960 it was reported that Derek planned to concentrate on racing Nortons in the 350 and 500cc classes in 1961, and the successful combination of Steve Lancefield and Hallets would continue. He also said he had no plans to race Bianchi or any other works machines. And although still 'troubled' by his injuries, he was riding his Norman in local trials.

Into 1961

What would 1961 hold for Derek? It was a big question, and only time would tell. But because he had already decided to carry on with the same entrant and tuner for his Nortons, Derek was able to start the season in fine form – and the winter lay-off had seen him successfully recover from the knocks he received the previous year.

In a by-now traditional fashion, the start of the British short circuit season for Derek comprised Brands Hatch on Good Friday 30 March, Snetterton on Sunday 2 April and Oulton Park on Monday 3 April.

The Motor Cycle asked: 'Who's the king of Brands Hatch now?', after an inconclusive set of results at this, Derek's first meeting of the new season, which saw him beaten in the 350cc race by Mike Hailwood, Read and Hartle; finish runner-up in one 1000cc and win the other 1000cc event. But it should be explained that in the 350cc race he made an awful start, leaving simply too much ground to be made up. Then in the two 1000cc races honours were shared, with Hailwood first and Derek runner-up in one, while Derek won the other with Phil Read runner-up. Just to affirm how close things were on the day, both Mike and Derek shared the fastest lap at 87.68mph – a new joint record.

Break even again at Snetterton

At Snetterton a couple of days later, Mike and Derek continued their Good Friday battles. The results were another three-fifty win for Hailwood's AJS and 500cc honours for Derek's Norton. Again in the 350cc race the two riders shared the fastest lap at 88.37mph. Derek not only won the 500cc class, but set a new outright motorcycle lap record for the Norfolk circuit at 94.9mph.

Then the two rivals split up – Mike went to Thruxton, while Derek travelled in the opposite direction to Oulton Park in Cheshire.

An early morning warning that there was ice on the circuit greeted the riders as they woke up at Oulton, before going out on the circuit for practice at the Wirral Hundred Club's international Easter Trophy Meeting. Although the day was cold, the frost soon cleared, and Derek was able to conclude the racing holiday weekend programme in style, with two wins and two lap records in the bag.

Of Derek's two races, the 500cc came first, and even though the starting grid contained a galaxy of stars – Bob McIntyre, Alastair King, John Hartle and Phil Read to name but four – it was Derek who immediately stamped his authority on the race, drawing ever further ahead to push the lap record first to 89.06mph, then to 89.22mph.

A similar pattern emerged as the evening shadows lengthened across the track for the last race of the programme, the 350cc – and the second part of the Minter double – with victory and a new class lap record of 87.19mph.

500cc Oulton Park – 19 laps – 51.3 miles
1st   D.W. Minter (Norton)
2nd   P.W. Read (Norton)
3rd   F.A. Neville (Matchless)

350cc Oulton Park – 19 laps – 51.3 miles
1st   D.W. Minter (Norton)
2nd   P.W. Read (Norton)
3rd   J. Hartle (Norton)

More success at Silverstone

After Oulton came Silverstone only five days later on Saturday 8 April, with Derek back in more hectic action. *The Motor Cycle* described the 350cc race:

> Excitement mounted when John Hartle and Derek Minter (Nortons) came to grips. Lap after lurid lap they swapped places, swapped again and tried all they knew to pull out an advantage of a yard rather than of inches. Eventually Hartle tried just that bit too hard and slid off at Copse – without injury – leaving Minter to canter home a long way ahead of Phil Read, also on a Norton. Derek set the fastest lap at 96.99mph.

In the 500cc race, after setting a joint fastest lap (a new record) with John

Hartle at 101.51mph, Derek was forced into retirement when his engine cut out on the 11th lap, leaving Hartle to eventually take the victory from Bob McIntyre and Fred Neville.

BMCRC 350cc Championship – 15 laps – 43.5 miles

1st D.W. Minter (Norton)
2nd P.W. Read (Norton)
3rd A. Shepherd (AJS)

Brakes the answer

Derek had certainly got off to a barnstorming start to the 1961 season. It was noticeable that he was frequently outbraking the opposition – notably in his close battles with John Hartle at Silverstone. New Oldani brakes were widely seen as the answer. Externally these appeared similar to those used the previous year, but they were of stiffer construction and featured heavier duty shrunk-in liners. Derek also commented that he had found no signs of the drum cracking problems he and other riders had experienced with the earlier Oldani brakes. At the same time he added that, after his unfortunate experiences on continental European bikes, he was concentrating upon his Lancefield-tuned Nortons. Although he would have very much 'liked a crack at all the classics, the cost of competing on the continent is high and my livelihood depends upon my racing successes.'

Another double at Brands

Any thoughts Mike Hailwood had of beating Derek at the Brands Hatch international meeting over the 'long' circuit on Sunday 1 May 1961 were swept aside by Mr Minter getting back into his once-familiar 350 and 500cc groove. But in the smaller class it was Phil Read who proved the main challenger, with Phil and Derek sharing a new lap record of 86.41mph. Then in the 500cc race Derek's determination simply 'wore his challengers down' (*The Motor Cycle*). And his victory was easier still once Read's rear tyre went flat and pitched him off.

Six days later, on 6 May, Derek's form took a dip when he crashed in the 500cc race at the North West 200. Lying fourth at the time (behind Bob McIntyre, Tommy Robb and Phil Read), Derek slid off, fortunately without any injury, on the fast S-bend near Millburn. This was after he had earlier finished fourth behind McIntyre (AJS), Read (Norton) and Fred Neville (AJS) in the 350cc event.

Back to winning ways

But if anyone thought that Derek's form might suffer from his indifferent results in Northern Ireland, this was certainly not the case, because at

Thruxton on Bank Holiday Monday he bounded back to winning ways, with four victories comprising heat and final wins in both the 350 and 500cc races. And for good measure he also set a new lap record of 80.29mph in the 350cc and equalled (with Roy Mayhew) the 500cc record with a speed of 82.89mph. *The Motor Cycle* called it: 'Minter's Day Out' and 'Canterbury Star in Record shattering Form at Thruxton.' In both finals the runner-up was Phil Read.

TT fortnight
Derek journeyed with his bikes – and Steve Lancefield – to the Isle of Man for the annual TT fortnight. Throughout the practice period he was on the leaderboard and sometimes topped it.

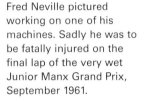

Fred Neville pictured working on one of his machines. Sadly he was to be fatally injured on the final lap of the very wet Junior Manx Grand Prix, September 1961.

An experimental Avon front tyre with 10 ribs in place of the usual 12 appeared on Derek's Senior Norton. The ribs, and two medial interrupted treads, were broader than on the standard pattern.

With the previous year's fastest Norton lap to his credit, Derek was seen as a potential winner should MV's lone rider, Gary Hocking, strike trouble.

This year Derek's racing numbers for the TT were: Junior: 3; Senior: 9.

In the Junior race Derek was consistent throughout the entire six laps, in fourth position. The final finishing order was: Phil Read, Gary Hocking (MV), Ralph Rensen and the 'Mint'. Actually, Derek's Norton engine was inexplicably short of revs and it was very much a case of hanging on, rather than challenging for a top-three finish. In the author's opinion, Derek, rather than Phil Read, could well have been in contention for victory, but it was not to be. As it was Derek averaged 93.50mph, against Read's winning speed of 95.10mph.

Before the start of the Senior race, and while the remaining 73 riders were busy warming up their engines, Derek was in something of a panic. His Norton's special light-alloy fuel tank was leaking. Fortunately, Manchester entrant/dealer Reg Dearden was able to produce a standard replacement in a matter of minutes.

And things did not get any better in the race, with *The Motor Cycle* commenting: 'As on Wednesday, Minter was a trifle disappointing: he was lapping at 97mph when 100mph stuff of last year was expected, and he dropped a place (second lap) to ninth.' Then on the next lap Derek slid back some more – to 11th.

And as *The Motor Cycle* race report of 23 June 1961 says:

Minter rounded off the day with a touch of heroics. He took on slightly too little fuel on filling and paid the penalty of a dry tank at Creg-ny-Baa. By coasting and pushing the three-and-a-half miles to the line, he made 30th place and a richly deserved second-class replica. The race was won by Mike Hailwood (Norton) and of the original 74 starters, 45 finished.'

Sadly Ralph Rensen, who had finished in front of Derek in the Junior a couple of days before, had crashed fatally at the 11th Milestone.

From Lancefield to factory

The 1961 TT signalled the end of the Lancefield involvement, brought on, Derek says, mainly due to Steve 'not being pleased that the Norton factory did not invite him to a dinner in honour of my 100mph lap the previous year.'

And so there was a gap of almost a month before Derek was back in the saddle. This time he had the use of some Norton factory models, most notably an experimental short-stroke three-fifty with a low-boy Domiracer-type chassis. The other machine at Derek's disposal was a standard 499cc Manx production racer.

The first outing for this new set-up (still with Hallet involvement) came at Brands Hatch on Sunday 9 July.

In the 350cc event Phil Read dashed into the lead from the start with Mike Hailwood (AJS), Fred Neville and Derek (on the experimental bike) pressing close. By the fourth lap Neville and Derek had displaced Hailwood – and Neville was within yards of Read. Lap 8 saw the pair in line abreast past the pits. Read finally pulled away to win a 'great race' (*The Motor Cycle*) and set a new class lap record at 85.48mph. However, although quick enough, the new Norton was not handling as it should, which placed Derek at a distinct disadvantage.

In the two other races that day in which Derek took part, *The Motor Cycle* comment 'Minter Once Again Top Dog at Brands Hatch' was certainly true, as he won both in 'sizzling' form – from an entry which included Mike Hailwood, Phil Read and John Hartle.

The experimental three-fifty

Details of the experimental three-fifty included the concept of cutting height and weight, and so the three-fifty had a similar frame to that of the 500 Domiracer twin that Tom Phillis had ridden to third place in the Senior TT the previous month. The bike, as with the twin, was the work of Norton's development engineer Doug Hele and his team at the factory's development shop in Birmingham.

The tyre size (compared to the standard Manx) was reduced from 19 to 18-inch diameter, with 3.25 and 2.75-inch section rubber.

Bore and stroke were standard at 76 x 76.7mm, but a shorter connecting rod was used, thus enabling the engine to fit the new, compact frame. Additionally, the engine was lower slung than usual between the bottom frame tubes and closer coupled to the gearbox. This had been made possible by dispensing with the magneto to make way for the coupling plates. Coil ignition was employed with the contact breaker outboard of the oil pump. The battery and coil were suspended from a rubber diaphragm on the offside (right) top frame tube, in much the same way as the Manx float chambers were hung on the nearside (left). A factory spokesman said that 'inside the engine are other experimental features at present on the secret list.'

Storming Castle Combe

As *The Motor Cycle* explained, 'lightning flickering across the sky, occasional heavy downpours and intermittent bright sunshine provided a chequered backcloth for an exciting day's racing at Castle Combe last Saturday [16 July 1961].'

Having equalled his own lap record in his heat, Derek, riding the experimental Norton single (with modifications to improve its handling), passed virtually everyone on the first lap – and on a wet track too! Another lap and he was in the lead, never to be headed. Mike Hailwood, riding his new twin-cylinder Ducati Desmo, found it to be a real handful on the slippery, bumpy track and was out of the hunt. The runner-up went to Tony Godfrey.

In the 500cc final it was Derek's turn to finish runner-up, this time behind Mike Hailwood (Norton). But with the fastest lap (as he had done in the 350cc event) Derek was the quickest rider out on the circuit, only a terrible start ensuring a Hailwood, not Minter, victory.

The handling problems encountered by Derek with the new 350 had been cured by altering the characteristics of the rear suspension units.

Snetterton

Derek knocked his own lap record for six in the 500cc final at Snetterton on Sunday 31 July. He clocked 94.35mph – a 1.44mph increase over his own existing figure. Any challenge Derek might have had fizzled out when Phil Read's Norton suffered a persistent misfire.

In the 350cc final Read emerged as the victor. The large crowd had expected another Minter victory, but contact breaker trouble in the first heat meant that Derek did not qualify for the final.

British Champion once again

After setting a new 350cc class lap record at the Oulton Park British Championship meeting on August Bank Holiday Monday, 8 August 1961, *The Motor Cycle* reported 'Minter was well ahead, with a lap record into the bargain. It seemed all over bar the shouting. But with only two more laps remaining Minter went out, his engine locked.'

Then, in the 500cc British Championship race, over 30 laps of the Cheshire circuit, Derek was simply unbeatable – nobody from the cream of British racing could live with him.

500cc British Championship – 30 laps – 81 miles
1st   D.W. Minter (Norton)
2nd   F. Neville (Matchless)
3rd   S.M.B. Hailwood (Norton)
4th   A. King (Norton)

Derek talking to Alastair King at Oulton Park in 1961.

5th   A. Shepherd (Matchless)
6th   P.W. Read (Norton)

Later in the 10-lap non-Championship Les Graham Memorial Race, Derek (in finishing runner-up to Alastair King) hoisted the outright circuit motorcycle lap record to 90.03mph – the first-ever 'ninety' figure for the Cheshire circuit.

Thirteen days later, on Sunday 21 August, Derek was at Brands Hatch, but after grounding his machine at South Bank bend on lap 2 of the 350cc event, he was forced to sit out the remainder of the race, which was ultimately won by Mike Hailwood from Fred Neville. Then in the 500cc race Derek and Phil Read fought a wheel-to-wheel battle throughout the entire 12-lap distance, with Read finally getting the verdict by some two machine lengths.

Sadly, after setting fastest laps in both the 250 and 1000cc races, the up-and-coming Fred Neville was to meet his death a couple of weeks later when leading on the final lap of the Junior (350cc) Manx Grand Prix, in terribly wet conditions.

Skating at Snetterton
One commentator described the 4 September 1961 Snetterton national road races as: 'A dish of cold porridge with the most exquisite *crêpe suzette* to follow.' The weather alternated between downpours and warm sunshine, which turned the 2.7-mile Norfolk circuit into what *The Motor Cycle* described as a 'skating rink'. And 'nearly 300 riders slithered, wobbled, took to the rough or simply fell off.'

After winning his heat, Derek scored yet another race victory in the 350cc class on the experimental Norton, and also set the fastest lap at 88.5mph, but a retirement in his 500cc heat meant no more action in the bigger class. At least he stayed clear of the many spills which occurred that day in the treacherous conditions.

His throne regained
For any one of the doubters, Derek truly regained – if he had ever lost it in the first place – his Brands Hatch crown on 18 September 1961. And he did it in stunning fashion when he won the three big races on three different Nortons; the 350cc and two 1000cc events over the long 2.65-mile Grand Prix course. The machines he used that day were the works developmental 350, a 500 Manx and a Domiracer twin. Derek's main opposition included Phil Read, Roy Mayhew, Lewis Young, Dan Shorey and a star of the future, Chris Conn.

Aintree Century
Having a rare outing on Joe Ehrlich's EMC, Derek won the five-lap 125cc at the international Aintree Century meeting up near Liverpool on Saturday 1

October 1961. But in the larger 350 and 500cc classes Derek could only come fourth in the latter and fifth in the former, having something of an off day after a string of outstanding performances on Nortons.

A busy final weekend

Then came a busy final weekend of the 1961 British road race scene, with Oulton Park on Saturday 8 October and Brands Hatch the following day.

At Oulton, Derek experienced mixed fortunes with a victory in the 150cc event on the EMC and a record-breaking lap of 78.89mph, then, after setting the fastest lap in the 350cc race on the experimental Norton, he was forced out with ignition troubles. Finally, in the 500cc outing on one of the Norton Domiracer twins he was hampered by a back-row grid position. This, added to Derek's traditional less-than-perfect start, saw him come home behind Mike Hailwood, Phil Read and Alan Shepherd.

A spring 1961 advertisement showing Derek aboard the new 250cc B4 twin. The Ashford, Kent-based firm had close connections with Derek, as explained in the text, 729 LKJ being Derek's personal machine.

150cc Oulton Park – 6 laps – 17.4 miles
1st   D.W. Minter (EMC)
2nd   D.F. Shorey (Bultaco)
3rd   R.J.G. Dickinson (Ducati)

Then it was the overnight journey down south to Brands, where it would be true to say that Derek remained King of Brands, as he virtually monopolised the day on the 2.65-mile Kent circuit.

First the 'Mint' won the five-lap 125cc race on the EMC, in the process setting a new class lap record of 80.03mph.

Next he took the 350cc race, followed by the 500cc event. In fact, the only race he did not win that day was the 1000cc class, in which he finished second to Phil Read (496cc Matchless), riding a 597cc Norton Domiracer.

125cc Brands Hatch – 5 laps – 13.25 miles
1st   D.W. Minter (EMC)
2nd   R.A. Avery (EMC)
3rd   D.F. Shorey (Bultaco)

350cc Brands Hatch – 10 laps – 26.5 miles
1st   D.W. Minter (Norton)

Talking about Derek's new Peugeot car with Ray Hallet on the forecourt of the Hallet dealership in Canterbury.

2nd P.W. Read (AJS)
3rd M.A. Duff (AJS)

500cc Brands Hatch – 10 laps – 26.5 miles
1st D.W. Minter (Norton)
2nd P.W. Read (Norton)
3rd S.M.B. Hailwood (Norton)

Little did Derek know it at the time, but he was on the verge of his greatest ever year – 1962 – when not only would he achieve his long-held ambition of winning an Isle of Man TT, but he would also ride Japanese machines for the first time.

He would form a partnership with another Norton tuner, which would last for the remainder of his professional career, and would most effectively replace the departed Steve Lancefield.

Chapter 4

Broadening the Horizons

Although Derek had ridden a variety of bikes – BSA Gold Star, Manx Norton, the Ron Harris MVs, Bob Geeson's REG twin and Joe Ehrlich's EMC – it was not until mid-1959 that he got his first full works ride on Continental European machinery.

MZ and Moto Morini

When the chance eventually came, not one but two factories were interested in obtaining Derek's services: MZ and Moto Morini. His debut for both marques came during the Dutch TT at Assen on Saturday 27 June 1959.

The MZ, at that time, was seen as fast but rather fragile. For the 1959 season MZ, directed by the brilliant engineer Walter Kaaden, had obtained the services of a foreign rider for the first time, the widely travelled Swiss star Luigi Taveri. And it was Taveri who had come up with the idea of fitting British Norton front forks – mainly in an attempt to improve the road-holding of the fast MZ two-fifty twin. But Derek only rode the one-two-five single – fearing the two-fifty was 'seizure prone'.

Technically speaking

Technically, another major change adopted by MZ in 1959 was a third transfer port (bridged like its two companions to prevent the single Dyke-type piston ring fouling). Perhaps equally important, however, was the side effect of this improved cylinder filling and extra power, which was the much superior lubrication of what was rapidly becoming a source of unreliability, the caged Ina needle-roller small end bearing. Another change was the

One of the disc-valve single-cylinder 125cc MZ two-strokes as raced by Derek in 1959. A problem with oil contracts prevented the partnership continuing.

substitution of the aluminium-alloy dolphin fairing for a much cheaper and easier to construct fibreglass version.

Through 1959, the MZs became ever quicker and more effective as viable top-class Grand Prix machines. The season had started well when Taveri finished runner-up in the 125cc Isle of Man TT, with his teammate, the East German Horst Fugner, supplying excellent support in fourth place. When one considers that Taveri was sandwiched between Tarquinio Provini and Mike Hailwood (on MV Agusta and Ducati respectively), this was a really impressive result. But in the Lightweight (250cc) TT, things were very different, as although well placed initially, the MZ trio of Ernst Degner, Fugner and Taveri were all forced out with mechanical trouble.

Next stop on the Championship trail was Hockenheim, for the West German GP, where Degner came home sixth in the 125 race, and Fugner fourth in the 250.

But Taveri was rapidly becoming unsettled. He much preferred four-strokes to two-strokes and returned to Ducati, whom he had ridden for in 1958; finishing third in the 125cc World Championships.

And so to the Dutch round, and Derek's arrival in the MZ team. He rode in the 125cc category for the East German firm, for two reasons. One was that he had already agreed to ride for the Italian company Moto Morini in the 250cc class and also that he was 'worried' about the ongoing reliability issue with the larger MZ.

Mastering the MZ

As Derek told *The Motor Cycle* journalist David Dixon later in 1959, he had 'quickly mastered' the two-stroke MZ 125. And the 'East German folk were so pleased with my performance, that I kept my place in the team'; subsequently gaining a couple of fourth places in the Belgian and Italian rounds after his initial fifth position in Holland.

125cc Dutch TT, Assen

1st	C. Ubbiali	(MV Agusta)
2nd	B. Spaggiari	(Ducati)
3rd	S.M.B. Hailwood	(Ducati)
4th	H. Fugner	(MZ)
5th	D.W. Minter	(MZ)
6th	K. Kavanagh	(Ducati)

125cc Belgian GP, Spa Francorchamps

1st	C. Ubbiali	(MV Agusta)
2nd	T. Provini	(MV Agusta)

MZ

Before World War Two, the East German Saxony town of Zschopau was home to the most advanced two-stroke motorcycles in the world. DKW had earned the respect of other, predominantly four-stroke, manufacturers with its ultra-quick racing bikes in the years leading up to the outbreak of hostilities in September 1939. When the conflict was over, the DKW works was nothing but rubble, and Zschopau found itself under the occupation of the Red Army. DKW, therefore, set up shop anew in Ingolstadt, in the western sector, resuming its pre-war activities as best it could.

Meanwhile, from the ashes of the old plant in Zschopau arose a new addition to the ranks of the world's motorcycle manufacturers: MZ, or to give its full title, VEB Motorraderwerke Zschopau. The prototype racing MZ (entered as an IFA) appeared in 1950, four years after the first production model roadster left the factory. Like its street-going brother, the track bike was a rather unexciting 125cc single with piston-port induction and a three-speed gearbox. Then, in 1951, a private German tuner, Daniel Zimmermann, modified his home-built IFA racer by means of a crankshaft-driven rotary disc valve. Thus was ushered in a new era of two-stroke technology.

Zimmermann's modifications were so successful that MZ quickly took out patents, and subsequently development of the concept was taken over by the engineer Walter Kaaden, who had joined MZ at the end of 1952. And so Kaaden began the development of what was to become the forerunner of the famous MZ Grand Prix machines which spanned the mid-1950s until the mid-1970s. At the beginning of the 1953 season, the MZ 125 racing engine was giving 9bhp at 7,800rpm, but by the end of the year it was pumping out 12bhp at over 8,000rpm – a healthy 25 per cent increase. Much of the extra power came from extensive changes to the transfer and exhaust ports, the compression ratio and the exhaust system. In fact, it was this last area that was to be Kaaden's most significant achievement. It was he who recognised the importance of a highly resonant exhaust system, combined with the extended port timing made possible by disc-valve induction, coupled with multiple transfer ports and a squish-type combustion chamber.

The MZ works at Zschopau in eastern Germany; actually MZ stood for Motorraderwerke Zschopau.

By 1955, Kaaden had developed the disc-valve single cylinder engine to a point where it was almost competitive with the very best of the twin-cam four-strokes, such as MV Agusta and FB Mondial. But a major problem was that MZ suffered, as did other East German companies, from the effects of the 'Cold War'. Not only were they denied the currency to enable them to improve its machines by way of Western components, but staff were also often denied the necessary visas for foreign travel.

During the winter of 1953–54, first drawings had been made of a completely new MZ, a two-fifty twin. The broad strategy was to experiment on the one-two-five, then transfer the technology to the twin. The two-fifty was actually two one-two-fifties with crankshafts spliced to a common primary drive. It also utilised the square 54 x 54mm bore and

The brilliant MZ engineer Walter Kaaden with works rider Derek Woodman at the East German Grand Prix at the Sachsenring, July 1967.

stroke dimensions of the one-two-five. But Kaaden encountered many teething troubles with the larger engine and it was not really ready until the spring of 1958. By then output of both units was impressive to say the least, with a power output of 160bhp/litre, the one-two-five producing 20bhp and the two-fifty 36bhp. This also coincided with the factory deciding to take in as many of that year's World Championship events as possible.

MZ also scored its first GP victory in 1958, when Horst Fugner won the 250cc class at the Swedish round. But the year had also shown up another problem – the lack of foreign racing talent. Unfortunately, except for Ernst Degner, the other East German riders were simply not good enough at world level. Also local riders often hit the visa problem (as did the support staff, including Kaaden).

For 1959, MZ obtained the services of its first foreign rider, in the shape of the Swiss Lightweight star Luigi Taveri. Then Derek Minter joined the team. But Derek only rode the one-two-five single, as he was also contracted to ride for the Italian Moto Morini factory in the 250cc class. As detailed in the main text, Derek only had a few rides for MZ and never raced the two-fifty twin. MZ were keen for him to continue, but having different oil companies always seemed to keep them apart. This, in the author's opinion, was a pity because, particularly on the larger MZ, Derek could have won at GP level. And by 1961, the one-two-five single and two-fifty twin were offering the equivalent of 200bhp per litre, an amazing figure for the time, and MZ looked like taking the world by storm. But it was not to be. Their chief rider, Ernst Degner, defected to the West (after the 1961 Swedish GP) and went to work for Suzuki (who coincidentally won their first-ever World Championship title the following year, 1962). Walter Kaaden had been approached earlier, but had refused Suzuki's advances, putting his family and country before personal freedom or wealth. And from that time Kaaden's research was to be reflected in all subsequent racing two-strokes, not just those from Suzuki, but also from the rest of the industry. Walter Kaaden died on 3 March 1996, but his technology was to act as a reminder of the man who is universally acclaimed today as 'the Father of the Modern Two-Stroke'.

3rd	L. Taveri (Ducati)
4th	D.W. Minter (MZ)
5th	K. Kavanagh (Ducati)
6th	K. Kronmuller (Ducati)

125cc Italian GP, Monza – 18 laps – 64.31 miles

1st	E. Degner (MZ)
2nd	C. Ubbiali (MV Agusta)
3rd	L. Taveri (Ducati)
4th	D.W. Minter (MZ)
5th	T. Provini (MV Agusta)
6th	G. Hocking (MV Agusta)

The 1957 500cc World Champion Libero Liberati testing one of the Moto Morini 250 GP bikes at Monza in March 1959. However, Morini chose Derek Minter instead.

The Monza Race

Of Derek's three outings on the 125 MZ, his performance at Monza was probably the best. Here is an extract from the race report in *The Motor Cycle* dated 10 September 1959:

> There has seldom been such fierce and sustained battling as distinguished the 125cc race. At the end only 2.6 seconds bracketed the first five riders and that was typical of the elbow rubbing which went on from start to finish. A different rider led on each of the initial three laps. First it was young Gary Hocking, making his debut for MV Agusta, then his teammate Tarquinio Provini, and then Derek Minter (MZ). Summoned from Belfast at the eleventh hour to ride an MZ, Tommy Robb was prominent early but went out at Vialone with engine seizure on lap 5. Minter held his lead for five laps closely followed by Degner, while Luigi Taveri on a desmodronic Ducati twin traded places furiously with Ubbiali, Provini and Hocking, with young Alberto Pagani (MV Agusta) and Mike Hailwood (Ducati single). Hailwood's machine lacked the speed to hold the pace, and he gradually fell away to finish eighth, but up front the excitement never waned.

The Italian job

The Moto Morini two-fifty used a double overhead camshaft single-cylinder engine. And as Derek told the author, 'it was certainly faster than my three-fifty Norton.' In fact, although he only raced it twice, Derek has high regard for the Italian job.

His first race on the Morini came, as with the MZ, at Assen on 27 June 1959. And as Derek said: 'I came a good third on the Morini.' He continued: 'What a bicycle that Morini was. I'm convinced I could have won the race, but the bicycle had been undergeared. The wind had changed since my final practice the previous day, but the mechanic would not be convinced the machine wanted attention, still, I led for seven laps.'

His second, and as it happened final race on the Morini came at Monza on 6 September 1959. Derek again: 'On the first lap the rear brake of my Morini snapped, but I managed to keep third place until the very last lap when a rear wheel spindle broke and the Italian rider Emilio Mendogni nosed me out of third, though we were both given the same time. He was also riding a Morini.'

250cc Dutch TT, Assen – 17 laps – 81.38 miles

1st	T. Provini (MV Agusta)	
2nd	C. Ubbiali (MV Agusta)	
3rd	D.W. Minter (Moto Morini)	
4th	S.M.B. Hailwood (FB Mondial)	
5th	H. Fugner (MZ)	
6th	E. Degner (MZ)	

250cc Italian GP, Monza – 22 laps – 78.6 miles

1st	C. Ubbiali (MV Agusta)	
2nd	E. Degner (MZ)	
3rd	E. Mendogni (Moto Morini)	
4th	D.W. Minter (Moto Morini)	
5th	L. Taveri (MZ)	
6th	T.H. Robb (MZ)	

The politics

Derek had made a very favourable impression and both MZ and Moto Morini were keen to extend Derek's appearances for them. So why did it not happen? Well, MZ and Derek were contracted to different oil companies, so this was the reason why it did not go ahead, even though Dipl. Ing. Walter Kaaden, MZ chief engineer and team manager, was all for it.

As late as January 1963 Derek, then the triple British racing champion, received a firm offer from East Germany to ride works MZ machines the next season. In a letter from the *VEB Motorraderwerke Zschopau*, technical director Walter Kaaden said: 'You can be sure I will give you the best water-cooled two-fifty and one-two-five works machines. The 250cc water-cooled twin cylinder engine is very reliable and the power is good enough to beat the Hondas in 1963.'

Kaaden concluded the offer by saying that the MZ factory now had a scheme to overcome the difficulties experienced in 1962 (Kaaden and other personnel were refused visas for travel to the West, due to the political situation – remember the Cold War and the Cuban Missile Crisis were current at that time).

Derek, though obviously delighted to receive such a 'tempting offer' (*MCN*), was unfortunately not able to take it up, due as before to him and MZ being contracted to different oil companies.

While in Moto Morini's case, although the Bologna factory and Derek were both happy, Morini's number 1 rider Emilio Mendogni was certainly not. He was dead against the idea. As Derek says: 'Mendogni knew I could beat him…'

Bianchi

In early January 1960, it was finally announced that Moto Morini would not be offering Derek a contract for the new racing season. Then, in a surprise move in mid-March, Derek travelled to Italy and signed to ride for the Bianchi factory on Friday 18 March. This was despite the fact that later the same day the all-new 250cc Bianchi twin-cylinder racer that he was trying at Monza seized up, throwing Derek off while travelling 'full bore' at an estimated 130mph.

A pair of Moto Morini two-fifties being prepared by the company's chief development engineer, Dante Lambertini, in the factory race shop, spring 1959.

Bianchi

Founded by Eduardo Bianchi in Milan during 1885, the marque which bore his name was destined to become the very first company to manufacture motorcycles in Italy. Versatility was its byword in those pioneering days; first came surgical instruments, then bicycles, tricycles and finally, in 1897, motorcycles. However, it was not until 1920 that the Milanese works began to take a serious interest in speed events. It was in that year that Carlo Maffeis, riding a 500cc overhead-valve V-twin Bianchi, established a new flying kilometre world record at 77.6mph, on a stretch of road near Gallerate (later the home of the legendary MV Agusta brand). Even then, it was not a full factory effort, as the engine had been prepared by Carlo and his brothers, Miro and Nando, who later marketed their own Maffeis machine powered by British-made Blackburne or JAP power units. Riding his record-breaking Bianchi V-twin in the following year's Brescia road race, Carlo Maffeis crashed heavily and was fatally injured.

A Bianchi Formula 3 racer at Monza in 1957. Derek Minter later rode a development of this machine to victory at Brands Hatch in spring 1962.

Bianchi designer Lino Tonti
(right), with the factory's
motocross star Emilio
Ostorero, Italian
Champion in 1960.

Following this tragedy, Bianchi took no further part in racing until 1925, when it became necessary to counter the challenge being made to its market position by the likes of Moto Guzzi and Garelli. Both these latter firms were winning races and thus gaining valuable publicity which, of course, was not so with Bianchi. Initially Bianchi chose the 350cc class which, in Italy, was then dominated by the all-conquering Garelli split-single two-stroke. The new machine was designed by Ing. Mario Baldi and incorporated several innovative features with double overhead camshafts, it displaced 348cc (74 x 81mm). A rarity in those days was that the camshafts and valve gear were enclosed in an oil-tight compartment.

Known as the Frecia Celeste (Blue Arrow), the design proved both fast and reliable and was ridden to many victories by the likes of Achille Varzi and the great Tazio Nuvolari. But by the end of 1930, the Frecia Celeste had had its day. After such a run of success, and the additional sales it had generated, Bianchi had no desire to stop racing. So Ing. Baldi went back to his drawing office and, in 1932, a new 500cc dohc single made its bow. The larger-engined bike was not destined to be as successful as its older, smaller brother, even though it was victorious in the 1933 Milano-Napoli and 1934 Italian events. However, in full Grand Prix events it was not speedy enough against the latest Moto Guzzi V-twins or British Nortons.

Against this background, Bianchi instructed Baldi to design a brand-new multi-cylinder machine. The result was the breathtaking supercharged 493cc across-the-frame four, which first saw the light of day towards the end of 1939. Developing some 75bhp at 9,000rpm, this impressive motorcycle would have been a true challenger to the existing Gilera fours and BMW twins which had dominated international racing in the months preceding the outbreak of war in September 1939. So sadly Bianchi's multi came too late and by the end of the conflict in 1945 Baldi was dead and the FIM banned supercharging.

During the late 1940s and early 1950s Bianchi concentrated its efforts purely on series production roadsters. However, by the mid-1950s the company was back in the sport, with several successes in the long-distance races of the day and in dirt bike racing, taking the Italian Moto Cross Championship title in 1958, 1959 and 1960. It had even gained a number of world speed records at Monza in November 1957, using a fully streamlined machine derived from the production 175ohc Tonale.

In mid-1958 Bianchi had appointed the talented designer Lino Tonti to create a new series of racing and off-road models. At first the road racers employed 174 and 248cc single-cylinder engines based on the moto cross units. But in March 1960 came news of a brand new dohc two-fifty parallel twin. Without doubt the engine was an impressive looking assembly. It was a built-in unit with a six-speed gearbox mounted in a 9kg (20lb) all-welded duplex frame. A striking feature of the latter was its use of small diameter tubing and also an oval sectioned brace that extended from the top/rear of the steering head to the centre of the frame in the area towards the rear of the fuel tank.

A train of gears between the cylinders transferred drive from the intermediate gear to the inlet camshaft, while a further train led forward from there to the exhaust camshaft. Extensive use was made of electron alloy, including the cam boxes, clutch housing and integral 2.25-litre (half-gallon) oil sump; however, the vertically-split crankcases, cylinder barrels and heads were of aluminium alloy.

Each cylinder head housed twin 12mm spark plugs, which fired simultaneously courtesy of a pair of Bosch 6-volt double-ended coils. There were a total of four contact-breakers, which were driven from the offside end of the crankshaft. The two 27mm Dell'Orto SSI carburettors employed separate float chambers. A pair of oil pumps were used; one fed the crankshaft bearings, the other the valve gear. Other features of the design are detailed in the main text, but suffice to say Derek Minter's time as a works Bianchi rider was not a successful one, not because of his riding abilities on the Italian bike, but because of the development problems which he, and other team riders, experienced at the time. Later, after Derek was no longer involved, the design (in 350 and eventually 500cc guises) was transformed into a much more competitive and reliable motorcycle.

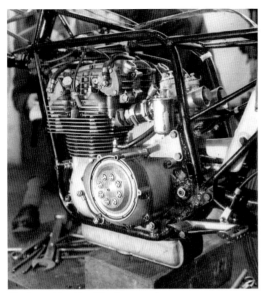

Designed by Lino Tonti, the Bianchi 249cc (55x52.5mm) dohc twin was launched at a press conference on 31 March 1960.

Frame from the 1960 Bianchi two-fifty twin. Note the use of small diameter tubing and the double-ended ignition coil.

Although Derek had got the clutch in, the thrust mechanism gave way and the clutch re-engaged with a bang, causing the rear wheel to lock and Derek was unable to control the resulting slide. He then parted company with the Bianchi and slid across the track, catching his shoulder on an iron fence as he came to a standstill. He was taken to hospital and treated for a broken right collarbone and a bruised right leg, but was fit enough to fly back to England a couple of days later. On the Monday morning he visited his local Kent and Canterbury Hospital. The bone specialist there said: 'If you were a horse jockey you'd be fit to ride in 10 days, but as you're a motorcyclist it will take a few more days.'

In mid-April at the Italian Championship event at Cesenatico the 250cc race included entries from MV Agusta, Moto Morini, Benelli and Bianchi.

Although Derek was not there this meeting would serve as an early indication of the potential problems existing at Bianchi. Carlo Ubbiali and Gary Hocking went straight into the lead on their twin-cylinder MVs, ahead of Tarquinio Provini (who was now to be the sole Moto Morini rider that year) and Emilio Mendogni (who had switched from Morini to MV). The leading two MVs proceeded to draw steadily away from Provini to win easily, over the 2.5-mile street circuit in pouring rain. Meanwhile Mendogni and both works single-cylinder Benellis – ridden by Bruno Spaggiari and Silvio Grassetti – were slowed by ignition problems caused by the flooded track. As for the Bianchi twins ridden by development riders Osvaldo Perfetti and Giancarlo Muscio, one Italian race report stated: 'These were not impressive and are obviously still in the experimental stage.' Perfetti crashed out, leaving Muscio to finish fifth.

In early May, Derek received a cable from Bianchi to say no machine would be available for him to ride in the North West 200. But MCN's Mick Woollett rang Terry Hill in Belfast, the latter being responsible for entering Bianchi riders in British events, and he told Mick that he was still expecting the Bianchis to arrive. All arrangements had been made to meet the Bianchi van off the boat, and to accommodate the mechanics and Bianchi race chief Lino Tonti, who was due to fly over.

Moto Morini

To many historians the double overhead camshaft 250 Moto Morini, which reached its peak in 1963, when the might of Honda only just managed to vanquish the lone Italian single with Tarquinio Provini in the saddle, was the most outstanding design of its type ever conceived. And it was certainly the fastest single-cylinder four-stroke of its engine size ever made.

To trace the machine's history, it is necessary to go back to the period just prior to the outbreak of World War One. It was then that Alfonso Morini, after serving an apprenticeship with a local smithy, set up a tiny motorcycle repair shop near his home in the central Italian industrial town of Bologna. Then came the war and at its end he was able to return to his Bologna workshop with sufficient experience to undertake a more ambitious business venture. No longer satisfied with repairing machines, Morini realised that the time was ripe for manufacturing. To this end, he joined up in a partnership with Mario Mezzetti, thus creating the MM marque. Throughout the inter-war years of the 1920s and 1930s MM became one of Italy's premier motorcycle brands; certainly where quality of construction and reliability in service came into things.

But in 1938 Morini and Mezzetti split up. Always something of an individualist, Morini wished to establish a factory of his own. But although by mid-1939 he was ready to produce motorcycles, World War Two came along to

A 1958 Moto Morini dohc single, the forerunner of the machine raced by Derek Minter the following year.

interfere with these plans. So it was not until 1946 that he could begin to do this. In fact he was one of the very first Italian manufacturers to put a new model into production after the end of the hostilities. This was a 125cc single-cylinder piston-port two-stroke, and a three-speed, in-unit gearbox, wet clutch and magneto ignition. And it was not long before tuned versions were giving an excellent account of themselves – even at the highest level. One of the first to make himself a name on one of the Morinis was a certain Umberto Masetti, later to become a double 500cc World Champion with the famous Gilera team.

But by the beginning of the 1950s Morini had switched to four-strokes with a new 125cc single overhead cam engine. For 1954, Morini produced an enlarged one-two-five, on which Emilio Mendogni won the 175cc class of the Italian Senior Championship. This led to the 175 Settebello, but with pushrod operated valves. The Settebello not only won races, but also sold in many thousands. But although the Settebello was an excellent sports bike, for top line racing the company needed something else. What it got was the Rebello which, unlike the Settebello, featured a chain-driven sohc engine of particularly advanced design. Another feature was its use of a five-speed transmission, which was extremely rare in those days. The 172.4cc (60 x 61mm) motor produced 22bhp at 9,000rpm.

A Rebello won the 1955 Milano-Taranto and Giro d'Italia long-distance races, thus proving not only its speed but its stamina too. In fact the bike proved such a fine motorcycle that a larger two-fifty version with double-overhead cams was constructed for GP-type events, making its debut at the 1957 Italian Grand Prix. Against a hoard of pukka works bikes from FB Mondial, Moto Guzzi and MV Agusta, rider Emilio Mendogni lay an impressive third for some considerable time, before being forced out through a minor technical problem. After this impressive debut, Alfonso Morini immediately authorised an extension of the development programme. The prototype used by Mendogni had used chain-driven camshafts (as per the Rebello). However, tests soon showed that a system using spur gears was superior in several respects. The actual engine displacement on both engines was the same, 247.7cc (69 x 66mm), with maximum power being quoted at 30bhp at 10,000rpm (120bhp/litre) on a compression ratio of 9.5:1. The special steel connecting rod was heavily webbed at both ends, while the big-end consisted of a series of hardened steel rollers retained within a light-alloy cage. Lubrication was by the traditional Morini dry-sump, with a double-gear pump circulating the lubricating oil. Two ignition systems were tried: battery/coil and magneto. The former was eventually chosen as it proved superior; both employed twin spark plugs. Like the Rebello, the gearbox was five-speed and built in with the engine.

Intense development took place and, exactly 12 months later, Morini burst back onto the international stage with a sensational victory in the 250cc Italian GP. The latest engine, producing 32bhp and with gear-driven cams, featured many changes compared to the prototype assemblies, not the least of these being a six-speed gearbox.

In 1959 Morini signed its first foreign rider in the shape of Derek Minter, who made up the team with the existing members Mendogni and Gianpiero Zubani. But largely because of new twin-cylinder machines from MV Agusta and MZ, whose machines were producing considerably more power, success was not as great as it could have been expected to be. However, the Morini certainly impressed Derek and if political problems within the team had not surfaced, the 'Mint' would have very much liked to have continued riding for the Bologna factory. As it was, Tarquinio Provini joined from rivals MV Agusta, being the sole Morini rider in Grand Prix events. He stayed with the company until the end of 1963 when he quit to join Benelli.

The final development of this speedy double-knocker single came in 1967, when Angelo Bergamonti rode the machine to victory in the Italian Senior Championship. By then it had gained some 6bhp and 500rpm. During this time, the bore and stroke had been changed to 72 x 61mm, giving 248.36cc. Although three and four-valve heads and desmodromic valve operation were tried, the simplicity of the original two-valve system was found best. What had really made the 250 Morini such an excellent racer was that it was a complete motorcycle: fast, reliable, great handling and lightweight.

Monza, September 1963. Morini rider Tarquinio Provini waves to jubilant fans after winning the 250cc Italian GP. A happy Alfonso Morini shares in the glory.

Irrespective of whether the Bianchis arrived in Northern Ireland (which they did not), Derek would ride his Nortons in the 350 and 500cc classes of the North West. Then he would fly to Italy on 17 May to test ride the latest 250 Bianchi twin, in preparation for the forthcoming TT. And *Motor Cycle News* reported: 'Minter will test the Bianchis at Monza. After the poor performance at Cesenatico and Imola, the factory have been working hard to improve the machines.'

Then in *MCN*, dated 25 May 1960, Mick Woollett wrote: 'Derek Minter is back from Italy with news that the 250cc Bianchi twin is much improved. He was riding it at Monza last week, unfortunately the machine will not be at Silverstone on Saturday; the factory is determined to have all the machines perfect for the TT. Derek tells me he saw the new "three-fifty" version while he was at the factory: it is not complete yet but it will be on the Island.'

And so to the Isle of Man for the TT fortnight. Besides Derek (number 15), Bianchi had a number of other riders in the programme for the Lightweight (250cc) event on 13 June: Jack Brett (16), Osvaldo Perfetti (19), Ernesto Brambilla (22), Giancarlo Muscio (25), Ray Fay (27) and Peter Middleton (34), making a total of seven riders. In retrospect, this was probably the last thing that should have happened bearing in mind the newness of the design, the problems already encountered and the difficult nature of the event. Even the date, the 13th, was not a good omen!

Derek, practising with his new machine on the evening of 7 June, did not get off to the best of starts as his Bianchi seized when flat out on the Sulby straight. As *MCN* said: 'Derek's second experience of this failing of the

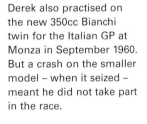

Derek also practised on the new 350cc Bianchi twin for the Italian GP at Monza in September 1960. But a crash on the smaller model – when it seized – meant he did not take part in the race.

Bianchi was not so disastrous as the first when he crashed at Monza, breaking his collarbone – this time he managed to pull up safely.'

As for the race itself, only two of the pale blue Bianchis actually started: Derek plus Osvaldo Perfetti. But although Derek was 'well up' (*MCN*) his Bianchi had gone quiet by the time he reached Sulby Bridge and he coasted in to retire with a seized engine.

By the end of the third lap Osvaldo Perfetti was in 12th position, the top three being Gary Hocking (MV), Tarquinio Provini (Moto Morini) and Carlo Ubbiali (MV). At the end of the fifth and final lap, Perfetti had moved up to 9th, while Provini and Ubbiali had swapped places. Of the original 43 starters (from 66 entries) only 17 finished.

It was later revealed that apart from the engine seizure problems, the Bianchi twins had been plagued by valve spring breakages throughout the practice week. But 'useful lessons' had been learned by designer Lino Tonti in the Island.

Following its dismal showing, Bianchi did not have any machines ready for Derek until the Italian Grand Prix at Monza, some three months later. And after racing his own Nortons at Snetterton on Sunday 4 September, Derek flew to Milan to prepare himself for the Italian GP at Monza seven days later.

However, as the *Motor Cycle News* reported in its 14 September 1960 issue:

The practising on this 3.57-mile ultra-fast boomerang shaped circuit has been marred by a crash which eliminates Derek Minter from today's races. Derek had set third fastest time in the 350cc training on the much improved works twin cylinder Bianchi and was practising on the 250cc model when it seized when laid over for a corner – a repetition of the accident he suffered earlier this year when testing a Bianchi at Monza. At first Derek's injuries were said only to be a cut forehead and extensive bruising. But were later diagnosed as a broken nose, black eye, elbow and shoulder problems – plus a return of his painful ankle injury sustained at the first meeting on the new extended 2.65-mile Brands Hatch GP circuit in July that year.

In the 5 October 1960 issue of *MCN*, Mick Woollett, writing in his *Paddock Gossip* column, had this to say: 'The "Mint" is as tough as they come. He's now out of hospital following an operation to put his broken nose right and if his other Monza injuries continue to heal satisfactorily he'll be at Brands to fight the last battle of the year with Mike Hailwood to decide just who is "the King".' But, as detailed in chapter three, Derek was not at his best and could clearly be seen to still be suffering the effects of his Bianchi crash. And so ended what can only be described as a disastrous period in Derek's racing career. And one which was to make him wary of future Continental European overtures.

Strangely, Derek was to have one successful race on a Bianchi; this coming on 13 May 1962 when he won the 250cc race at Brands Hatch. However, this was not a twin, but one of the small number of 235cc sohc singles made by the Italian firm, with an engine similar to the Tonale 175 series production model. This bike had originally been owned by Peter Doncaster before being acquired by Shrewsbury rider/dealer Fron Purslow. For the Brands meeting Derek was originally down to ride one of Fron's Benellis, but this broke down and the Bianchi was rushed down to Brands. In fact, as Peter Doncaster told *Motor Cycle News*: 'It still had the gearing for Cadwell Park where it made its last appearance.' He continued: 'I think that if it had been properly geared Minter would have had a chance of getting the Honda record. I spent a year working on the bike and I know it will really go.'

And go it did! Unusually for Derek, he got a quick start on the Bianchi single and in complete contrast to the factory's twin-cylinder models he had ridden for a couple of years, the ex-Doncaster single proved not only quick, but reliable too. Derek won comfortably at an average speed of 78.1mph – only slightly slower than his Easter victory on the four-cylinder Honda (see chapter six).

250cc Brands Hatch – 8 laps – 21.2 miles

1st	D.W. Minter (Bianchi single)
2nd	B. Clark (Ducati)
3rd	A.S. Pavey (NSU)
4th	B.T. Osborne (NSU)
5th	D.F. Hardy (REG)

The ex-Peter Doncaster 235cc Bianchi single which Derek rode to victory at Brands Hatch in the 250cc race on 13 May 1962, entered by Fron Purslow.

Chapter 5

Man of the Year

As the year 1962 arrived, Derek and his new wife Marion (the couple had got married in December 1961) were in demand for various club functions. Typical was *MCN's Paddock Gossip*, which reported thus in its 31 January 1962 issue: 'The King of Brands, Derek Minter, together with his wife Marion will be guests of honour at the Kettering Motorcycle Club dinner due to be held at Wickstead Park Pavilion, Kettering, on Tuesday, February 20.'

In past years Derek had been none too keen on the Mallory Park circuit in Leicestershire. And with the 1962 season only weeks away the 'Mint' was to be found practising towards the end of February, having decided that his career demanded that he now needed to take in the more important Mallory events, including the big money Race of the Year in September.

Racing plans

It certainly looked as if Derek would have his hands full, with offers of machinery coming from various directions. Besides the works development Norton and his own three-fifty and five-hundred Nortons (which he had retained following the break with Steve Lancefield), he had also tied up a deal with the British Honda importers, Hondis Ltd (owned by Maico UK). This would see him loaned what could be described as a 1961 works 250 four, plus the use of a CB72 roadster for the long-distance sports machine races at Silverstone and Thruxton. Finally, in the TT he would ride Hondas in the 50, 125 and 250cc classes.

Derek also had an agreement with Joe Ehrlich to ride the 125cc EMC in certain races, at home and abroad.

Another possibility (although nothing was to come of it) was that now Bob McIntyre had signed for

Programme cover for the 1 April 1962 Brands Hatch road races – with Derek (57) and Mike Hailwood in action on the approach to Druids Hill bend.

OFFICIAL PROGRAMME   **I'-**

BRANDS HATCH

Motor Cycle Road Racing
Sunday 1 April 1962

ORGANISED BY THE BRANDS HATCH RACING COMMITTEE

THE MOTOR CYCLE

ALWAYS OUT IN FRONT · THURSDAY 9d.

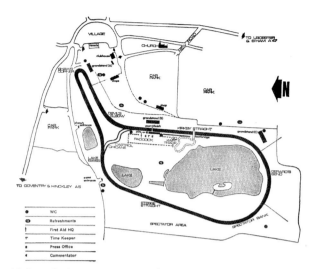

Mallory Park.

Honda, Bianchi might offer Derek their revamped twins. Although in truth, had the offer come, he would probably have turned it down following his disastrous experiences in 1960 with the Italian factory.

One other piece of information was that Derek had joined forces with Cove, Farnborough, Hampshire tuner Ray Petty to look after the engines of his own Nortons. This was to prove a particularly long-lasting and happy relationship.

Musical chairs

The week before the start of the road race season, on Sunday 1 April at Mallory Park, the situation about who would ride what could only be compared to a game of musical chairs!

The front page of *Motor Cycle News* tells the story:

Four days to go to the opening of the road racing season at Mallory Park on Sunday. And what has been going on behind the scenes is nobody's business. 250cc World Champion, Mike Hailwood, entered at Mallory on Bill Webster's Aermacchi, will now be riding Fron Purslow's 1961 ex-works Benelli. Derek Minter, who was to have ridden the Benelli in place of injured John Hartle, has now stepped down in favour of Hailwood, and so will have no ride at Mallory in the two-fifty class – unless he takes over Webster's Aermacchi!

As for the Hondis Ltd-sponsored works four, as detailed in chapter six, this was in the process of being dispatched by air from Japan. At the same time Derek said he would now not be racing the 125cc EMC in 1962 (actually he did ride the bike at a few meetings during the year). And with his plans to race the Honda four, the works development 350 and 500cc Nortons, plus the 650cc Domiracer and his own Ray Petty-tuned Nortons, Derek felt he had 'almost enough on my plate.'

Charlie Rous of *MCN* commented: 'He must be one of the few road racers who could cheerfully give up riding on a works Benelli and works EMC and still feel happy about things!'

Certainly, at the beginning of the 1962 season, Derek was at the very top of his career curve and, as events were to prove, 1962 was to be 'his' year.

No Fool's Day

1 April 1962 was not Fool's Day for Derek, as he romped home to victory in the 350cc final at the Mallory Park national road races and also won his heat and set up the fastest lap in 57 seconds, a speed of 85.26mph.

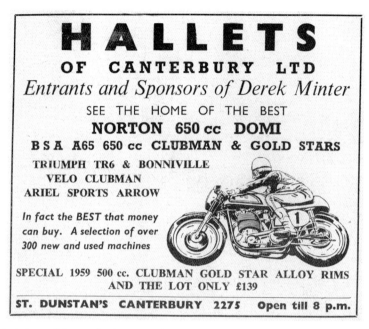

Hallets of Canterbury advertisement proclaiming: 'Entrants and Sponsors of Derek Minter', spring 1962.

This is how *Motor Cycle News* described the race:

Derek Minter's progress on his own Ray Petty tuned Norton in the 350 final was fantastic. He dropped it at the start and then riding as if he was possessed he cut his way right through the field, which from the start had been led by Alan Shepherd (AJS). That Minter caught Shepherd at all was fantastic, for the AJS rider too was flying, but Minter cut down on him and once he was past, cleared off alone and won the race by over nine seconds at 82.84, the fastest speed of the day.

Then, after winning his heat, Derek was to finish third in the 500cc final, behind Mike Hailwood (Norton) and Alan Shepherd (Matchless). Considering his lack of knowledge of the Leicestershire circuit, Derek's performances that day were fantastic.

350cc final, Mallory Park – 20 laps – 26 miles

1st	D.W. Minter (Norton)
2nd	A. Shepherd (AJS)
3rd	A. King (AJS)
4th	P.W. Read (Norton)
5th	P. Middleton (Norton)
6th	L.P. Young (AJS)

Silverstone

In contrast to what had been said before, EMC was out in force at the big international Silverstone meeting scheduled for Saturday 7 April 1962. Mike

Hailwood, Rex Avery and Derek were all to be seen practising at the Northamptonshire circuit the previous Monday, 3 April.

Derek and Mike were riding the older 1961 machines, while Rex (the development rider for the parent company, de Havilland) was aboard the brand new 1962 machine.

MCN's reporter Charlie Rous reported: 'Joe [Ehrlich] tells me he hopes Mike will be riding the machine during this season. Minter had had second thoughts after his decision last week not to ride.'

The Saturday meeting was in fact the 30th Hutchinson 100, organised by Bemsee. The first race (for 125s) saw Mike Hailwood and Derek battle it out at the front for the duration of the eight-lap distance. As *MCN* said: 'Their EMC machines were never more than four lengths apart, and their positions changed frequently.'

Then, on the final lap, Mike led by what was described as 'a short fairing-nose', but by Stowe they were side by side, with 'Derek falling back a little as they rounded Club Corner and the Abbey Curve.' Mike pulled ahead to sweep into Woodcote seemingly almost two lengths in the lead, but as they cranked their machines to round the timekeeper's box on the apex of the corner, Derek 'blasted round the outside of Mike to win by the narrowest of margins' (*MCN*).

125cc Silverstone – 8 laps – 23.2 miles
1st   D.W. Minter (EMC)
2nd   S.M.B. Hailwood (EMC)
3rd   R.A. Avery (EMC)
4th   D.F. Shorey (Bultaco)
5th   A.F. Wheeler (Ducati)

In typical fashion, Derek was slow to get his Norton away at the beginning of the 350cc event; even so, as in the 125cc race, Derek emerged the victor over Mike Hailwood, with the two men sharing the fastest lap in 1m 51.6s, a speed of 94.42mph. But Derek's victory over Mike was much more impressive – by some seven seconds.

350cc Silverstone – 15 laps – 43.5 miles
1st   D.W. Minter (Norton)
2nd   S.M.B. Hailwood (AJS)
3rd   A. Shepherd (AJS)
4th   H.M. Anderson (AJS)
5th   A.M. Godfrey (Norton)

The 500cc race began with 'a surprise' (*MCN*) when Derek was 'left struggling to get his machine started' as the pack disappeared towards Copse Corner. This bad luck continued into the race when he was forced to retire with magneto trouble.

The Easter Weekend

In the two-week period between Silverstone and the Easter Weekend programme, Derek was able to test the recently arrived 250 Honda four. His experiences (at Oulton Park) are fully described in chapter six.

At Brands Hatch on Good Friday, 20 April 1962, he left little doubt in the minds of the 45,000 plus spectators that he was still 'King' of the Kentish circuit.

With winning debut rides on the works Honda four and works development 650 Norton Domiracer twin, he 'shattered' (*MCN*) all opposition in both the 250 and 1000cc events – and completed a hat-trick by taking the 500cc class on his own Ray Petty-tuned Manx Norton. But Derek also lost out twice – to Dan Shorey (Bultaco) in the 125cc event and to Mike Hailwood (AJS) in the 350cc; in both cases finishing runner-up.

500cc Brands Hatch – 10 laps – 26.5 miles
1st	D.W. Minter (Norton)
2nd	P.W. Read (Norton)
3rd	H.M. Anderson (Matchless)
4th	A. Shepherd (Matchless)
5th	S.M.B. Hailwood (Norton)
6th	R. Mayhew (Matchless)

1000cc Brands Hatch – 15 laps – 39.75 miles
1st	D.W. Minter (647cc Norton Domiracer)
2nd	S.M.B. Hailwood (Norton)
3rd	A. Shepherd (Matchless)
4th	R. Mayhew (Matchless)
5th	A.M. Godfrey (Norton)
6th	J. Cripps (Norton)

With poor starts – and Mike Hailwood mounted on his works four-cylinder MV – Derek had a slightly disappointing day at Snetterton on Easter Sunday. *MCN* said: 'Derek had to fight his way through from about tenth position in each of his four races.' He did gain a second in the 350cc heat and third in the 500cc heat and his third place in the 350cc final was

EMC

To trace the origin of EMC, one must go back to 1937 when Dr Joseph Ehrlich, then in his twenties, arrived in Great Britain from Austria seeking to further his career in the field of two-stroke engineering. Two years later he produced the first of his engines, but it took a further seven years of research to come up with a machine which would be a viable proposition in quantity production, and attract the City money that was needed to start the ball rolling. With the necessary backing acquired, Dr Ehrlich went into production in 1947 with his 350cc split-single two-stroke, which at the time was priced at a very competitive £157.

Operating from a factory in Park Royal, north-west London, EMC Ltd (Ehrlich Motor Company) produced a modest 10 to 12 machines per week. But even though the 80mph 350cc EMC – using an air-cooled single-cylinder engine with squared-off cylinder finning, four-speed Burman footchange gearbox, telescopic front forks and duplex frame – had for its day an impressive specification (there was even an auto-oiling system), sales never reached more than 500 units per year. The bike was simply too radical for the austerity of the immediate post-war era, and production was brought to a close in late 1952. The company folded in March 1953.

However, this was far from the end of either Dr Joe or EMC. The first EMC racer had appeared in 1946, with Les Archer riding a 250cc EMC winning the coveted Mellano Trophy in 1947. The first in a long line of 125cc EMC racers was introduced in 1952, with use being made of an Austrian Puch air-cooled split-single two-stroke engine. The short open megaphone exhaust was responsible for an incredible din, and E.H. Burman, who finished sixth in the 1952 Ultra-Lightweight TT, could be heard approaching from a distance of over five miles! Disillusioned by the lack of success attained by his motorcycle manufacturing enterprise, Dr Joe then joined the Austin car company to assist with new vehicle development. While

Dr Joe Ehrlich second left, with his team at the de Havilland Small Engine Division, 1960. Development rider Rex Avery is seated on the machine.

there he designed a twin split-single featuring four pistons for the then revolutionary Austin Mini. But Ehrlich's engine was deemed 'too revolutionary' by the Austin board and so never passed the prototype stage.

During the late 1950s, the British aircraft industry, due to a substantial fall-off in both military and commercial sales, was looking to diversify production into other fields. And like many others, the de Havilland company decided to move into the production of small capacity industrial engines, designing a 150cc two-stroke unit that proved a total disaster. The man brought in to solve the problem was Dr Ehrlich. And in this he was successful, achieving results that de Havilland had previously thought to be unobtainable. Operating from the de Havilland works at Leavesden, north Watford, and promoted to small engine division chief, Dr Ehrlich proceeded to develop a series of small two-stroke engines. Based on a single-cylinder from the DKW three-cylinder, he adapted the design to suit a whole range of prototype vehicles, which included a 150cc 80mph bike, a 150cc scooter, a 150cc outboard motor and even a two-stroke dumper truck. The primary aim was to rival Villiers in commercial and motorcycle engine sales.

Then, in early 1959, the development team came up with a 125cc rotary disc induction engine of advanced design. This was clearly modelled around the existing MZ design. However, the liquid-cooled engine was equipped with a finned cylinder, as opposed to the bald MZ component, and this was produced at the local foundry, Browns of Hitchin. In spring 1959 Dr Joe fitted this still experimental engine into one of the antiquated Puch frames that were last seen in the mid-1950s, but despite the indifferent handling, early tests proved extremely promising.

All that was needed was a good development rider, and Dr Joe found his man working as a toolmaker not 200 yards away in the main de Havilland factory. Rex Avery, an established Norton rider, was only too pleased to transfer to the small engine division and became the unofficial works rider. Derek Minter also had occasional outings that year on the two-stroke machine. The 54 x 54mm six-speed engine was a winner almost immediately and in original form put out a healthy 23.5bhp fitted with a 'C' (factory coding) barrel. This proved virtually unbeatable on the British short circuits with Rex Avery aboard throughout the 1960 season, at least when Mike Hailwood was not riding his works Ducati Desmo single.

During 1961 and 1962 Mike rode the 125cc EMC liquid-cooled two-stroke single, making his debut at the Spanish GP on 23 April 1961. After leading the race and setting a new lap record, Mike eventually finished fourth after the EMC's exhaust split. However, its potential was evident to everyone and, with a bit more good fortune, EMC could have been a major force, even at the highest level. Mike finished fifth in the 125cc World Championship table in 1962. Also, from October 1961, Derek Minter rejoined the EMC team for the occasional outing, enjoying some considerable success. The original engine had an effective powerband of 2,000rpm, but later engines, although giving 27bhp, had powerbands of only 800rpm making them extremely difficult to ride. Another problem was vibration, which of course did not help reliability.

The highpoint of the EMC single came in the 1962 Belgian GP, where Dr Joe's team finished a magnificent third, fourth and fifth (Paddy Driver,

Derek Minter's EMC teammate on occasions, Mike Hailwood, seen here at the West German GP in 1962. He finished third against a horde of Japanese works machinery.

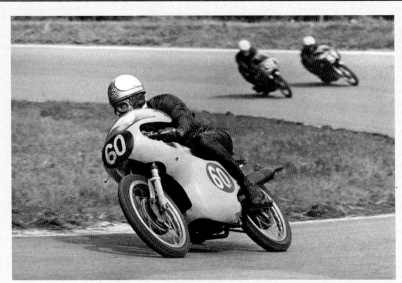

Mike Hailwood and Rex Avery), with Mike taking third the following week in the West German Grand Prix. In 1963 the Japanese development went into overdrive, resulting in exotic designs such as a five-cylinder one-two-five Honda, a Suzuki twin and ultimately a 41bhp Yamaha V4. Dr Joe did build a twin to replace the single, but this proved unsuccessful. During his stay at Leavesden, Dr Erlich produced, on a consultancy basis, designs for other factories. He also sketched out a 500cc liquid-cooled rotary disc induction square-four two-stroke. The drawing of this still survives to prove its existence on paper.

In 1965 the de Havilland group of companies was taken over by aero engine giants Rolls-Royce. This left Dr Ehrlich and his team high and dry, as one of the first moves Rolls-Royce made was to dissolve the small engine division. This meant Dr Joe now had to finance his own two-stroke research or retire. So he set up in his own small factory unit at Bletchley, Buckinghamshire. From there he carried out a number of development contracts, including racing outboard engines and even an engine for a lawn mower. Then came a period in the 1970s when Dr Ehrlich turned his attention to Formula 3 racing cars, before returning once more in the next decade to his original love, motorcycles.

After a short-lived association with the ill-fated Waddon enterprise, Dr Joe was to taste perhaps his greatest moment of glory when English rider Andy Watts took his EMC-Rotax powered inline twin to a brilliant runner-up spot in the 1984 250cc British Grand Prix at Silverstone.

Dr Josef Ehrlich passed away in 2001.

well deserved, but after reaching fourth place on the fifth lap of the 500cc final, he could not gain any further ground on the three leaders, who were well ahead (Hailwood, Mayhew and Godfrey).

And his results were, except for victory on the Honda in the 250cc race, not much different when the circus journeyed to Oulton Park for the Easter Monday meeting. However, he did have the satisfaction of breaking the

125cc lap record for the Cheshire circuit, before a leaking radiator caused his engine to overheat on the EMC.

Practising his starts!

As the saying goes 'practice makes perfect'. And as *Motor Cycle News* journalist Charlie Rous told readers in the newspaper's 2 May 1962 issue 'Derek Minter's trouble just lately has been starting.' He continued: 'not once this season has the Mint been the first away at the drop of the flag; more generally he's been way down the field and has had to carve his way through to head the field.' Although this had always been Derek's weak spot, as Charlie pointed out: 'there's no doubt at all his bad starts have cost him several wins.'

So at Brands Hatch the previous Saturday, Derek spent much of the day attempting, as he said at the time, 'to brush up my technique in this area.'

The trouble, it seemed, was not lack of pushing power entirely. Together, Derek and Ray Petty had gone right through the bikes and found that the remote float chambers for the Amal GP carburettors had been set wrongly. Derek said: 'I take the can for this.' So, having corrected the fuel levels and the like, the pair came to the practice outing – hence Brands as it was the most local venue. And the first test of their work came the following day at Mallory Park.

Just to make sure of things Derek fitted new plugs before the start of each race and, at least in the 350cc class, he was swiftly away. But the bigger Norton, *MCN* said, 'hedged a bit and was troublesome all the way through with misfiring.'

350cc Mallory Park – 20 laps – 26 miles

1st	R. McIntyre (285cc Honda four)
2nd	A. Shepherd (AJS)
3rd	D.W. Minter (Norton)
4th	R. Mayhew (AJS)
5th	P.W. Read (Norton)

More short circuit action

Then came three meetings in two weeks – and no less than 13 straight victories!

This began with heat and final wins at Castle Combe on Saturday 5 May 1965, in the 350 and 500cc classes on Derek's Ray Petty-tuned Nortons.

DEREK MINTER

One of Britains greatest ever short-circuit kings writes HIS story of today's racing – ONLY in next week's Motor Cycle News Order YOUR copy with your newsagent

Motor Cycle News

EVERY WEDNESDAY NINEPENCE

By now Derek was seen as the undisputed King of Brands and also one of Britain's greatest-ever short circuit kings.

Next, at Brands Hatch on Sunday 13 May, he consolidated his position as 'King of Brands', winning all four races for which he was entered. As *Motor Cycle News* reported: 'his riding and the added interest of his debut on the ex-Peter Doncaster now Fron Purslow Bianchi "single" [for the full story of this incident see chapter four], added warmth and sparkle to a bitterly cold day for the 10,000 fans.' Derek's other victories came in the 350, 500 (Redex Trophy) and 1000cc races, all on his Petty Nortons.

At Snetterton a week later, on 20 May, as *MCN* began its race report: 'Derek Minter can now claim another title – "King of Snetterton". Riding at the top of his form on Sunday at the first International meeting to be held at the popular 2.7-mile Norfolk circuit [at which the author was a spectator], he won every race he entered.'

Even though he failed to better the 350 and 500cc lap records set up by Mike Hailwood on MV4s the previous month, Derek became the first man to lap at over 90mph on a two-fifty (on the Honda four, see chapter six).

Derek in action on the 125cc EMC at Brands Hatch on 20 April 1962.

Alastair King

Both Alastair King and fellow Scotsman Bob McIntyre were great friends of Derek Minter, even though they came from different ends of the British Isles. Born in 1927, Alastair's first race was on a Norton International at Errol Aerodrome in spring 1951. Contrary to regulations, he had managed to reach the starting grid without completing a single lap of practice and astonished himself by not only reaching the final, but also coming home in sixth position.

For the 1952 season a more serious approach was made, with the purchase of a Velocette KTT Mark VIII. But against the latest AJS 7R and Featherbed Manx Nortons, which were beginning to appear north of the border, Alastair found it extremely difficult to find success that year. 1953 saw a new machine and a change in fortune. He purchased a Featherbed-framed International and, entered by the Glasgow Mercury Club, he finished fifth in the Senior Clubman's TT, averaging 81.77mph.

Alastair King was another Scottish rider who was a good friend of Derek Minter's. Alastair is seen here on the MZ stand at the Earls Court Show, London, November 1960.

Following his Isle of Man result, he was offered the loan of an AJS 7R from Troon dealers Cooper Brothers, for the Manx Grand Prix in September 1953. However, the result was not what everyone had hoped for; far from it in fact. Not content with falling from the bike within a mile of the start on the first lap at Quarter Bridge, some helpful spectator removed the spark plug lead in an effort to prevent the engine over-revving. With surplus fuel all over the place, it would be an understatement to say that Alastair's dreams of success went up in smoke. The resultant pyre was, as one commentator described it, 'second only to Hiroshima', and the fire even found its way, by photograph, to the following day's *Daily Express* newspaper. But into 1954 Cooper Brothers remained loyal, and this faith was repaid by a string of victories both north and south of the border. In addition, Alastair won the Senior Clubman's TT (on a BSA Gold Star), but success in the Manx GP was again not to be his, even though he seemed destined for victory in the Junior (on an AJS 7R) before being forced out on the final lap with a seized engine. He did have the satisfaction of setting a new class lap record.

1955 was a 'year to forget', when injuries and mechanical woes were the order of the day. Then, in 1956, Alastair had a brilliant year, with success after success in his native Scotland. Again luck deserted him in the Manx, with yet another retirement, but a new Senior lap record of 91.07mph was to stand for several years thereafter. For 1957, Alastair joined the Joe Potts stable, which made him a teammate of Bob McIntyre, although the two men had been close friends for a number of years and members of the same Glasgow-based Mercury Club. With the Potts-tuned bikes, Alastair scored many victories in Scotland, as well as at Brough, Silverstone and Oulton Park. This year too saw him compete in the TT for the first time. After valve gremlins in the Junior, Alastair brought his Potts Norton home to a magnificent seventh position in the Senior TT (the eight-lap Jubilee affair won by Bob McIntyre on a Gilera four) and was rewarded with his first replica.

Alastair King astride one of the Joe Potts Nortons, signing an autograph for a young fan.

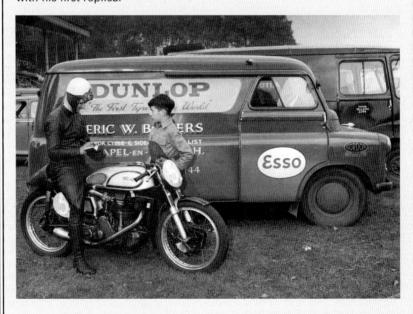

Potts machinery was again the order of the day for 1958, with early successes including victory at Oulton Park, where he had the scalp of Geoff Duke, among others. But again the Isle of Man caused problems. After finishing sixth in the Junior, disaster struck at Kirkmichael, where Alastair crashed heavily, causing damage to his elbow that resulted in three months enforced rest.

Back in the saddle during September 1958, he immediately sprang to form – for example, at Oulton Park only John Surtees on the MV four could stay in front of the speedy Scot. Easter Monday 1959, again at Oulton Park, saw Alastair score a triple, winning the 250, 350 and 500cc finals, a feat enjoyed by only the really talented riders. Then came the TT, with truly magnificent performances: a third in the Junior behind the MVs of Surtees and Hartle, and one better in the Senior, when he came home runner-up behind the Surtees/MV combination. He also won the newly instigated 350cc Formula 1 TT. But it was not until 1961 that he was to repeat this sort of form, with a fourth in the Senior TT, third in the 500cc Ulster GP (behind Hocking's MV and Hailwood's Norton) and runner-up in the 350cc race riding a works Bianchi (again behind Hocking's MV). Then came Alastair's finest Continental Grand Prix result, runner-up to Mike Hailwood in the 500cc Italian GP at Monza in September 1961.

In August 1962 Alastair's great friend Bob McIntyre crashed fatally at Oulton Park. Following this tragic event, Alastair rode (in a demonstration) Bob's Matchless G50 Special at the Remembrance Meeting, run at Oulton in October 1962, then hung up his leathers for good.

Sadly, Alastair suffered a fatal car accident in his native Scotland during the early 1970s.

In winning their 350cc heats, both Derek and Tony Godfrey (Norton) lapped at 89.83mph, so it seemed very likely that these two would be well up in the final. Alastair King suffered suspected big-end failure on his AJS and was a non-starter, but with Continental stars such as the Austrian duo of Bertie Schneider and Rudi Thalhammer, the competition was fierce.

The 20,000-plus crowd was treated to a great battle up front, with Derek winning from Godfrey. But there were many private battles behind, including the one that involved Peter Darvill, Dan Shorey and Thalhammer, this trio 'riding nose to nose for lap after lap' (*MCN*).

350cc Snetterton – 10 laps – 27 miles

1st	D.W. Minter (Norton)
2nd	A.M. Godfrey (Norton)
3rd	D.F. Shorey (Norton)
4th	R. Thalhammer (Norton)
5th	P. Darvill (AJS)
6th	D. Degens (Norton)

The main race, the Molyslip trophy for 500cc machines, again saw Godfrey as Derek's main challenge. And the former 'shot ahead at the flag, leaving Minter to sort his way through the pack after a slow start.' At the end of the first circuit, as *MCN* describes: 'Godfrey already had an impressive lead, but Minter was already lying second.' The report continued: 'Almost imperceptibly, Minter began to close the gap, and by the end of lap five that Minter magic had done the trick, and Godfrey was once more watching "the Mint's" rear wheel.'

500cc Molyslip Trophy, Snetterton – 10 laps – 27 miles

1st   D.W. Minter (Norton)
2nd   A.M. Godfrey (Norton)
3rd   D. Degens (Matchless)
4th   A. King (Norton)
5th   D.F. Shorey (Norton)
6th   P.W. Read (Norton)

Back to the Island

Next came the Isle of Man TT. The following is an interesting extract from the Wednesday 30 May 1962 issue of *Motor Cycle News*:

> Every year the Manx authorities do a little something to improve the circuit and this year is no exception. When Derek Minter arrived we took him around in a car for a quick look, and when we got to the Highlander his immediate comment was: "I just don't know this place." And having now gone out for practice a few times, he considers the circuit to be at least six seconds faster than last year. At Braddon Bridge, where the famous hump has been flattened and the road widened slightly on the exit, he feels this section is now at least two mph faster. Union Mills is also faster, but most of all here the passage through is not so dicey. He thinks the section is at least three mph quicker, but most of all it's faster for everybody and not just the brave few. The only slight criticism he has is of the work carried out from Hillbury to Signpost, in that although it is a very good surface, it's still very bumpy. One stretch that never fails to delight Derek is the run down from Creg-ny-Baa to Brandish Corner. For him, and perhaps others, this is the smoothest and fastest leg of the course.

1962 was to be Derek's busiest ever TT, as he was competing in every solo class, 50cc, 125cc, 250cc, 350cc and 500cc, on Hondas (see chapter six) and Nortons. Interestingly, Derek was entered for the 500cc (Senior) on

With the works
development 500cc
Norton Domiracer at
Oulton Park, Easter
Monday 23 April 1962.

the works development Domiracer, but actually rode his own private Norton single in the race.

Derek practised on two Domiracers. Both engines, Norton said, were 'fitted in standard Manx frames.' One engine was essentially the 1961 model with which Tom Phillis finished third in the Senior that year, while the other one was brand new. The latter differed from the original Domiracer by being fitted with a light alloy cylinder barrel. The only outward differences from the series production engine were the oil feeds to the modified valve gear, and an external oil feed to the exhaust camshaft, plus shorter, larger diameter megaphones. But although Derek finished on all his three Honda machines (see chapter six for full details) his Norton experiences were just the reverse – a retirement in the 350 and a crash in the 500.

On the first lap of the Junior, Derek experienced a 'hair-raising slide' (*MCN*) at the Mountain Box, easing up afterwards and later retiring at the pits when he discovered the rear end of his Norton dripping oil.

In 1960, Derek had become the first man to lap the TT circuit at over 100mph on a single-cylinder machine. And he did it again on the second lap

Technique

As Derek once told Dennis May, when he was interviewed in 1961, 'so far as the actual knack or art or what-have-you of riding technique is concerned, I'd better admit I've never learned much from the experts' teaching and I don't believe this is something that you can put across in words. You have it in you or you don't, like tightrope walking.'

However, Derek firmly believed that there were certain things one could do to improve one's performance, saying 'for instance, experience teaches you how hard and in what way to train.' As for Derek himself, 'Personally, where to draw the line between too much and too little racing practice, when to stick your neck out and when to play it canny, whether to have a go at non-racing competition and so on.' Derek certainly understood the importance of the correct mental approach, saying 'the condition you're aiming for isn't just a matter of bodily tune – it's a state of mind too.' Derek did not smoke or drink, and also eating correctly and regular exercising were important.

Derek also pointed out that self-confidence was really important – and should certainly not be confused with deceit – pointing out 'they are two different things', and that 'you get absolutely nowhere without the first.' Generally, Derek was of the opinion that too much practising 'only wears your bikes out and shows the opposition your hand.' And certainly 'if you have ambitions to go professional, or even semi-pro in a serious way, it's no use thinking you can win, and go on winning, if you saddle yourself with your own engine building and tuning.' Continuing 'Even if you are equally hot as a rider and an engine man – an unusual combination, goodness knows – there simply isn't time to devote the necessary attention to the machinery.'

Derek also acknowledged the debt he owed to firstly Steve Lancefield and latterly Ray Petty for his success. This is how Derek once described Lancefield's role: 'Steve's own self-confidence is magnificent, as it should be. He hasn't a test bench at his place at Norwood, so when he builds an engine for my Norton it isn't run before I get it for installation. I don't run it at my end either – on his say – thus it normally doesn't fire until we get to the circuit. And as I do only the necessary minimum of practice at some circuits, it will probably have run for no more than three or four minutes before racing starts.'

Throughout his career, Derek would be the first to admit that he looked after the 'preparation of cycle parts, but not the engines.' And during his time racing Manx Nortons, Derek rode trials bikes during the winter months (at first Norman and later Cotton machines). He quoted a specific instance where he experienced the value of this 'trials training', as he described it. This happened at Kirkmichael in the 1960 Senior TT, saying 'though I say it myself, I was really getting a shift on – up to second place on the fourth lap, split the two MV fours [of Surtees and Hartle]. Suddenly the back wheel broke away due, as it transpired, to oil on the tyre wall from a split tank. I was flat-out in second (meaning about 80mph) and laid hard over at the time. Well, that was a real lulu of a slide – genuine speedway stuff. Nothing will convince me it was anything but trials experience, and the sense of balance it gives you, that enabled me to hold and snuff such a broadside.'

'About the only useful tip on the subject of cornering methods that I know,' said Derek, 'never go into corners in a big hairy rush – enter with restraint and you'll come out on the right line, which is the important thing. Bill Lomas taught me that one – Guzzis carried out some very careful tests, stop-watch timed to get the thing buttoned up, back when he was riding for them.'

Ken Hayward was portrayed by *Motor Cycle News* in November 1973 as Derek's biggest fan, and he explained this technique by saying 'what I liked about Derek, as opposed to later racers, was that he braked early going into bends and went for power coming out. I think this was what upset him in 1965 and 1966 when the scratchers came in, who braked hard right into the bends cutting him out and then Derek was having to wait for them coming out of the bend.' That was also a reason why Derek was always good in the Isle of Man 'he could ride his own race'.

Derek certainly took safety seriously, both from a riding angle – he never liked Mallory Park for instance – finding the Devil's Elbow section 'dangerous' for example. While machine preparation was described in the following manner: 'Never settle for anything less than 100%.' And, certainly, 'never trust to tyres that you wouldn't send your own mother out on!'

of the 1962 Senior. But, unfortunately, on the very next lap at Quarry Bends he crashed out of the race at an estimated 130mph.

This meant that not only was Derek out of the TT, but he was also forced to withdraw from racing at Brands Hatch the following Monday. In addition to a badly bruised left foot, Derek had also suffered burning where his foot had scraped along the road and a minor infection had set in. So his doctor advised him against racing for a few days.

Although Derek had hoped to compete at Snetterton on Sunday 17 June, it was not until the following weekend – on Saturday 23 June – that he was back in the saddle. And as fully detailed in chapter six, this was at Thruxton, the scene of the famous 500-miler for production motorcycles. Here, partnered by Bill Smith, Derek rode a Honda CB72 Super Sports to a class victory. And of course, as with the pukka racing Hondas, much of Derek's success in 1962 came from his many Honda outings on a number of different machines.

'Classics a waste of time'

In 1962 'Classics' meant meetings counting towards World Championship points – not old motorcycles. And as Charlie Rous explained in a feature on Derek in the 27 June 1962 issue of *Motor Cycle News*: 'World Champion…sounds great doesn't it, but have you any idea what it means to a professional racing rider? Next to nothing! Well, certainly as far as Derek Minter is concerned, and that in a nutshell is why he does not contest the full round of world Championship race meetings.'

Perhaps this might sound rather strong, but to Derek, whose livelihood and business was racing motorcycles, the world classic events were, as he told *MCN* 'an absolute waste of time.' The cost of being away from home for perhaps weeks was nowhere near met by the amount of money he could hope to earn. As Derek explained: 'Take the TT as an example. I was in the Island for nearly three weeks and my expenses came to more than £200, and for winning the 250cc Lightweight race I won £100, and this plus bonuses still did not cover my costs.'

The Rous article also revealed that, prior to the start of the 1962 season, Derek did have thoughts of racing at foreign events and he said from the Spanish GP organisers had come the offer of £50 starting money. From the French GP, which followed over the next weekend, was an offer of £14. As Charlie Rous pointed out: 'Obviously he couldn't have hoped to win at any of these races, so the prize money forthcoming would have been quite low, and into the bargain he would have been away for about three weeks and would have travelled more than 2000 miles.' So Derek had decided 'to remain in England and race at a couple of home meetings' – which netted in a sum in the region of £200 with an outlay of just £25.

Charlie Rous pointed out: 'Perhaps this sounds extremely mercenary, but after all this is a business and one in which the main commodity – the competitors – appear to be fair game.'

However, Derek did have one exception, saying: 'but I am going to the Dutch TT. This is the one big meeting left which has atmosphere and is fun in which to ride. But I'm not going to the Belgian; I'm coming home to ride at Brands on July 8 – because although racing is my living, I still like to enjoy it, and as far as I'm concerned that can only be done at home.'

The Dutch

Just why the Dutch TT was such a favourite with Derek is perhaps explained by Geoff Duke writing in the 4 July 1962 issue of *Motor Cycle News*, commenting: 'there is little doubt that the organisers have produced a short circuits exponents' "paradise", and riders of the calibre of Mike Hailwood, Derek Minter and Phil Read are in their element.'

But even though he had won in the Isle of Man TT, Derek was unable to get an entry for his Honda four in the 250cc class of the Dutch TT. So it was left to his 350 and 500cc Petty-tuned Nortons, entered by Hallets of Canterbury.

The 350cc race opened the programme – in cold blustery weather on Saturday 30 June – but fortunately rain held off, much to the relief of the massive crowd of 130,000 spectators. Works bikes filled the first few places: from Honda, MV Agusta, Bianchi and Jawa. But Derek managed to head the privateers at the finish of the 95.7-mile race.

350cc Dutch TT – 20 laps – 95.7 miles

1st	J. Redman (285cc Honda)
2nd	S.M.B. Hailwood (MV Agusta)
3rd	S. Grassetti (Bianchi)
4th	F. Stastny (Jawa)
5th	D.W. Minter (Norton)
6th	P.W. Read (Norton)
7th	A. Shepherd (AJS)
8th	A.M. Godfrey (Norton)

No one expected the combination of Mike Hailwood and MV not to win the 500cc race, so there was no surprise when Mike led from flag to flag. Silvio Grassetti dropped his bigger Bianchi twin in what *MCN* described as 'a curve that was impossible to negotiate at full throttle and that's where the Bianchi was stuck!' Grassetti was lucky to be unhurt except for the odd scratch or two – even though the bike was extensively damaged.

And so Derek, on his Hallets-entered Norton, was able to secure second spot after a tussle with Phil Read (Norton). Alan Shepherd (Matchless) was never far behind and they all finished in that order, thus giving Derek probably his best continental result for several years on a Norton.

500cc Dutch TT – 20 laps – 95.7 miles

1st	S.M.B. Hailwood (MV Agusta)
2nd	D.W. Minter (Norton)
3rd	P.W. Read (Norton)
4th	A. Shepherd (Matchless)
5th	B. Schneider (Norton)
6th	A.M. Godfrey (Norton)
7th	J. Ahearn (Norton)
8th	F. Stastny (Jawa)

Mike Hailwood racing an unfaired Manx Norton three-fifty at Brands Hatch, *c*.1958.

Mike Hailwood

Many consider S.M.B. (Stanley Michael Bailey) Hailwood to have been the greatest motorcycle racer of all time. He was born in Oxford on 2 April 1940, the son of a self-made millionaire motorcycle dealer. His father Stan had competed pre-war on two, three and four wheels, before going on to build up the largest grouping of dealerships seen up to that time in Great Britain. Mike began his racing career aboard an MV Agusta 125 single overhead camshaft production racer loaned to him by family friend Bill Webster (also a close friend of Count Domenico Agusta). This debut occurred on Easter Monday 22 April 1957, at Oulton Park in Cheshire, only a few miles from Webster's base.

In stark contrast to Derek Minter's early racing days, there is absolutely no doubt that Stan Hailwood went about buying success for his son, with the best bikes, the best tuners and a huge media hype. However, in fairness, Mike did not really need this vast support as he had natural talent in abundance. An example of Stan Hailwood's methods is displayed by a story concerning the NSU Sportmax Mike rode during the early part of his career. In 1955 John Surtees had raced the new German bike thanks to his employers Vincent (who were the British NSU distributors). John was given a bike, plus a spare engine. Then, towards the end of 1957, John received a phone call from Stan asking: 'Can we borrow the NSU for Mike to use in South Africa this winter?' John agreed, and the machine went to the Hailwood équipe. Later another call from Stan: 'Can we have the engine too?' Again John was approached and agreed to lend the spare engine. Now Stan had both bike and engine – and John was never to see either again because Stan conveniently became an NSU dealer. The 'deal' with the new London-based importers meant that King's of Oxford would only become agents if Stan could keep the racer and the engine – even though it had been given to Surtees!

In many ways, Mike was embarrassed by his father's wheeler dealings, and as soon as he could, he became self-sufficient – his race results giving him freedom from his father's overpowering attention. In fact, Mike nicknamed his father 'Stan the Wallet'. But this was not before Stan had bought bikes such as a 125 Paton, a 125 Grand Prix Ducati, various Desmo Ducati twins and singles for the 125, 250 and 350cc classes, a couple of ex-works FB Mondial 250 singles, a squadron of Manx Nortons and an AJS 7R. In 1958 Mike was able to score a trio of British ACU Star titles (125, 250 and 350cc).

Mike's first Grand Prix victory came aboard a factory 125 Ducati Desmo single during the 1959 Ulster – the man he beat that day was none other than his future teammate at MV Agusta, Gary Hocking (riding an MZ). That year he also won all four ACU Stars, adding the 500cc to the classes he had retained for a second year. He repeated this feat the following year and it is one which no man before or since has equalled. For 1961, Mike

Mike, seen here with the 1949 125cc World Champion Nello Pagani during a visit to Italy in 1962. The machine is an Aermacchi Harley-Davidson 250cc Sprint H bound for the American market.

rode 125 and 250cc works Hondas, plus a 350cc AJS 7R and a 500cc Manx Norton. He gained his first world title, the 250cc, on the four-cylinder Honda and took the 125 and 250cc Isle of Man TTs and the Senior race on his Norton. On the latter machine (tuned by Bill Lacey) Mike averaged over 100mph for the six-lap, 226-mile race.

At the end of 1961 he signed for MV Agusta – going on to win the 500cc world title four years in a row (1962–65). In 1964 Mike set a new one-hour world speed record (at Daytona), thus breaking the existing record set by Bob McIntyre on a 350cc Gilera four at Monza in November 1957. In 1966 Mike rejoined Honda, winning both the 250 and 350cc classes on the new six-cylinder models, equalling this feat the following year before switching his attention to four wheels. But even he could not tame the wayward 500cc four-cylinder Honda, with MV (ridden by Giacomo Agostini) retaining the title.

For more than a decade Mike largely stayed away from bikes (except for a couple of outings on BSA and Yamaha machines) before making a historic comeback TT victory on a Ducati V-twin in 1978. The following year, 1979, he rode a Suzuki to a final TT victory. Then he retired once more, becoming a partner in the Hailwood & Gould business (with fellow World Champion Rod Gould). By a twist of fate, the premises they used had formally been the home of the Birmingham branch of King's of Oxford (part of father Stan's dealership chain).

Mike died tragically (with his younger daughter Michelle) while driving home in his Rover car after collecting a fish and chip supper on 14 March 1981.

Back to Brands

After Holland it was back to Brands Hatch on Sunday 20 July 1962, over the full 2.65-mile Grand Prix circuit. Besides his Norton, Derek was also down to ride the 250 four-cylinder Honda on which he had scored his TT victory. In all 254 riders would be taking part, in nine separate events.

And the *MCN* headline, in its 11 July 1962 issue, read: 'Derek Minter Takes Five'. He marked his return to the Kentish circuit 'with a vengeance' taking part in five races, with five wins and five records.

Derek tumbled the 125cc and 250cc all-time records riding two Hondas – the prototype production twin (which would emerge as the CR93 for the 1963 season) and the four-cylinder two-fifty. The other wins and records were set by his own two Nortons and the 647cc works development Domiracer.

John Phillips, writing for *MCN*, said: 'His performance must rate as his best at the Kentish circuit and probably one of his finest ever. He was in fantastic form and in all five races completely dominated the entry.' Derek won the 125, 250, 350, 500 and 1000cc races. He also set an all-time record for the 2.65-mile long circuit in the latter on the 647cc works developed Domiracer, at 89.32mph.

1000cc Brands Hatch – 10 laps – 26.5 miles

1st   D.W. Minter (647cc Norton)
2nd   P.W. Read (Norton)
3rd   L.P. Young (Matchless)
4th   J. Dunphy (Norton)
5th   T. Thorp (Norton)
6th   C.R. Conn (Norton)

In luck

Derek was very much in luck at Castle Combe on 21 July when, after winning both his heat and final in the 350cc class, he found the inlet valve spring of his Norton broken. It was of the coil type (hairpins were standard on the production Manx) and was broken in two places. Derek said that the engine was 'down on revs' from the start of the final and could therefore only conclude that it was broken before he started. But even this potential problem did not stop Derek winning comfortably.

Like his Brands performances, his riding at Castle Combe was truly fabulous. Just listen to the opening section of *MCN's* race report:

> A King slipped out of his domain on Saturday and conquered another territory. Brands Hatch master Derek Minter slammed the star-studded opposition at Castle Combe road races by brilliantly winning the two major events of the day and creating a new 500cc lap record.

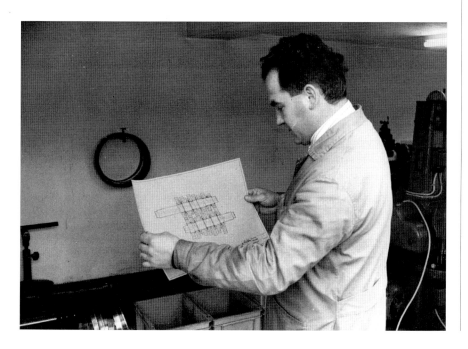

The factory development Nortons now had five-speed gearboxes, manufactured by the Austrian engineer Michael Shaftleitner. This tie-up came about thanks to the Austrian racer Rudi Thalhammer.

500cc Castle Combe – 10 laps – 19 miles
1st   D.W. Minter (Norton)
2nd   S.M.B. Hailwood (Norton)
3rd   A.M. Godfrey (Norton)
4th   C.R. Conn (Norton)
5th   J.N.P. Wright (Norton)
6th   C.J. Williams (Norton)

Out of luck

If Derek had been in luck with his smaller Norton a week before at Castle Combe, it was certainly not the case at Snetterton eight days later on Sunday 29 July 1962 when, after catching and passing both Mike Hailwood and Phil Read (Nortons), and looking set for what seemed certain victory, his ignition failed and he had to sit by and watch Read take the flag in the 350cc final.

Conditions were so bad by the time the 500cc finalists came to the line that the race distance was reduced from 10 laps to seven. And *MCN* reported: 'Riders had difficulty not only in finding wheel grip but in seeing where they were going through the rain and spray – another hazard was the high wind experienced on the exposed former airfield circuit.' But, amazingly, Derek, adjudged to be 'riding carefully, and always picking the best path' (*MCN*), was still fast enough to be only just outside Mike Hailwood's record time for the 2.7-mile Norfolk circuit. And the track was so slippery that marshals lost count of the number of riders who fell off, including Mike Hailwood! But Derek seemed, that day, simply head and shoulders above the opposition. I can still remember watching him and marvelling at the 'Mint's' ability in the wet.

Triple British Champion

Already acknowledged in 1962 as the King of Brands, crowned King of Mallory, conqueror of Snetterton and Castle Combe, on August Bank Holiday, 6 August, Derek became 250, 350 and 500cc British Champion at Oulton Park, Cheshire, in what *Motor Cycle News* said was 'breathtaking fashion'. The three races will long be remembered by the 45,000-strong crowd. Again, the author was there that day himself.

On the Hondis Ltd-entered Honda four, Derek carved his way through a glittering array of star names to shatter the existing lap records for not only the 250, but also the 350 class. And in the process he lapped everyone except 250cc World Champion elect Jim Redman.

Then, in a race-long duel in the 350cc race, Derek succeeded in holding off Mike Hailwood (AJS).

350cc British Championship, Oulton Park – 30 laps – 87 miles
1st   D.W. Minter (Norton)
2nd   S.M.B. Hailwood (AJS)
3rd   P.W. Read (Norton)
4th   R.H. Anderson (AJS)
5th   A. Shepherd (AJS)
6th   M.A. Duff (AJS)

Then came a truly bittersweet race for Derek, but even though he was to emerge the victor and score his third title that historic day, his joy was tarnished by the news that his great rival and friend Bob McIntyre had been seriously injured in the rain-lashed race.

After a fine morning, torrential rain came down in the afternoon. Derek had what *MCN* described as a 'very comfortable' 500cc win and in splashing his way to victory lapped everyone but second man Phil Read. Derek also set the fastest lap at 82.69mph – slower than his earlier 250cc win.

500cc British Championship, Oulton Park – 30 laps – 87 miles
1st   D.W. Minter (Norton)
2nd   P.W. Read (Norton)
3rd   S.M.B. Hailwood (Norton)
4th   F.J. Stevens (Norton)
5th   H.R. Anderson (Matchless)
6th   M.A. Duff (Matchless)

As detailed in the companion volume *Bob McIntyre – The Flying Scot* (Breedon), Bob McIntyre sadly passed away just over a week after the Oulton Park meeting.

A crash in Ulster
Just to show how fickle success can be in racing, Derek, in taking over Mike Hailwood's ride on the EMC in the 125cc Ulster GP at Dundrod on Saturday 11 August, crashed himself. It happened in the following manner: he had just taken over the lead from the factory Hondas of Jim Redman and Luigi Taveri, when he hit a patch of water, aquaplaned, and lost the fight to stay aboard. Derek was taken to hospital for treatment on a broken finger and eight stitches for a head injury – his helmet prevented a more serious injury, and he was discharged the following morning.

As the 125cc race was the first in the programme, Derek did not take part in the other races in which he was entered – 250, 350 and 500cc.

The Ulster crash put Derek out of action for some six weeks – but he made a triumphant return on Sunday 23 September when, still suffering from the after effects of the accident – plus more poor starts – he still managed to 'shatter all opposition' at Brands Hatch, winning the 250, 350, 500 and 1000cc classes. Derek's only comment about the badly bent third finger of his left hand, which bled profusely while racing, was 'it helps me to hold on.' But joking apart, Derek's return after weeks out of the saddle was really impressive. As one commentator described it: 'Is there anyone to approach him? Derek Minter, racing for the first time since his Ulster GP crash in August, scored the limit – four rides, four wins.' Again, I, the author, was there that day. And to me, at that time Derek was the greatest rider in the world – and even today as I write these words 45 years later, my view hasn't changed. On **equal** machinery, Derek Minter, in 1962, was fully capable of beating anyone. Certainly, when he met up with the official World Champions of that year (Jim Redman and Mike Hailwood) Derek would come out on top…

Beating Read

Another top line rider – Phil Read (who would ultimately win no fewer than eight World Championship titles) – was at Brands Hatch that day, and Phil could not hold that man Minter, even though in the 500cc event the two riders tied for setting a new lap record at 89.83mph. Otherwise, in each of Derek's four races, once in front that was the end as far as the opposition was concerned.

The Brands meeting was also notable as it saw Derek make his debut on the JSD (John Surtees Ducati) in the 250cc race. Essentially this machine was the combination of one of the Desmodromic twin-cylinder engines mounted in a special frame commissioned by John Surtees and manufactured by Reynolds Tubing in Birmingham. The bike also employed a Reynolds-made leading link front fork assembly and Oldani brakes front and rear. In its original form (but later with an Ernie Earles frame) the engine had been raced by Mike Hailwood during 1960 and 1961. There were a small number of two-fifty and three-fifty machines, these having been commissioned by Stan Hailwood from Ducati – the engines being designed by Ing. Fabio Taglioni. John Surtees had acquired the various machines from the Hailwood équipe in lieu of payment for stock from his West Wickham showroom sold to the King's Group, of which Stan Hailwood was managing director when the former was closed. The full story of the bikes and the politics is detailed in *John Surtees – Motorcycle Maestro* (Breedon).

250cc Brands Hatch – 8 laps – 21.2 miles

1st	D.W. Minter (JSD)
2nd	D.F. Shorey (Bultaco)
3rd	N. Surtees (Aermacchi)
4th	F.D. Hardy (NSU)
5th	B.T. Osborne (NSU)
6th	T. Grotefeld (Aermacchi)

Derek seen here at South Bank Bend, Brands Hatch on 23 September 1962, winning on the works development 647cc Norton Domiracer.

After winning both the 350 and 500cc races, for the Fred Neville Memorial and Redex trophies respectively, on his Petty-tuned Nortons, Derek's final race of the day was in the 15-lap 1000cc event. This time he was mounted on his 647cc Domiracer. Again he scored what *MCN* described as a 'runaway win.' But as the paper also said, 'the second day star was Dave Downer on Paul Dunstall's 650cc Dominator.' Sixth the first time round, Downer was chasing Read, Godfrey, Driver and Shorey, and within two laps passed them all and built up an appreciable second-place lead by the end.

It was to be this combination of rider and machine which was to be involved on the same 2.65-mile Brands circuit the following year. The outcome then would be Downer's death and serious injury for Derek – which would completely alter the course of events and, ultimately, the 'Mint's' racing career.

1000cc Brands Hatch – 15 laps – 39.75mph

1st	D.W. Minter (647cc Norton)
2nd	D. Downer (647cc Norton)
3rd	P.W. Read (Norton)
4th	A.M. Godfrey (Norton)
5th	D.F. Shorey (Matchless)
6th	R.F. Driver (Norton)

Another fabulous weekend

Then came another fabulous weekend, with more highly acclaimed performances at Aintree on Saturday 29 September and Mallory Park the following day.

At Aintree *MCN* were able to headline 'Minter Slays That Aintree Hoodoo.' The north-west circuit had previously not been a happy hunting

Ray Petty in his Cove,
Farnborough, Hampshire,
workshop, inspecting a
Manx Norton cylinder
barrel.

Ray Petty

The latter part of Derek Minter's Norton racing career is very much
associated with the famous Farnborough, Hampshire tuner, Ray Petty. But
Ray was much more than simply someone who tuned Manx Nortons.
Besides being a first-class engineer, he was also a racer, sprinter and trials
rider of no mean ability: he was even responsible for building some
innovative specials.

Ray began racing at Brooklands during 1939 on a two-fifty New
Imperial, but had only appeared at three meetings before war was
declared at the beginning of September that year. By then his
apprenticeship as a fitter in a local Farnborough garage had been
completed. Ray was then sent to an engineering company, where he was
employed as a detail fitter making small components to drawings.
Promotion brought a clerical job, which he detested, so he moved on to
the tank design department of Vivien Lloyd. From there he moved on to the
Vickers Armstrong experimental shop at Fox Warren, not far from his
home, where he stayed from 1942 until 1946, working on aircraft engine
installation. It was here that he met the legendary Francis Beart, at the time
employed by the Bristol company as their technical representative. His job
was to check that engines, some of them installed by Petty, were behaving
correctly.

So it was that in 1946, released from Government work, Ray Petty
joined Beart in preparing Norton engines for racing. This was a full-time
job, involving many long hours on the bench. But even so Ray managed
to squeeze in a considerable amount of racing on his own account with
various machines, including an AJS 7R and, later, a couple of Manx
Nortons. He also still managed to compete in another branch of the sport,
one-day trials. Many thought he could have gone to the very top as a mud
plugger – he even won a gold medal in the ISDT.

Ray Petty pictured in November 1963 working on Derek Minter's 350 Reverse Head Norton.

From 1955, Ray entered the tuning business on his own account, operating a workshop behind his parents' house in Farnborough, helped by his first wife Peggy. The list of riders who could count themselves as Petty customers reads like a *Who's Who* of Norton racing and includes the likes of Dan Shorey, John Cooper, Bob Keeler, Geoff Tanner, Jack Ahearn, Billie Nelson, Bertie Schneider and, of course, Derek Minter himself. And Derek is the first man to acknowledge the debt of gratitude for the friendship and high level of engine preparation that Ray provided to him during their association. In fact, Ray Petty was involved with his beloved double-knocker Nortons until the very last, in more ways than one. For a Petty-tuned Norton took the final British Championship title won by a single, in 1971 (Percy May), and he was still preparing them for classic racing enthusiasts almost until the very end, when he died from cancer in 1987.

In the final analysis, Ray Petty even eclipsed his former employer, Francis Beart, with more victories and race records to his credit than anyone, except perhaps the factory and Joe Craig. What better tribute to this highly capable and friendly man could there be than this?

ground – since 1957 Derek had only won two races there (a 250 and a 350cc).

But in 1962, in what were perfect conditions for racing, Derek put in a 'scintillating' (*MCN*) performance to win the premier award of the day, the 21-lap Aintree Century, and the Aintree Senior.

Since his Ulster crash, unbeknown to his many fans, Derek had been riding with his ribs in a plaster cast, and at Aintree he revealed to *MCN* journalist John Phillips: 'I think I've broken one.'

Derek, riding the JSD for the second time, had the 250cc race in the bag until the final lap, when the engine went on one cylinder and he crossed the line third behind the winner Tommy Robb (Aermacchi) and Dan Shorey (Bultaco). Then, after winning his heat, Derek came home runner-up behind Shorey in the Junior (350cc) event.

Aintree Century – 21 laps – 56.7 miles

1st	D.W. Minter (Norton)
2nd	A. Shepherd (Matchless)
3rd	F.J. Stevens (Norton)
4th	R. Fitton (Norton)
5th	T.F. Phillips (Norton)
6th	C.R. Conn (Norton)

Minter in the money

At Mallory Park on Sunday 30 September 1962, the prize money fund (the richest in racing at the time) exceeded £2,000, of which £1,725 was at stake in the Race of the Year. And after winning the 250 and 500cc races, plus a fourth in the 350cc event, Derek made sure that he took home the big prize.

And, except for Mike Hailwood, just about everyone who was anyone took part – Read, Redman, Shepherd, Cooper, Dunphy, Conn, Shorey – the list was almost endless.

Jim Redman (beaten by Derek in the 250cc race) used his two-fifty Honda four against the 500s favoured by the majority of other riders in the Race of the Year event.

At the start, it was in fact Redman and Read who got away best, Derek having to battle his way through the field as usual. And it was Read who set the pace for the first 10 laps. By this time Derek was pressing him hard, and then the 'Mint' got past. Four laps later Read crashed at Shaw Corner, knocking himself out. It had taken Derek six laps to overhaul the flying Redman. Shepherd was the next rider to overhaul the little Honda which, following Read's mishap, was going well in third place. Then Cooper became a serious challenger and thundered past Redman. At the 30-lap stage the leaders were: Derek, Shepherd, Cooper and Redman, followed by Shorey and Brian Setchell. As *MCN* said: 'All had seen Minter's bellowing Norton go past.' The race pattern was now fixed. And at the flag Derek had scored a famous victory; only Shepherd, Cooper and Redman remained unlapped. And with a cheque for over £1,200 (including bonuses for a 90mph + lap), Derek was to say afterwards: 'I've never made so much money in my life.'

Race of the Year, Mallory Park – 40 laps – 54 miles

1st   D.W. Minter (Norton)
2nd   A. Shepherd (Matchless)
3rd   J. Cooper (Norton)
4th   J. Redman (Honda)
5th   D. Shorey (Matchless)
6th   B.R. Setchell (Norton)
7th   C.R. Conn (Norton)
8th   G.A. Jenkins (Norton)
9th   R. Butcher (Norton)
10th   B.L. Denehy (Norton)
11th   J.C. Simmonds (Matchless)
12th   R.J. Langston (Norton)

The Bob McIntyre Remembrance Meeting

On Sunday 6 October 1962, some two months after Bob McIntyre's fatal accident, the Oulton Park circuit staged the Bob McIntyre Remembrance Meeting, in memory of the Scottish star. And it was perhaps fitting that his great friend and rival Derek Minter should be the highlight of a full programme of races for all classes by winning the 350 and 500cc races. In the 350cc race Derek broke Bob's existing record by almost two seconds, hoisting the lap speed from 88.59 to 89.87mph.

But perhaps more significant than Derek or anyone else could have realised at the time was the fact that six-times World Champion Geoff Duke received a tremendous reception from the Oulton Park crowd (estimated to have been over 60,000 strong) when he paraded a 1957 dustbin-faired Gilera; a machine similar to that on which Bob McIntyre became the first man to cover the Isle of Man Mountain Circuit at over 100mph.

350cc Oulton Park – 10 laps – 27.6 miles

1st   D.W. Minter (Norton)
2nd   F.J. Stevens (Norton)
3rd   D.F. Shorey (AJS)
4th   F. Fisher (Norton)
5th   M.A. Duff (Norton)
6th   D.L. Downer (Norton)

500cc Oulton Park – 10 laps – 27.6 miles
1st   D.W. Minter (Norton)
2nd   M.A. Duff (Norton)

3rd	D.F. Shorey (Matchless)
4th	A.R.C. Hunter (Norton)
5th	R. Fitton (Norton)
6th	J.R. Cripps (Norton)

Derek's chances of virtually 'clean sweeping' (*MCN*) the 1962 Brands Hatch season were spoiled at the final meeting on Sunday 14 October, when he was brought down during a pile-up in the 125cc race. Derek, who was riding an EMC, was not seriously injured but suffered 'a severe shaking', (*MCN*) which caused his retirement from the remainder of the meeting. But this came after he had clinched the opening 350cc race on his Petty-tuned Norton at 84.62mph.

As for the 125cc crash, this is what transpired: with Derek (EMC) and Jim Redman (Honda) on the line, the crowd, *MCN* said, 'was fully expecting to witness racing of a calibre that would make a world classic look like a picnic.' But, unfortunately, this match fizzled out – first Redman's machine refused to start and, as the field went out of sight at South Bank bend, Rex Avery, Derek's EMC teammate, overslid and struck Bill Ivy's Honda. The two of them fell, bringing Derek down with them.

350cc Brands Hatch – 10 laps – 26.5 miles

1st	D.W. Minter (Norton)
2nd	A.M. Godfrey (Norton)
3rd	M. Duff (AJS)
4th	E. Driver (AJS)
5th	C.R. Conn (Norton)
6th	J. Cripps (Norton)

Top Man

Back at the beginning of October, *Motor Cycle News* had said:

> Minter...Minter...Minter...Time and again this season the name of Derek Minter has headed the results of races in this country. He's had a wonderful season and deserves every penny his dashing skill has earned him. Thousands of race followers will vote him their Man of the Year.

Then some three weeks later *MCN* asked its readers: 'Who is your Man of the Year?' Among the leading contenders from all branches of the sport came a wide array of talent, including Jeff Smith, Mike Hailwood, Don Rickman, Jim Redman and Dave Bickers. But as *MCN* said: 'Who will receive top votes is anybody's guess, but of the many names to have hit the headlines in the past year there are two which have got a good start on the others: road racing "King" Derek Minter and trials wizard, Ulsterman Sammy Miller.'

In its 14 November 1962 issue *MCN* announced that Derek was its Man of the Year. The final voting in the poll being: Minter, Dave Bickers, Mike Hailwood and Sammy Miller, in that order.

Derek received his award at the London Earls Court Show on Wednesday 14 November 1962.

What of the future?

Derek's tremendous season had put him firmly in the limelight, and the press was quick to come up with who they thought he might be riding for in 1963. But the big news was that during late November Derek had been riding a four-cylinder Gilera at Mallory Park. The official version of the story was that the try-out on the Gilera came because Geoff Duke was engaged on tyre testing for Avon tyres and had invited Derek to assist him. *MCN* said: 'Derek, despite icy conditions, went round faster than he has ever lapped Mallory before on any machine.'

Finally, in the 28 November 1962 issue, *MCN's* Charlie Rous, writing in the *Paddock Gossip* column, said: 'forget about the Gilera for a minute…Geoff Duke tells me he will be sponsoring Derek Minter next season in the production machine races at Thruxton and Silverstone, on a 250 Royal Enfield (Geoff acted as a consultant for the Redditch marque).'

As events were to prove, Geoff Duke and Derek were to join forces in 1963. But this was very much in the future as 1962 drew to a close.

Chapter 6

The Honda Saga

After their success in 1961, when they won the 125 and 250cc World Championship titles (Tom Phillis and Mike Hailwood respectively), the name Honda was on everyone's lips during the closed season of 1961–62.

It seemed that just about everyone who was anyone in the racing world at this time was being associated with the Japanese marque – including not only Phillis and Hailwood, but also Jim Redman, Bob McIntyre and John Hartle.

Then in mid-February 1962 came news that the British Honda importer Hondis Ltd, owned by the London-based Maico concessionaires company, had acquired the use of a 'pukka works 250 four,' for 'all international meetings beginning with the Hutchinson 100 at Silverstone on 7 April.'

But who would the rider be? On this subject Maico Ltd was tight-lipped. However, *The Motor Cycle* in its 15 February 1962 issue got it right: 'A little bird whispering hints here and there is making cheeps that, translated, could read Derek Minter.'

Three weeks later *Motor Cycle News' Paddock Gossip* column, compiled by Charlie Rous, had the following as its lead story: 'It is confirmed that Derek Minter will be riding a privately entered Honda four this season.' It continued: 'His first outing on the Nip four will be at Silverstone on Saturday 7 April, at BMCRC's Hutchinson 100 meeting and this will be followed by eight further outings at Brands Hatch twice, Oulton Park twice, Snetterton and Mallory Park, plus the Isle of Man Lightweight TT and the Ulster Grand Prix. Besides racing the only non-works Honda four out of captivity in this country, Derek will also compete in the production races at Silverstone and Thruxton on a standard 250 Honda Super Sports twin [the CB72].'

Towards the end of March the Hondis Ltd-sponsored Honda four that Derek had signed to ride in the selected meetings mentioned above was dispatched by air from Tokyo. But even so he was a non-starter at Silverstone on 7 April.

One of the four-cylinder 250 Hondas pictured in Japan during 1961. The power output was a claimed 40bhp at 14,000rpm.

Honda 250 Four

Honda's first four-cylinder model, the RC160, made its debut at the Mount Asama circuit during a race meeting which took in three days – 22, 23 and 24 August 1959. And what a debut it was too. At the end of the 16-lap race, those machines filled five of the top six places.

Sharing the same 44 x 41mm bore and stroke dimensions as the 125cc twins which had made their European debut in the Isle of Man TT (winning the team prize) a couple of months earlier, the double overhead camshaft four displaced 249.2cc and ran on a compression ration of 10.5:1. It produced 35bhp at a heady 14,000rpm. On optimum gearing, this related to a maximum speed of approaching 130mph. Unlike the twin of the same era, which featured inclined cylinders, the RC160 had upright cylinders. Drive to the camshaft was on the offside and, unlike the 125cc twin of 1959, the four relied upon shaft and bevel gears. In fact, Soichiro Honda used this system, having been impressed by the German NSU marque using this layout in its works racers of the mid-1950s, following Honda's visit to Europe in the summer of 1954. A particularly interesting feature of the RC160 was its first use by Honda of four-valves-per-cylinder technology.

Many of this first four-cylinder Honda's features were also found on the 1959 one-two-five twin, including the leading link front fork layout. However, because of the four's superior speed, it had not simply been a case of 'make do', but instead virtually everything was re-engineered to take account of the additional speed of the heavier machine.

The RC160 was never raced in Europe; but it was a significant engineering achievement and was to lead directly to Honda's 250cc Grand Prix entry the following year, 1960. This later design, coded RC161, was an entirely new motorcycle and, except for features such as the 44 x 41mm bore and stroke, dohc, four-valves-per-cylinder and horizontally-split crankcases, owed nothing to the RC160.

For 1960, Honda planned new, much improved machinery. Gone were the upright cylinders, bevel camshaft drive and leading link front suspension. In their place came inclined cylinders, central gear drive (the one-two-five twin retained the bevel cam for the year) and telescopic front forks. The RC161 produced 38bhp at 13,500rpm, but could be revved to an incredible 17,000rpm before bursting. Throughout the season development continued apace, resulting in ever-improving race results. The 1961 machines were considerably different from the 1960 version. Although the bore and stroke was again unchanged, the cylinders of the new RC162 were less steeply inclined, although they still tilted forward at an angle of 30 degrees from the vertical. The engine had also been modified from wet to dry-sump lubrication and was claimed to produce in excess of 40bhp at 14,000rpm. It also featured an entirely new tubular frame, which the press claimed was modelled on MV lines, although in Honda's case it dispensed with front down-tubes. The new four also incorporated a fresh ignition system, employing one coil for each pair of cylinders and producing sparks on the compression and exhaust strokes; some bikes were also equipped with a Kokusan Denki magneto. Honda sources quoted maximum speed as being 145mph. 1961 saw Honda win both the 125cc (Tom Phillis) and 250cc (Mike Hailwood) World Championship titles.

For the 1962 season Honda produced the RC163, but, as explained elsewhere, the 'private' RC162 raced by Derek Minter for the British importers Hondis Ltd caused huge controversy when Derek beat the entire works squad on the latest RC163s in the Isle of Man, including team captain and forthcoming 250cc World Champion Jim Redman. And in addition, Honda expanded its presence for the 1962 season by also contesting the 350 and 50cc classes (the latter newly introduced for that year). The 'three-fifty' was actually a 285cc variant of the existing 250, achieved by boring out the cylinders to 47mm.

Not only did Jim Redman win the 250cc title in 1962, but the same rider went on to also take the 350cc crown. Redman then also won the 350cc title in 1963, 1964 and 1965, plus another 250cc one in 1963. As for the man who beat him in that controversial 1962 TT, Derek Minter was sadly ignored by the Japanese company.

A 1961 RC162 with the fairing removed, showing the engine, carburettors, frame and hydraulic steering damper.

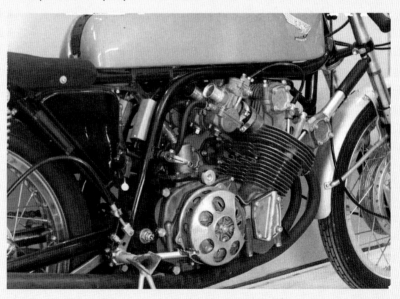

In the 18 April issue of *Motor Cycle News* Derek told readers: 'My 350 Norton is the fastest 350 I have ever ridden.' And he continued: 'But after trying the 250 Honda four, I can only say this machine is miles an hour faster.' This came after Derek had ridden the bike for the first time, at Oulton Park. 'The power comes in at 8,000 revs' he said, 'and then streaks up to the 13,000 mark just like that. I was reaching 13,000 from Esso Corner to Knicker Brook.'

The bike also appeared 'a shade undergeared,' but this did not stop Derek from lapping the Cheshire circuit in precisely two minutes.

Debut day at Brands

Derek's debut on the two-fifty Honda came on Good Friday, 20 April, in front of an estimated 45,000 at Brands Hatch. And as *Motor Cycle News* reported: 'the race everybody was waiting for was Minter on the Honda four, and he didn't let them down. This was the only race [of a day when he also rode a 125 EMC and 350, 500 and 650 Nortons] he led from start to finish and for a rider who had never raced a four-cylinder machine before, his handling of the Honda was superb, averaging 80.92mph with an unofficial lap record of 82.38mph. That's just about all one can say – the spectators saw him, but certainly none of the other competitors.'

250cc Brands Hatch – 8 laps – 21.2 miles
1st   D.W. Minter (Honda)
2nd   D.F. Shorey (Bultaco)
3rd   N. Surtees (JSD)
4th   B. Clark (Ducati)
5th   F.D. Hardy (REG)
6th   A. Pavey (NSU)

Another ride, another win

Four days later, at Oulton Park on Easter Monday, 23 April, in front of 52,000 spectators, Derek had his second race on the Honda and another victory. As *MCN* said: 'He did not break any records, but this was not surprising for he was never challenged and finished an astounding 1 minute 2 seconds ahead of Alan Shepherd (Aermacchi). In fact Derek lapped all but the second and third place men – third spot being taken by Alastair King riding Fron Purslow's ex-works single-cylinder Benelli.'

250cc Oulton Park – 19 laps – 55 miles
1st   D.W. Minter (Honda)
2nd   A. Shepherd (Aermacchi)

Derek on his way to victory at Oulton Park, Easter Monday April 1962.

3rd	A. King (Benelli)
4th	S. Graham (Aermacchi)
5th	E. Cheers (Aermacchi)
6th	G. Leigh (NSU)

Record breaking at Snetterton

It was record breaking time at the international Snetterton road races on 20 May 1962. As *Motor Cycle News* said: 'The Minter Magic was at work again on Sunday. Riding the 250cc Honda four, Derek became the first rider to lap Snetterton at over 90mph on a 250, pushing the record up to 91.01mph.'

As chapter five reveals, he also won the 350 and 500cc events – in fact every race for which he had entered. I well remember riding my Ducati 250 Daytona to Snetterton, my local circuit, and watching Derek dominate the meeting. He knocked Mike Hailwood's lap record 'for six' (*MCN*). He broke it on his second lap, did even better on the third, and on lap 5 he pushed his speed to over 91mph – just over 4mph faster than Mike's speed on the Mondial. As *MCN* said: 'Minter's Honda, the only four in the race, made everything else look painfully slow. He gained some 10 seconds in every lap, and crossed the line only a fraction less than one minute ahead of Clark on the Ducati, who robbed Norman Surtees of second place on the final circuit.'

250cc Snetterton – 6 laps – 16.2 miles
1st   D.W. Minter (Honda)
2nd   B. Clark (Ducati)
3rd   N. Surtees (JSD)
4th   D. Warren (GMS)
5th   T. Grotefeld (Aermacchi)
6th   R. Cowles (Velocette)

Unknown to many spectators at Snetterton, Derek had the previous day been competing at Silverstone in the 1000 Kilometre race for series production bikes on the Hondis Ltd-entered CB72. The event was held in truly vile conditions of rain, high wind and extreme cold – it had seemed more like mid-winter than mid-May! But Derek, partnered by Joe Dunn, was forced to retire towards the end of the second hour – after the pair suffered their second flat tyre.

Isle of Man TT practice
After Snetterton came the Isle of Man TT, where for the first time in his career Derek was entered in all solo classes, which in 1962 meant 50, 125, 250, 350 and 500cc – the three smaller capacity ones being on Honda machinery provided by Hondis Ltd.

The first practice session of that year's TT began on Saturday morning, 26 May, and consisted of 125 and 250cc machines. *Motor Cycle News* reported: 'The 125cc class brought the first outing of the recently announced Honda twin production racers. Three of them were tweaked around in the hands of Tom Phillis, Derek Minter and Shimazaki.' Phillis was fastest in 28m 52s, a speed of 78.44mph. Shimazaki was next with 77.02mph and then Minter with 76.07mph. Overall the three riders were fourth, fifth and sixth fastest in this session, behind the factory Honda riders (on full works machines) in the shape of Luigi Taveri, Kunimitsu Takahashi and Jim Redman. But in the evening session the same day Derek was second quickest, going around in 26m 1.2s and was obviously more in tune with the bike. *MCN* commented:

> The performance that really got people talking and thinking of the future was Derek Minter's on the production race 125cc Honda twin. He howled it around at 87mph! The only man who was faster was Takahashi, who with 88.23mph was just four seconds away from the record – but on a works machine of course.

That Derek was a serious contender in the 250cc class became evident as practice week unfolded. And on Thursday evening, 31 May, he headed the leaderboard with a lap in 23m 44.8s, a speed of 95.33mph. Next came fellow Honda riders Bob McIntyre and Mitsu Katano, plus Mike Hailwood (Benelli).

King of the Island
On 4 June 1962 – for a single day – the 'King of Brands' became 'King of the Island', when he took on and defeated the might of the entire works Honda team, with its hand-picked squadron of stars, and won the Lightweight (250cc) TT.

Derek began the six-lap, 226.38-mile race with the number 1 plate, but was passed on the road by Bob McIntyre on one of the 'official' Hondas. But Bob, after setting a fantastic 99.06mph lap from a standing start, found his machine running on only two cylinders shortly afterwards and was forced into retirement at Baaregarroo on the second lap.

The race then developed into a dramatic struggle between Jim Redman, then leading the World Championship, and Derek. And the *MCN* race report commented: 'The "Mint" was certainly on his way. Reports from around the course told us he was going around the corners quicker than anybody else...and has cut Redman's lead to six seconds.' So, after two laps the leaders were: Redman, Derek, Mike Hailwood (Benelli) and Alan Shepherd (Aermacchi). At Keppel Gate, on the third lap, Derek was in the lead – with an estimate that Redman was now 11 seconds adrift.

After three laps Derek came in for fuel and proceeded to overshoot his pit 'by a few yards' (*MCN*). He was forced to wheel his bike back to his Hondis mechanic, who 'calmly' (*MCN*) tended the Honda. Derek got away just as Redman (who had a large tank enabling him to go through the race non-stop) flashed past. As *MCN* said: 'The race for first place was now to begin.' But the fuel stop had cost Derek no less than 52 seconds!

Derek's speed after three laps was 97.07mph, with Redman averaging 96.98mph. But Derek was back in front at Kerroo Mooar, having caught and passed the Honda team captain.

After the completion of four laps, Redman was in the lead and Derek was leading on the road at Sulby Bridge. Then Derek received something of a bonus, as Redman came into the pits and took on more fuel. But even without Redman's stop, which cost him 22 seconds, Derek would still have won.

After the race Derek commented that he had become 'bored' when he was out in front, but paid a special tribute to Stan Hailwood for the use of his telephone line 'which served to keep him accurately informed of his position at all times.'

Derek completed the race in 2 hours 20 minutes 30 seconds, at an average speed of 96.68mph, compared to Redman's figures of 2 hours 22 minutes 23.6 seconds, 95.40mph.

Lightweight (250cc) Isle of Man TT – 6 laps – 226.38 miles

1st	D.W. Minter (Honda)
2nd	J. Redman (Honda)
3rd	T. Phillis (Honda)
4th	A.F. Wheeler (Moto Guzzi)
5th	A. Pagani (Aermacchi)
6th	D.F. Shorey (Bultaco)

Riding the smaller Hondas

Derek then had two more Honda rides on the Island; the 125cc on 6 June and the 50cc on 8 June. In the former he again had the satisfaction of beating Redman. And when one considers that Derek came home fourth on an obviously slower bike than the official Honda works machines, this was a

With his first wife Marian after victory in the Lightweight (250cc) TT on the Hondis Ltd privately entered four-cylinder Honda.

tremendous performance. His race average speed was 87.24mph, compared to the winner, Luigi Taveri's figure of 89.88mph.

Ultra Lightweight (125cc) Isle of Man TT – 3 laps – 113.19 miles

1st	L. Taveri (Honda)
2nd	T. Robb (Honda)
3rd	T. Phillis (Honda)
4th	D.W. Minter (Honda)
5th	J. Redman (Honda)
6th	R.A. Avery (EMC)

Derek pictured after his famous 1962 Lightweight TT success.

A Castrol advertisement showing Derek's 250cc TT win.

Derek rode a prototype production Honda single like this in the inaugural 50cc TT, held in June 1962, coming home ninth at an average speed of 70.61mph.

Derek also rode in the 50cc event (his only ever race on this size of machine), coming home ninth at an average speed of 70.61mph (compared to the winner, Ernst Degner riding a Suzuki, who averaged 75.12mph for the two-lap, 75.46-mile race).

Later the same day, Derek crashed in the Senior race on his 499cc Petty Norton, putting himself out of action for a couple of weeks.

Victory in the Thruxton marathon

Derek showed he was back to full fitness again, when, partnered by Bill Smith, he won the Lightweight (250cc) class and finished ninth overall in the Thruxton 500-miler on Saturday 23 June. Unlike the Silverstone race of a few weeks before, when he was forced out while leading with tyre trouble, Derek and his new partner, Bill Smith, had a relatively stress-free ride, completing 212 laps of the new 2.2-mile Thruxton circuit at an average speed of 70.98mph. The overall victors were Phil Read and Brian Setchell on the Lawton & Wilson-entered Norton 650SS, who completed 228 laps, averaging 76.45mph. When one considers this machine had an additional 300cc, Derek and Bill Smith's efforts were, as *Motor Cycle News* said, 'a great performance.' Another journal called it 'staggering'.

The biggest problem experienced was a lack of ground clearance, with the silencers taking a real bashing. Watched by 'a large crowd of enthusiasts who came to see how "their" machine fared,' the

Honda teammates Jim Redman (5) leading Tom Phillis (4) on their two-fifty four-cylinder models, out of the hairpin at Mallory Park, September 1961.

Jim Redman

Jim Redman was a rider who never seemed to hit the headlines in quite the same way as other world champions and, in truth, never had the fan base of men such as Mike Hailwood or Derek Minter. However, in terms of results and influence he was a huge success. And in any case, with six world titles (two 250 and four 350cc) he was certainly no dummy on the track. As journalist Gerard Periam wrote in 1964: 'the reason probably is that Jim Redman's approach to motorcycle racing is purely professional. No more and no less than is required to win. No unnecessary records, no unnecessary fastest laps'.

Jim was born in Hampstead on 8 November 1931 and attended primary school in Greenford, Middlesex. He passed his 11-plus and went to grammar school. But he had to leave at 15 'because the family needed the money'. He found a job as a motor mechanic, but was 'disappointed, as I wanted to stay on at school to take exams'. And his garage job was 'a bit of a comedown'. When he was just over 16, Jim's father died – and to make matters even worse, his mother passed away within a month. There was a sister, Jacqueline, a year older than Jim, and twins Peter and Wendy, 10 years old. Before she died, their mother had urged them to 'stick together as a family'. Aunts and uncles offered to take the children. Welfare authorities wanted to put them in homes. This was one of Jim's first brushes with authority. However, the family stood firm, 'determined to stick together'. Money was obviously tight. Jim wanted a bike and took on additional work in the evenings to pay for an ex-WD Matchless G3/L single, later swapped for a Triumph twin.

National service was still in place and Jim faced an exemption tribunal. But the crisis was solved in two ways. Sister Jackie married

The 1962 250cc World Champion Jim Redman. However, Derek beat Jim Redman every time the pair clashed on Honda fours that year.

and she and her husband took on responsibility for the twins. And Jim had a friend in Bulawayo, so off to Southern Rhodesia (now Zimbabwe) he went, as going there meant that he did not have to do his national service. Jim got a job as a mechanic and later moved into a government transport department. At first, Jim sent money home for the family and later he paid for them to come over to Rhodesia.

At this stage the reader should be aware of the considerable responsibilities and sacrifices for a teenager. And also the reason for Jim's 'professional' way of doing things in his racing career. Jim's first race came via a friend, John Love, who loaned him a Triumph Grand Prix. This was followed by an International Norton. Then in 1955 he purchased a 1951 AJS 7R and it was on this bike that Jim scored his first big victory. Meanwhile, a sign was going up over a new business

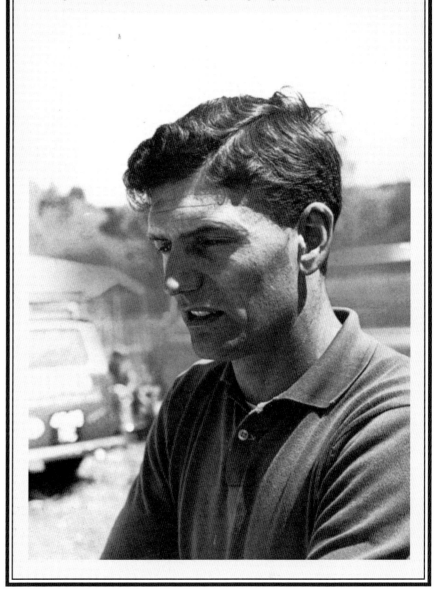

in Bulawayo – Love and Redman Motor Cycles. Jim then set his sights on winning the South African 500cc Championship, but in 1957 was just pipped by the highly experienced Borro Castellani. The Championship was important to Jim, who was keen to go to Europe along with his pal Paddy Driver. Actually Jim had not realised that in fact he had won a Championship title – the 350cc on the faithful 7R! Then came 1958, and it was Jim who stunned everyone, when that Easter weekend he created headlines in the British press by finishing runner-up to Derek Minter at Brands Hatch – behind him were the likes of Bob McIntyre, Alastair King...and Mike Hailwood. Other similar results followed riding a brace of Nortons and a 125cc Ducati.

Jim's first ride for Honda came in the 1960 Dutch TT, when Tom Phillis was unfit. At that time the Hondas were 'not terrifically quick and not many of the top runners wanted to know them'. When Hondas really began to perform and the company wanted to plan their full-scale assault in the GPs, Tom Phillis and Jim were summoned to Tokyo. On Honda's desk the pair saw 'letters from some of the biggest names in motorcycling wanting to ride Hondas'. But Honda's view was 'Tom and Jim rode when they were slow. Tom and Jim will ride them now they are quick'. And there is no doubt whatsoever that Jim Redman was Honda's most loyal servant, and this is why he was subsequently made captain of the Honda works team. The family thing shows through in the following words he uttered after having got to the top and won several world titles: 'I'll always remember 1962 as a hard year. I lost my best friends, Tom Phillis, Bob McIntyre and Gary Hocking. Bob hadn't been in the Honda team long, but we had taken a liking to each other and he fitted in well.'

As for his Honda performances, Jim's first Grand Prix victory came aboard one of the revised fours in the 250cc Belgian event. Then in 1962 he won six of the 10 rounds counting towards the 250cc Championship, thus winning the title. He also finished runner-up (behind Luigi Taveri) in the 125cc class. But the big surprise was winning the 350cc crown, a feat he was to repeat in 1963, 1964 and 1965. He also won the 250cc title again in 1963, after a season-long battle with Italian challenger Tarquinio Provini on the Moto Morini. In 1964, he was runner-up to Phil Read (Yamaha) in the 250cc stakes.

Then came 1965 and the arrival of new boy Giacomo Agostini at MV. But even Ago and teammate Mike Hailwood could not stop Jim taking his sixth world title. At the beginning of 1966, now with Mike Hailwood in the Honda team, Jim took the new four-cylinder Honda to victory in the first round of the 500cc Championship at Hockenheim, with Agostini runner-up. In the Isle of Man it was Hailwood first, Agostini second. The third round at Assen saw Redman victorious with the Italian again runner-up.

Then came that fateful day in Belgium, when, during torrential driving rain, Jim crashed at Spa Francorchamps, breaking his arm. He subsequently returned to his home in Bulawayo and announced his retirement from the sport to become Yamaha importer for Rhodesia. In recent years Jim has become a familiar figure, like many other stars of yesteryear, at historic racing events around the world.

Southampton club's annual event enjoyed a pleasant, not too hot June day, with a cool breeze blowing across the Hampshire airfield circuit. Again the author was there in person as a spectator.

250cc class Thruxton 500-miler results

1st	D.W. Minter – W. Smith (247cc Honda CB72)	212 laps
2nd	P. Inchley – R. Good (248cc Ariel Arrow)	209 laps
3rd	C.C. Sandford – M. O'Rourke (248cc Ariel Arrow)	207 laps
4th	D. Lee – D. Woodman (249cc BSA SS80)	202 laps
5th	D. Ellis – J. Somers (247cc Honda CB72)	201 laps
6th	G. Leigh – F.J. Stevens (247cc Honda CB72)	200 laps

Two record lap performances

Besides the TT, Derek's only other ride with the 125cc Honda production racer came at Brands Hatch on Sunday 8 July and with this machine and the 250 four Derek not only won both races, but also broke the lap record for both classes – add to this a further three wins and three fastest laps on Norton machinery (see chapter five) and his performance that day can only be described as out of this world. *MCN* said: 'Minter's amazing score at Brands.' And, as the race report confirmed: 'the 250cc race was the most thrilling for Minter, on a Honda four, really getting it moving and broke Mike Hailwood's lap record of 84.12mph by over two and a half miles an hour. He recorded a speed of 86.72mph and a race record of 84.65. He shot away from the grid at the start and proceeded to pull away at a tremendous rate, and lapped everyone but the eighth man.'

In the 125cc event Derek's machine was reluctant to fire and he had an 'anxious moment at the start' (*MCN*). He was halfway down the field by the time it did come to life. By the end of the first lap he was in front and finished a full 15 seconds ahead of Michael O'Rourke (Bultaco). Derek also set up a new lap record time of 80.84mph and a race record of 77.71mph. In doing this he beat his own previous records of 80.83mph and 77.40mph respectively.

125cc Brands Hatch – 6 laps – 15.9 miles
1st   D.W. Minter (Honda)
2nd   M.P. O'Rourke (Bultaco)
3rd   F.D. Hardy (Bultaco)
4th   P.C. Preston (Bultaco)
5th   J. Russell (Ducati)
6th   B. Clark (Bultaco)

250cc Brands Hatch – 8 laps – 21.2 miles
1st   D.W. Minter (Honda)
2nd   B.T. Osborne (NSU)
3rd   F.D. Hardy (REG)
4th   A.S. Pavey (NSU)
5th   T.P. Grotefeld (Aermacchi)
6th   B. Lawton (Aermacchi)

M-I-N-T-E-R

This was the headline in the Wednesday 8 August 1962 issue of *Motor Cycle News*, together with a large photograph of Derek racing the 250 Honda four at Oulton Park the previous Monday, where he became triple British Champion (250cc plus 350cc and 500cc). As *MCN* also said: 'On the Hondis Ltd entered Honda "four" Minter carved his way through the star-studded field to shatter the old lap records for not only the 250, but also bettering the 350 record! And in the process lapped everyone in the race save second man Jim Redman!' He upped the lap record from 86.43mph to 89.55mph; the previous speed had been set, jointly, by Mike Hailwood and John Hartle, also both mounted on four-cylinder Hondas, 12 months before.

Quite simply no rider could match Mr Minter that day. Mike Hailwood on Fron Purslow's Benelli did not have a happy time and eventually went out with engine trouble, while Tommy Robb was also out of luck. After holding third place for most of the race, he dropped out on the last lap.

250cc British Championship, Oulton Park – 20 laps – 56 miles

1st   D.W. Minter (Honda)

2nd   J.A. Redman (Honda)

3rd   F. Fisher (FB Mondial)

4th   D.F. Shorey (Bultaco)

5th   P.H. Tait (Aermacchi)

6th   B. Clark (Aermacchi)

Derek winning one of the three British Championship titles he gained in a single day at Oulton Park, Bank Holiday Monday 6 August 1962.

After Oulton Park, Derek crossed the Irish Sea to take part in the Ulster Grand Prix over the Dundrod road circuit. But after crashing on the EMC in the 125cc race, Derek was a non-starter for the rest of the meeting and thus did not ride the Honda four. His injuries, as detailed in chapter five, meant that Derek did not race again until late September, when he once again beat World Champion elect Jim Redman. This was at Mallory Park's Race of the Year meeting on 30 September, and Derek set a new 250cc lap record for the Leicestershire circuit in the process. Although Derek did not realise it at the time, he was destined never to race the Honda four (or for that matter any other Japanese bike) again.

No bike

The following is an extract from Charlie Rous's *Paddock Gossip* in *Motor Cycle News* dated 17 October 1962:

> Seems Derek Minter is not the most popular rider on earth – certainly not as far as the eastern hemisphere is concerned anyway. As had been mentioned, Derek was very hopeful and keen to make a trip to Japan for the meeting out there on 3 November. He has not been able to get any assistance at all to make the 9,000 odd mile trip. He won't be paid any starting money nor will he be helped towards his expenses. But most of all, Honda won't provide him with a bike...Could it be that because he won every time out on the 250 Honda this season, including the TT, it has not done him any good? Or is there another reason we don't know about?

Now, getting on for half a century after the events of 1962, here is Derek's own version of what really went on:

> Honda approached me at Oulton Park [August 1962] and asked if I would like to race in Japan and they would supply me with a bike. I said "no", as I wanted to ride the Hondis machine – but the Honda people replied that it was "not possible". I lost interest at that point, because I knew I would be provided with a slower machine and in fact I never heard anything more from Honda.

Chapter 7

Scuderia Gilera

With the headline 'Exclusive!' the 28 November 1962 front page of *Motor Cycle News* was dominated by one story. It read:

Guess who and on what? No prizes for the correct answer. It's *Motor Cycle News* 'Man of the Year' Derek Minter on the Gilera, tramping it round Mallory last week. And Derek, despite icy conditions, went round faster than he has ever lapped Mallory before on any machine! Derek got his chance to try out the Gilera four because Geoff Duke was engaged on tyre testing for Avons, and Duke invited Minter to assist him. Duke himself lapped Mallory – the first time he has ever ridden a motorcycle there – in less than a minute!

In demand

Having just completed his most successful season's racing ever, Derek was on the crest of a wave, with almost everyone, it seemed, talking about his exploits. Certainly in 1962 he had been virtually unbeatable, both on his own Nortons and the four-cylinder Honda. On the latter bike, privately entered by the British Honda importers, Hondis Ltd, Derek had won every race he had taken part in, and on more than one occasion had beaten the 1962 250cc World Champion Jim Redman, including of course Derek's legendary TT victory, where he had taken on and slain the entire Honda works team.

The rumours

As 1962 became 1963, the big news story was the prospect of a return to racing by the famous Gilera factory, with their four-cylinder machines which had not been raced since 1957. Rumour upon rumour had swept the motorcycling world that at last Gilera might be about to make a comeback. But whereas earlier stories had not had much foundation upon fact, this time the odds were on it to happen. Why? Well, it had

The big news at the beginning of 1963 was Gilera's return – via Geoff Duke – to racing. Here Derek (seated on one of the fours) chats to Geoff, while John Hartle cleans his goggles at Monza in early March that year.

all begun when Bob McIntyre – the first man to lap the TT course at 100mph on a Gilera in 1957 – had died after an accident at Oulton Park in August 1962. Then, when a Remembrance Meeting was held for Bob at Oulton in October 1962, not only had a record crowd for the Cheshire circuit attended, but six-time World Champion Geoff Duke had paraded one of the 1957 Gileras, which had received massive publicity. And it also inspired Geoff into attempting to persuade Gilera to make a return.

And so in the first week of 1963 the position was as follows: Gilera had not yet decided to make a racing comeback, but tests were to be carried out at the Monza circuit (near Gilera's Arcore factory on the outskirts of Milan) for the firm's bosses to determine for themselves if the 1957 machine's performance would be good enough to compete against their chief rivals, MV Agusta.

The machines involved in the testing would be a pair of 500s and a 350cc. But it was considered 'unlikely' at that stage that the three-fifty would actually be raced in 1963. And Duke was 'confident' that the performance of

Geoff Duke (left), Derek and journalist Charlie Rous (right), together during the Monza testing that preceded Gilera's comeback.

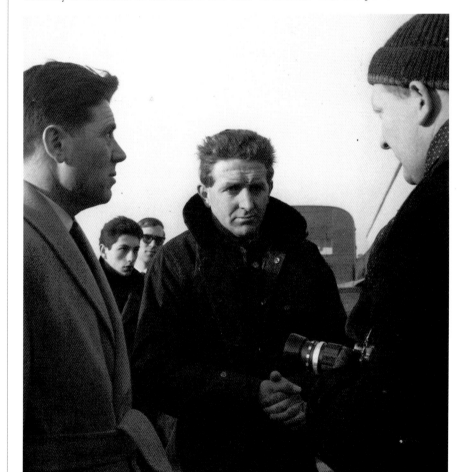

the 500s would convince the Gilera management that these two machines could resume racing that year.

Finally, at the Monza test session would be Derek and, *MCN* said, 'another rider whose name need not be divulged at the moment.' With them would be representatives from Avon Tyres, under, said *MCN*, 'the watchful eye of Geoff Duke, who would boss any future Gilera racing team.'

Motor Cycle News, in its 9 January 1963 issue, also published a photograph showing Geoff Duke (in racing leathers), Brian Heath, Avon's competition manager, Derek (also in leathers), two of Avon's 'backroom boys' and Giovanni Fumagalli, mechanic to Geoff Duke when Geoff won his world titles for Gilera. This picture, it is believed, was taken at the Mallory 'tyre testing' session described earlier.

The following is a typical news story published towards the end of January 1963 and gives a good insight into how the press viewed Mr Minter at that time:

> Derek Minter and Gilera. Tests at Monza soon will decide whether he will use the six-year-old Italian four-cylinder machine for Grand Prix racing. If he does, and the partnership is now more than a mere probability, Minter will be hard to beat in the 500cc World Championship series. He was the first man to average over 100mph on a Norton in the Senior TT. Last year, on a Honda-four, he won the Lightweight TT and also licked the Honda 250cc World Champion at Oulton and Mallory. King of the home circuits, Minter was last year's triple British Champion.

Testing at Monza

The actual testing at the Monza Autodrome took place over three days: Friday, Saturday and Sunday 1, 2 and 3 March 1963. And at these test sessions it was revealed that the 'other rider' was in fact the very experienced John Hartle, who had previously ridden for the Norton and MV factories and was a close friend of John Surtees. And on the strength of these tests Gilera agreed to make a return. However, unbeknown to everyone apart from those involved, it was not a full works return. Gilera themselves would only provide bikes and mechanics, while the rest of the funding for the project had to be found by Geoff Duke. And although several sponsors were verbally agreed, none in fact actually came forward with money. And so the Gilera comeback had problems even before it began the actual racing. In addition, Geoff Duke, through lack of funds, was forced to allow both Derek and John Hartle to ride other bikes when not riding Gileras. And this, as the reader will discover, was to prove the fatal flaw in the entire project…

John Hartle, Derek
Minter's Scuderia Duke
teammate in 1963. Unlike
Derek he was already fully
experienced on a 500cc
four-cylinder machine,
having ridden for MV
Agusta in many Grand
Prix.

John Hartle

Mike Hailwood's father Stan is on record as saying that John Hartle's 105mph lap from a standing start on the Scuderia Duke Gilera four in the 1963 Senior TT was one of John's finest performances.

Hailing from Chapel-en-le-Frith in the English Peak District, John Hartle was born in 1933. And in a career which spanned the early 1950s until the late 1960s he rode a variety of machinery, including not only four-cylinder MV Agustas and Gileras, but BSA, AJS, Norton and Aermacchi singles, plus Bob Geeson's REG twin and even being a TT winner for Triumph aboard a Thruxton Bonneville. For a couple of years after leaving school, John took a job in a local garage where, as he once described: 'I was required to delve into the internals of cars and lorries'. But his interest,

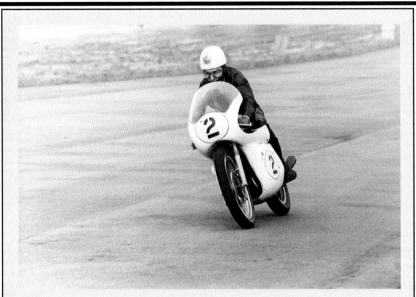

Hartle in action during the 500cc race at Silverstone in April 1963, where he finished runner-up to Derek Minter. Both were riding four-cylinder Gileras.

however, lay more with two wheels than four, and with a certain degree of what he described as 'hero worship' the young Hartle visited various trials and scrambles in which local star Eric Bowers was competing. The lure of motorcycle sport proved too strong to resist and so in 1950, then aged 17, John joined Bowers' Chapel-en-le-Frith dealership. By this time Bowers had retired from active competition, but was sponsoring a couple of road racers, including Eric Houseley; John was recruited as a 'weekend race mechanic'. When Houseley subsequently won the 1952 Junior Clubman's TT on a BSA Gold Star, the young Hartle was there to look after the spanners and pitboard.

The following year, John made his own race debut at Brough airfield circuit in East Yorkshire on a BSA single, alongside the likes of Houseley, Peter Davey and Ken Kavanagh (the latter on a works Norton). In September 1953 John found himself competing in the Manx Grand Prix, on an AJS 7R in the Junior and a Manx Norton in the Senior. But after refuelling the 7R in around 10th position, he braked too hard at Quarter Bridge and fell off. Undaunted he then remounted to come home 21st. In the Senior event he did better, finishing a respectable 15th on the Norton and, as a result of these two finishes, collected that year's Newcomer Award.

But even better was to come the following year, when not only did Eric Bowers provide new machinery (still an AJS and a Norton), but, after finishing third on the 7R in the 1954 Junior Manx GP, John led the Senior race in truly awful weather conditions until he suffered the huge disappointment of running out of fuel on the last lap. Later that same month he also had the distinction of finishing third behind Geoff Duke (Gilera) and Bob Keeler in the Hutchinson 100 meeting at Silverstone. These outstanding performances led to John being invited to join the Norton team alongside Jack Brett and John Surtees for 1955.

A close friendship between John Surtees and John Hartle transpired and this played a part in Hartle later joining Surtees in the MV Agusta team for the 1958 season. Prior to that he continued to ride for Norton in 1955 and 1956, while in 1957 he had the use of a fully streamlined Norton bike. His MV contract continued into 1959 and he rode for the Italian factory in the 1960 TT, but was subsequently sacked, which John Surtees told the author he thought 'unjust'. There is no doubt that Lady Luck seemed to desert Hartle during his MV days – he suffered more than his fair share of crashes, breakdowns and even a fire.

After MV John went back to racing as a privateer on his own Norton machinery. He was recalled as a works rider for the Geoff Duke Scuderia Gilera squad in 1963. Following Derek Minter's crash in May that year he became the main challenger to Mike Hailwood in the World Championship series. But the combination of Mike and the MV simply proved too strong; this resulted in the Scuderia team being disbanded at the end of 1963. Then it was back to Norton, but by the mid-1960s he had switched to Italian Aermacchis, riding for the British importer Syd Lawton. Afterwards came a period riding factory-supported Triumph production bikes. In 1967 he set up a racing spares service business, but was fatally injured while racing at Scarborough the following year, aged 34.

But when the announcement came, of course, the press made no mention of this, and in truth were probably completely in the dark on the issue. And what bold and enthusiastic headlines greeted the motorcycling public at the beginning of March 1963 when the story broke.

One journalist who knew more than most was Charlie Rous of *Motor Cycle News*, who had travelled to Italy with the two British riders and the Avon Tyre men, Ralph Newman and Brian Heath. They all flew out from London airport (Heathrow) in late February.

It is interesting to note that another Briton, Bill Jakeman, had designed and made the dolphin fairings that replaced the now-outlawed full streamlining that Gilera had used in 1957 when they had last raced and which was fitted on the machine Geoff Duke had ridden at Oulton Park in October 1962.

For three days at Monza it was bright, but very cold – between 32 and 40 degrees Fahrenheit. Even so Derek came within 0.59mph of shattering John Surtees's Monza lap record when he lapped the 3.57-mile Italian circuit at a record speed of 118.55mph on the final day. Surtees's 1959 record stood at 119.14mph, set on an MV Agusta four.

As Charlie Rous told *Motor Cycle News* readers: 'Minter's was a staggering performance. He had not ridden for four months, he was alone on the track, and it was only a degree above freezing point, and the Monza track was affected by oil and rubber deposited on it by a Ferrari three litre car being tested at the same time.' As it happened one of these drivers was none other than John Surtees.

Although the three-fifty was used only briefly, Derek managed to put in 11 laps on the machine and his best time of 1 minute 56.2 seconds stood up well against the class lap record, held by Libero Liberati in a time of 1 minute 52 seconds, established on a fully streamlined Gilera back in 1956.

Both Hartle and Derek rode under instructions from Geoff Duke and under the watchful eye of Massimo Gilera, grandson of the firm's boss Giuseppe Gilera, who had been unable to witness the proceedings himself due to illness (flu) and was only able to return to Arcore late on the Sunday evening. He then had a meeting with his grandson and Geoff Duke, analysing the results of the testing.

The Kreidler offer

Derek had had a phone call from the Kreidler factory in Stuttgart half an hour before he had left for Italy, on 28 February, offering him a 50cc works machine for the 1963 World Championship season. He told them of his Gilera trip and they asked him if he could call at the German factory on his way to Italy or on his way back. Then on Friday morning a cable arrived at his Italian hotel repeating the offer, but Derek said he could make no decision on the issue until he knew the outcome of the Gilera tests. And because of how the Gilera situation turned out, the following week Derek declined the Kreidler offer.

Both Derek and John Hartle had already returned home when the news came through that Gilera had given the green light to the project. At the same time it was revealed that besides taking in the early Italian meetings, the Gileras, with Derek and John aboard, would be at Silverstone on 6 April for the big Hutchinson 100 meeting.

As for the riders he had chosen, Geoff Duke described Derek in the following terms: 'an exceptionally talented rider regarded more as a short circuit ace, yet overlooked as a TT winner and the first rider to lap the TT at 100mph on a single cylinder machine.' And 'the very experienced John Hartle.'

Derek's impressions

The following is an extract from *Motor Cycle News* dated 13 March 1963, on Derek's impressions of the Italian trip:

> I think the Gilera fours are fabulous. I have never ridden a machine so fast, that handles so magnificently, and which stops (when you want it to!). Unlike John (Hartle), I have never ridden a 350 or 500cc four cylinder racer before. I have raced the 250cc Honda of course and if one could compare the 250cc Japanese machine with the 350cc Gilera, then I'm afraid, for the Honda, there is no comparison. The Gilera is in a class of its own. The 1957 Italian machine is miles an hour faster – certainly

more so than the 100cc difference, it is far more powerful and the steering and brakes are without doubt the best of any machine I have ever ridden. Unlike John, again, I have never ridden a five-hundred of any sort at Monza before, and going round on either of the Gilera models certainly had me on my toes. The five-hundred especially arrived at corners far faster than I have ever done so before, but thanks to the wonderful Arcore brakes, the machine eased up with room to spare. But I must say the racing I have done on the 250cc Honda four helped me enormously with riding the big Gileras. A four cylinder machine has a technique of its own – the power is either on or off – but one difference with the Gilera, when the power is on, it's really on! Having ridden the machines for just this three days training period, I cannot really go into any strong detail – I don't know enough about them yet myself. The weather wasn't particularly kind at Monza, but the thing that really impressed me was that down the back straight I managed to keep up with the new 1963 Ferrari sports racing car that was being tested and I gathered from John Surtees afterwards that these are capable of a full 165mph. Just let me say I am looking forward to the coming season!

In the same issue, *MCN's* Peter Howdle penned an article headed 'Who will be this year's 500cc champion? MV Agusta or Gilera.' Would it be, Howdle asked, 'Hailwood and Shepherd on MVs – Minter or Hartle on Gileras.' He considered 'Any one of those four aces could become the 500cc World Champion of 1963. Four supermen. Four superbikes. Fighting for supremacy over a series of nine big time races. What a season it's going to be!'

Of these 'aces', Derek, at 30, was the oldest, Hailwood was the youngest at 22, with Shepherd 28 and Hartle 29.

Peter Howdle's view of Derek was: 'The undisputed British short circuit champion, has already proved his ability to race a "four" in world classics. He won the 1962 Lightweight TT on a Honda. But the Kentish ace doesn't know all the European circuits.'

To set the scene, at that time, Gilera and MV Agusta had each won six 500cc world titles, while there were nine World Championship events scheduled for 500cc machines in 1963:

West German GP	Hockenheim	19 May
Senior TT	Isle of Man	14 June
Dutch TT	Assen	29 June
Belgian GP	Spa Francorchamps	7 July
East German GP	Sachsenring	18 August
Finnish GP	Tampere	1 September

Ulster GP	Dundrod	7 September
Italian GP	Monza	15 September
Argentine GP	Buenos Aires	13 October

First signs of problems

The first public sign of the lack of sponsorship which Geoff Duke had managed to acquire for his Gilera squad was published in *Motor Cycle News* when a tiny news story appeared in the 20 March 1963 issue. It read as follows:

> Although Derek Minter and John Hartle's main racing this year will be on the 'Scuderia Duke' Gileras, Geoff Duke has no objection to them riding their own Nortons in other events. Hence John's entry at Modena yesterday. Ray Petty has more or less completed the refitting of Derek's Nortons and his second-string machinery this year will be two 500s and a 350.

In the 3 April 1963 issue of *MCN*, Charlie Rous boldly predicted that 'Gileras should put 10mph on their old speed.' He went on to say: 'The Gileras arrive in England today and are at Silverstone on Saturday's British Motor Cycle Racing Club's Hutchinson 100 meeting, we shall see them – in the hands of Derek Minter and John Hartle – open a new phase in racing which should place the 500cc class back on top of the tree, where it belongs.'

Charlie Rous continued: 'Hartle and Minter hold jointly the Silverstone lap record on Nortons at 100.51mph and I fancy this figure is going to look rather sick when they wheel back into the paddock after the big race this weekend. I'm going to stick my neck out by forecasting a speed of 104mph. This will be exactly 10mph more than when a Gilera last raced on this circuit in 1955.'

The author, together with thousands of other enthusiasts, was at Silverstone on 6 April 1963 to witness the historic Gilera comeback.

Reality

But of course the British weather can play havoc with the best laid plans, and rain, hail and snowstorms all fell on the 31st Hutchinson 100 meeting at Silverstone during practice on Friday 5 April, and near gale-force winds buffeted the Northamptonshire airfield circuit on race day, Saturday 6 April 1963.

I, and thousands more, braved the foul weather to witness the Gilera return. And as *MCN* said: 'The first sound in race-anger of the fabulous Arcore Gilera since 1957 was enough to stir the most hardened enthusiasts.'

At the beginning of the 500cc Daily Express Trophy race Phil

Read (Norton) was first away, a position he held at the end of the first lap. But Derek Minter was not to be denied. And as Charlie Rous wrote in the race report: 'The sight of him at Stowe Corner was fantastic! He had all his work cut out hanging on to the Gilera which went into a violent wobble at this point on every lap. But Derek was master of the situation and he soon moved into a comfortable lead.'

Instead the real battle of the race centred on Read and Hartle. *MCN* again: 'Phil tried every trick in the book to hold the flying four and he managed to stick in the Gilera's slipstream for no less than 14 of the 18 laps.' But in the end Hartle managed to give him the slip and finished 12.8 seconds adrift of Derek, who won at an average speed of 97.54mph. The fastest lap was shared between the two Gilera riders at 99.41mph – so much for the Charlie Rous prediction. But more worryingly, even at this early stage, the Gileras did not appear the all-conquering projectiles everyone had expected...

500cc Daily Express/BMCRC Championship, Silverstone – 18 laps – 48.78 miles

1st	D.W. Minter (Gilera)
2nd	J. Hartle (Gilera)
3rd	P.W. Read (Norton)
4th	S.M.B. Hailwood (Norton)
5th	J. Dunphy (Norton)
6th	M. Duff (Matchless)
7th	D. Degens (Norton)
8th	J. Cooper (Norton)

In the early stages of the 500cc race Phil Read (Norton) led at Silverstone, followed by Joe Dunphy (Norton). In this photograph Derek had just gained third from John Cooper and Paddy Driver, with fellow Gilera teamster John Hartle back in sixth.

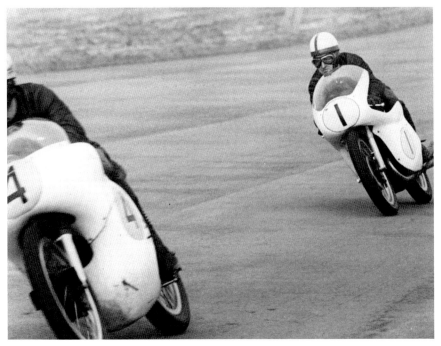

A lap later and Derek had almost caught Read and from then on assumed control of the race to give the Scuderia Duke team a debut victory.

Handling troubles

At Silverstone, under racing conditions, Derek (and to a lesser extent John Hartle) experienced handling problems. The problem was eventually traced to the front suspension. When the bikes had last been raced in 1957, full 'dustbin' shells were used, whereas in 1963 the much less aerodynamic 'dolphin' fairing was fitted. So in practice the front fork action was too stiff – almost solid in fact! In the six days between Silverstone and Brands Hatch, Gilera's chief mechanic Giovanni Fumagalli set about correcting the problem. And from Derek's comments he was successful. An interesting aside was that Giovanni had worked at the Arcore factory since 1922 – he started there at 12 and had been running around the factory complex since he was six! Giovanni had worked on all major Gilera projects, including the pre-war 90bhp supercharged liquid-cooled fours, and wielded the spanners for such famous names as Dorini Serafini and Piero Taruffi, to say nothing of Gilera's post-war stars such as Umberto Masetti and Geoff Duke.

Hailwood crashes – no Gilera-MV battle

Six days after Silverstone, I, like many others, travelled down to Brands Hatch on Good Friday expecting to see the much publicised Gilera–MV battle between Derek and Hailwood. But it was not to be. *MCN* takes up the story:

> If a man, like a cat, has nine lives, then Mike Hailwood surely forfeited one of his at Brands Hatch on Good Friday. He crashed his AJS at tremendous speed in a last bend dash while leading the 350cc

Phil Read (Kirby
Matchless) talking to
Tommy Robb, *c.*1964.

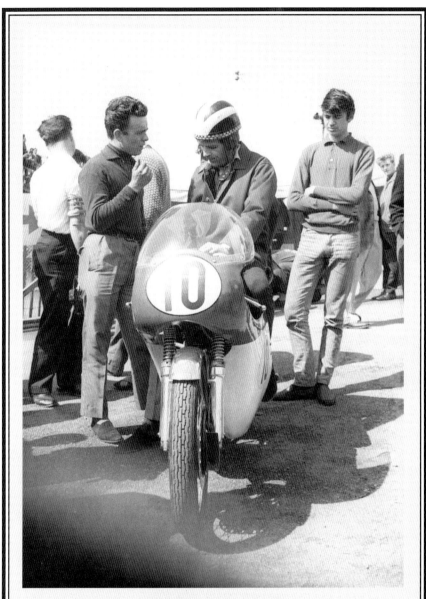

Phil Read

Phil Read was born in Luton, Bedfordshire, on 1 January 1939 and, together with John Hartle and Derek Minter, was part of the Scuderia Duke Gilera squad in 1963. Phil began racing (like Derek and many others) on a BSA Gold Star (encouraged by his mother) in 1957, but his really big break came when he won the Senior Manx Grand Prix on a Norton in September 1960. Then, again on a Norton, he won the Junior (350cc) TT the following June. Other excellent positions that year marked him out for future stardom.

During 1962 he mainly confined his activities to the British short circuits, winning many races. His results that year probably prompted

Geoff Duke to sign him up to support John Hartle in the Scuderia Gilera team, after Derek Minter was injured on his own Norton at Brands Hatch in May 1963. Although, as recounted elsewhere, the Gileras proved no match for Mike Hailwood and MV Agusta, Phil still did enough to attract an offer from Yamaha to race their air-cooled RD56 two-fifty twin, his first outing for the Japanese firm coming at the Japanese Grand Prix at Suzuka in October 1963.

In 1964, Phil was the top man in the 250cc World Championship title race, giving Yamaha its first world crown. It was also the first time a two-stroke had won the class. Phil's success broke a three-year stranglehold by rivals Honda. Phil retained his grip on the title the following year, then Honda signed Mike Hailwood and 'Mike-the-Bike' snatched the Championship from Read in 1966, after a season-long attempt by Phil to resolve teething glitches with the brand-new liquid-cooled four-cylinder Yamaha. These problems had been resolved in time for the 1967 season and Phil and Mike fought out probably the closest Championship in the history of the sport. Phil actually had a higher total of basic points, but was still adjudged to have been the runner-up, whereas Hailwood was crowned champion. Read also finished runner-up to teammate Bill Ivy in the 125cc title chase.

The following season, 1968, saw Phil win back both the 125 and 250cc titles. But even though both Honda and Suzuki had pulled out, this was no easy season, as a bitter rivalry erupted between Read and Ivy. In an effort to make peace, Yamaha ruled that Phil could win the 125cc, while Bill was pencilled in for the 250cc crown. However, the two riders had other plans, resulting in a season-long battle; at its end Phil had won both the titles, but in the process not only upset Ivy and Yamaha but also many race fans. For several years thereafter Yamaha were none too happy with the man who had given them their early successes, although all this is very much in the

Phil Read at the 1961 prize-giving after winning the Junior TT on his Norton.

past. Yamaha made Phil their star at the 1998 Centennial TT at Assen, for example.

Meanwhile, on a private Yamaha production racer, Phil won the 250cc title again in 1971, with an engine tuned by the German engineer/sidecar star Helmut Fath. In 1972 came the news that Read would be joining MV Agusta. At first this was to ride in the 350cc class, but for 1973 this was broadened to include the blue riband 500cc division too. As I described in the companion volume *Giacomo Agostini: Champion of Champions* (Breedon), this move was akin to putting a fox into a hen house. Phil and Giacomo both wanted to be number one. Ultimately, this led to Ago leaving to join Yamaha for the 1974 season. With Giacomo's departure the Englishman went on to retain the 500cc Championship in 1974, but he was not to be found in the 350cc results that year, for the simple reason that MV withdrew from the class. Giacomo Agostini took the title for his new team.

During 1975 a fierce battle developed between Read and Agostini for the 500cc Championship. Giacomo came out on top, even though the Italian rider had to wait until the last round to know the outcome of what can only be described as a titanic struggle. There is absolutely no doubt that both men wanted to win. It was to be Ago's final Championship, and MV Agusta were never again to win a world crown in Grand Prix racing. But it was certainly not the end of Phil Read, who continued to race for several more seasons, becoming Formula 1 World Champion on a Honda in 1977, his eighth and final title.

race, and Derek Minter, closing from behind (after another indifferent start), could not avoid the fallen rider. Luckily, Minter 'held it' and raced on to win, and luckier still, Hailwood 'walked away' to race another day.

Unfortunately, this untimely crash during the opening race of the Easter programme put paid to the hopes of the 60,000 crowd of seeing the 500cc World Champion matched for the first time on his 500 MV Agusta with the Scuderia Duke Gilera fours of Derek Minter and John Hartle.

And what a race it would have been, for in winning the major event Derek shattered his own lap record for the 2.65-mile Brands GP circuit with a speed of 90.34mph – the first time the Kentish circuit had been lapped at over 90mph by a motorcycle.

1000cc Brands Hatch – 15 laps – 39.75 miles

1st	D.W. Minter (Gilera)
2nd	J. Hartle (Gilera)
3rd	P.W. Read (Norton)
4th	M. Duff (Matchless)
5th	P. Driver (Matchless)
6th	G. Young (Norton)

Little did anyone realise, but this fabulous Brands performance, in retrospect, can be judged as the high water mark of Derek Minter's racing career. And one can only speculate on what might have transpired had not an incident happened at Derek's next (non-Gilera) outing at Brands Hatch some four weeks later.

But before this were to come a couple more vintage Minter performances on the reborn Gileras.

Three days later, at Oulton Park on Easter Monday, Derek is seen astride the Gilera in the Cheshire circuit's paddock.

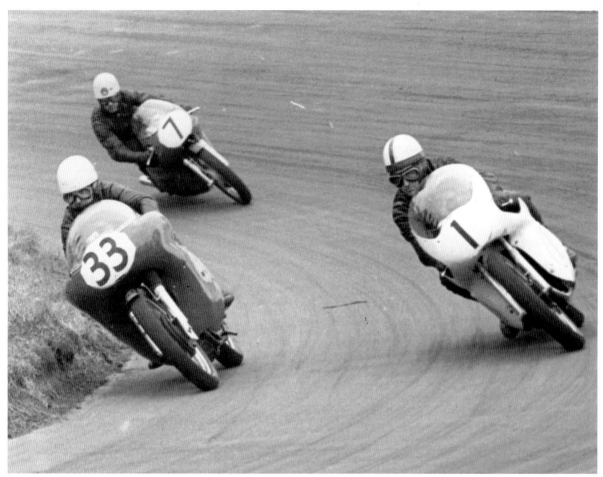

Derek sweeping around the outside on his way to another race win and record lap at Oulton Park on Easter Monday 1963.

The first was at Oulton Park, when a vast crowd (said to have been a record) turned up at the Cheshire circuit on Easter Monday, 15 April, to see both Derek and his teammate John Hartle break the existing lap record – Derek's speed being the best at 91.86mph compared to the old record of 90.36 set by Bob McIntyre – when the Gilera pairing finished first and second in the main race of the day for 500cc machines. Once again it was Phil Read (Norton) who was the main challenger.

500cc Oulton Park – 19 laps – 53.2 miles
1st   D.W. Minter (Gilera)
2nd   J. Hartle (Gilera)
3rd   P.W. Read (Norton)
4th   D. Downer (Norton)
5th   W. Smith (Matchless)
6th   D. Woodman (Matchless)
Note: fifth onwards only completed 18 laps.

First – and last – blood to Gilera

It was first (and, as it happened, last) blood to the Scuderia Duke Gileras of Derek and John Hartle at Imola on Thursday 24 April for the Shell Gold Cup, when the duo beat Mike Hailwood. Not only did first Derek and then John catch up and pass Mike, but Derek also set the fastest lap of the race at 91.40mph. It was an impressive performance and in the light of what happened later one must ask if Hailwood was entirely fit after his Brands crash of just under two weeks before.

Charlie Rous, writing for *Motor Cycle News* dated 1 May 1963, commented:

Nobody in their wildest moment could have forecast such a complete victory for the Gilera squad, which is best summed up in the words of Mike Hailwood, who told me after the race: 'Derek Minter's riding was fantastic. Even if my wrist injured in a crash at Brands Hatch on Good Friday was in perfect health, I doubt very much if I could have been able to beat him'.

But as the *MCN* report says:

The Oxford World Champion did not go down without fighting. From the start he was away like a rocket and built up a considerable lead and for over 11 laps was the horse ahead of the hounds. But Derek Minter's pursuit was relentless, and after four on the tail of his own teammate, John Hartle, Derek went ahead to grind his way to the kill. Minter, as he drew away from Hartle rode like a man inspired, and had the 40,000 crowd on its toes as he gradually narrowed the 'impossible' gap. It did not seem that he could do it, for Hailwood's pace, too, was terrific, but he did, and was with Mike after 11 circuits, and then went ahead on the twelfth lap.

Derek and Phil Read (42) on the startline at Oulton Park, Easter Monday.

At the international Shell Gold Cup meeting at Imola, Italy, on 24 April 1963, Derek's main opposition in the 350cc event came from Remo Venturi riding a works Bianchi twin. This ended in victory for the Italian after Derek crashed out on the smaller Gilera. However, he made amends by winning the 500cc race.

Gilera Four-Cylinder

The Gilera four-cylinder first hit the headlines in April 1937, when Piero Taruffi broke the one-hour speed record previously held by Norton and Jimmy Guthrie at 114mph. Taruffi raised this to 121.33mph over a 28-mile course comprising a section of the Bergamo-Brescia autostrada. The motorcycle the Italian piloted was a fully enclosed, liquid-cooled four-cylinder model developed from the earlier Rondine design, itself conceived from the air-cooled four of the mid-1920s. As for Gilera itself, the marque had been founded by Giuseppe Gilera in 1911. Signor Gilera had been shrewd enough to realise the Rondine's potential, with the basic design being steadily improved through an intensive racing and records programme until 1939. Gilera was on course to achieve supremacy in the all-important 500cc Grand Prix class. Twice during that year, rider Dorino Serafini achieved magnificent victories, beating BMW on its home ground in the German Grand Prix and winning the Ulster Grand Prix at record speed.

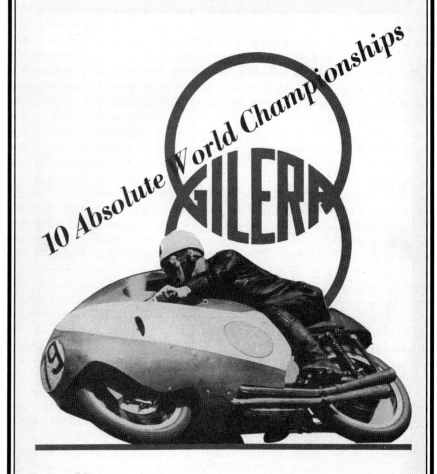

10 Absolute World Championships

GILERA

When racing resumed again after World War Two, the use of supercharging had been banned, so Gilera returned with new air-cooled fours designed by Ing. Piero Remor. Then, in late 1949, Remor quit to join rivals MV Agusta. However, Remor's exit left his former assistants at Gilera, Franco Passoni and Sandro Columbo, to carry out a redesign, which meant that in effect Gilera stayed ahead of MV, thanks to a lighter, more powerful engine during much of the 1950s.

Gilera's first world title came in 1950 (the second year of the FIM official Championship series) when Umberto Masetti took the crown. From then on success followed success, particularly after Englishman Geoff Duke joined the Arcore factory in the spring of 1953. Duke brought with him ideas for a new chassis which greatly improved the handling.

In eight seasons from 1950, Gilera riders Masetti, Duke and finally Libero Liberati won the 500cc Championship no less than six times, winning 31 races in the process. It was on a Gilera too that Bob McIntyre scored an historic Junior and Senior TT double in 1957 and became the first man to lap the legendary 37.73-mile Mountain course at over 100mph. In addition, there were also the performances of the sidecar ace Erole Frigero, who was consistently successful, but is today almost totally forgotten. For several years Frigero was second only to the great Eric Oliver (Norton) in the World Sidecar Championship.

The four-cylinder 500 Gilera, which ran from 1948, displaced 496.7cc (52 x 58mm) and was joined by a smaller three-fifty version in 1956. This latter engine displaced 349.7cc (46 x 52.6mm). As developed by Geoff Duke both sported five-speed gearboxes; telescopic front forks; duplex, steel cradle frames and twin shock, swinging arm, rear suspension. When Gilera retired from the sport it did so on a crest of a wave, with a series of record-breaking achievements at Monza in November 1957, crowned by Bob McIntyre's incredible 141.37 miles in a single hour on one of the 350cc four-cylinder models; the Monza surface for the speed bowl being in such poor condition at this time that riding the 500cc version was considered too dangerous. Although Gilera made a number of much-publicised comebacks during the next decade, notably with Scuderia Duke in 1963 and the diminutive Argentinian Benedicto Calderella a year later, the Arcore company was never to recapture its former dominance of the sport.

But the race was over 25 laps, almost 80 miles, and after putting a safe distance between himself and Hailwood, Derek seemed to slow the pace in the last few laps. This allowed Hartle, who had overtaken Hailwood on the 18th lap, to close up drastically. Then came drama as, on the last lap, Hartle caught and passed Derek.

MCN again: 'Nobody was more surprised than the "Mint", for with a superhuman effort which took him on the grass, he wrestled the lead back as they rounded the last bend, and headed his teammate over the line by less than one second, with Mike Hailwood coming home a further 26 seconds behind.'

It should also be remembered that this was Derek's first race over the 3.116-mile Imola course, whereas all the other leading riders had raced there several times.

500cc Imola Shell Gold Cup – 25 laps – 77.9 miles

1st   D.W. Minter (Gilera)
2nd   J. Hartle (Gilera)
3rd   S.M.B. Hailwood (MV Agusta)
4th   S. Grassetti (MV Agusta)
5th   R. Venturi (Bianchi)
6th   M. Duff (Matchless)

Note: sixth onwards only completed 24 laps.

Anti-climax

An anti-climax to the fabulous 500cc Gilera one-two came in the 350cc race, and here was also the closest battle of all. Derek and John Hartle, racing the 350 Gileras for the first time, both got flying starts, as did Remo Venturi (Bianchi). At the end of the first lap nothing separated Derek from the Italian rider, and this continued for lap after lap, with the timekeepers unable to separate the pair as they crossed the line. After 10 laps the position was still the same. Then came disaster for Derek, *MCN* commenting: 'Making a Brands Hatch style super-lean effort, he cranked the Gilera over to the point of no return and his foot brake pedal dug into the ground, flinging him off.' Luckily, he was not seriously injured, except for a badly grazed ankle, and he was able to walk back to the pits. The race eventually ended with victory for Venturi, with Hartle some 15 seconds in arrears and the only other rider unlapped by the winner.

And so everyone left Imola excited at the prospect of, at last after so many years, a true battle for the blue riband of the Grand Prix world – the 500cc Championship. The first round was to take place just over three weeks later on 19 May at Hockenheim, followed by the Isle of Man TT.

Fate takes a hand

Then, only seven days before Hockenheim, fate took a hand when, as fully documented in chapter nine, Derek was seriously injured while racing one of his own Norton singles at Brands Hatch on Sunday 12 May 1963. Of course, the reason he was even riding can be directly attributed to the Gilera/Geoff Duke set-up and the latter's inability to secure sponsorship needed to do the job properly. But, in the author's mind, one cannot blame Duke, but instead Gilera themselves, who simply refused to fund a pukka works team in the true spirit of the word.

To begin with, at least for public consumption, things did not seem too bad. For starters the Germans had decided to cancel the 500cc class at Hockenheim. And the press at least seemed to think Derek could be back in action as early as the TT. (It should also be noted that some of the dates as originally published had also been changed.)

But in practice, the TT fortnight came and went, and so did the Dutch TT and Belgian Grand Prix.

The most serious part of Derek's injuries concerned his back. The second of the two broken vertebrae sustained no more than a crack, but the other was crushed – and this required time to heal. And of course there were also the psychological problems to consider. Derek himself commented in *Motor Cycle News* dated 5 June 1963: 'I don't know how I shall feel when I first get on a bike. I'll have to wait and see.'

It was not until Sunday 14 July that Derek had his first ride on a motorcycle, this coming at Brands Hatch when he rode a marshal's Norton Dominator road bike. And at the same time it was revealed that he was due to fly out to Italy with Geoff Duke and would be testing a Gilera at Monza during the next few days.

And, subject to Derek's fitness, it was expected that he would be racing again at Oulton Park (the British Championships meeting) on August Bank Holiday Monday, 5 August, together with John Hartle – both would be Gilera mounted. From there the team would then travel to Northern Ireland for the Ulster Grand Prix.

A successful Monza experience

Things looked promising at Monza, when Derek unofficially broke the lap record on Monday 22 July with a time of 1 minute 46.4 seconds – a speed of 120.75mph. He had begun the practice session with two warm-up laps in hot, windless conditions. After changing spark plugs he then did his first flying lap in 1 minute 48.9 seconds and eventually reduced his lap time to 1 minute 47 seconds. Derek then went out again and, showing no ill effects from his Brands accident, unofficially cracked the record. As Charlie Rous reported: 'When Minter came in he was in perfect physical condition – with no aches or pains – and the whole Gilera camp were delighted with his performance.'

Then, the following day, Derek continued his Monza comeback tests and with another 50 laps got his time down still further – to 1 minute 46.1 seconds (121mph). The official lap record for the 3.75-mile Italian circuit then stood at 1 minute 47.9 seconds (119.14mph), which had been set by John Surtees (MV) during the 1959 Italian GP.

A record-breaking comeback

Derek made a record-breaking racing comeback at Oulton Park on Monday 5 August 1963 'in tremendous form' (*MCN*). Riding the Gilera, he became

After suffering a serious accident at Brands Hatch on one of his Nortons in May 1963, Derek made a record-breaking comeback at Oulton Park on Monday 5 August to win the 500cc British Championship title on the Gilera. Derek (37) and teammate John Hartle during pre-race scrutineering earlier that day.

the first rider to win the 500cc British Championship title three years running. And, in achieving this unique feat, he hoisted his own lap record from 91.86 to 92.86mph.

Peter Howdle of *Motor Cycle News* described the action:

During thirty windswept laps of the 2.76-mile Cheshire circuit, Minter gave a superb exhibition of high speed lappery. He picked off opposition in almost demoralising style. And when he took the chequered flag, he was within a few yards of overtaking second and third place men Phil Read (Lancefield Norton) and Alan Shepherd (Kirby Matchless). All this, mark you, by a man who is still a hospital out-patient! For despite his extraordinary recovery from a purler of a prang three months ago, Minter is required to attend a physiotherapy clinic four times a week!

Since he contested only the 500cc class, Derek relinquished his 250 and 350cc titles, but his lap records for those classes remained intact.

Earlier in the day, during the 10-lap Les Graham Memorial Race (which Derek also won), teammate John Hartle dropped his Gilera, thus putting himself out of the main race.

500cc British Championship, Oulton Park – 30 laps – 82.8 miles
1st   D.W. Minter (Gilera)
2nd   P.W. Read (Lancefield Norton)

3rd   A. Shepherd (Kirby Matchless)
4th   J. Findlay (McIntyre Matchless)
5th   M. Duff (Matchless)
6th   G. Marsovzky (Matchless)

The Ulster Grand Prix

Only five days after his Oulton Park success, Derek was racing in Northern Ireland. The Ulster was his first Grand Prix appearance of the season. And the task facing Derek was a tough one, for apart from this being his first GP race on the Gilera, it was still only his second outing in anger since his Brands crash in May – and his first appearance on a five-hundred at Dundrod since 1958. Conversely, Mike Hailwood, the current 500cc World Champion, was the race and lap record holder for the 7.45-mile road circuit.

In the race, Derek's combination of lack of fitness and circuit knowledge conspired against him and he ultimately came home in third position – teammate Phil Read had crashed out at Leathemstown Corner.

500cc Ulster GP – 17 laps – 128 miles
1st   S.M.B. Hailwood (MV Agusta)
2nd   J. Hartle (Gilera)
3rd   D.W. Minter (Gilera)
4th   A. Shepherd (Kirby Matchless)
5th   R. Bryans (Norton)
6th   M. Duff (Matchless)
Note: fourth onwards only completed 16 laps.

No rest

Only a week after Ulster came the East German Grand Prix at the Sachsenring. Again, Derek was at a disadvantage, never having seen the Iron Curtain circuit before. And again it was a natural road circuit, as in Northern Ireland, but measuring 5.25 miles to a lap. Also, with Mike Hailwood riding in no fewer than three events (500 and 350cc MV Agusta and 250cc MZ) Derek would also have only the single race. With Phil Read out of action, it meant that there were two Gileras – Derek, plus John Hartle. The latter's front mudguard came adrift, causing his retirement. So it was left to Derek to chase Mike around, but even though he averaged over 100mph (101.36mph) he finished nearly one minute behind the winner.

500cc East German GP – 17 laps – 92.1 miles
1st   S.M.B. Hailwood (MV Agusta)
2nd   D.W. Minter (Gilera)

3rd   A. Shepherd (Kirby Matchless)

4th   M. Duff (Matchless)

5th   J. Findlay (McIntyre Matchless)

6th   V. Cottle (Norton)

Note: fourth onwards only completed 16 laps.

The Benelli offer

In *Motor Cycle News*, dated 28 August 1963, the front page story was that Derek had agreed to race a 250cc four-cylinder Benelli at the Italian Grand Prix at Monza the following month. *MCN* said: 'He received a telegram offering the machine on Saturday and cabled his agreement to the factory on Sunday.'

Derek also said he had cancelled his entry for Snetterton on 8 September, because he was travelling to Italy, but hoped to spend the coming weekend practicing on his Norton at Brands Hatch. And this is what happened, as on Saturday 31 August he put in around 70 laps of the short circuit on his Ray Petty-tuned Nortons.

No luck in Italy

The Scuderia Duke Gilera squad, including Derek, did not have much luck in Italy. First John Hartle crashed during practice suffering slight concussion and breaking a little finger which prevented him from racing. Then, in the 250cc race, Derek's Benelli was reluctant to start, but after eventually getting away to rush through the field to fourth, his bike went sick and he retired. Then, in the 500cc race, after lying second to Mike Hailwood (MV), on lap 10 Derek was overtaken by the very fast 450cc Bianchi twin of Remo Venturi, before retiring on lap 13. Phil Read had already retired the other Gilera.

There is no doubt that this poor showing at Monza was to be instrumental in Gilera deciding not to continue with the Duke team at the end of that season. It had already showed the Gilera squad to be suffering from a combination of no ongoing development and poor reliability in front of its home supporters.

Home circuits

After winning his heat at Oliver's Mount, Scarborough, on 21 September, Derek suffered an embarrassing get-off on the very first corner (Mere Hairpin) in the 500cc final on the four-cylinder Gilera.

The following is how Charlie Rous described the incident: 'Nobody was more surprised than Derek Minter at Scarborough. The first thing which surprised him was the velocity of his getaway – "The man waved the flag and he was gone" says Phil Read. "He just disappeared out of sight while everyone else was still pushing."'

As far as Derek was concerned, this is what happened:

I arrived at the first corner miles too fast. I didn't realise the Gilera could reach such a terrific speed in such a short distance. It was only a couple of hundred yards or so from the start, but when I arrived at the corner I felt as if I was doing 200mph! In attempting to make the turn, I applied a little too much brake, skidded and came off. I picked the bike up before the rest of the field caught me, but I couldn't go on, the rear brake didn't feel right.

A day makes all the difference

The following day, Sunday 22 September, racing at Brands Hatch for the first time since his crash there in May, Derek returned to the Kentish circuit 'with all his old dash' (*MCN*) and won both Senior races on the Gilera, setting the fastest laps in both and also a new race record of 88.11mph.

And Scarborough race winner Phil Read, on the other Italian four-cylinder model, finished second to Derek on both occasions, but as *Motor Cycle News* said 'well behind the Canterbury ace'. This came after Read had led from the start in both outings.

1000cc Brands Hatch – 15 laps – 39.75 miles

1st	D.W. Minter (Gilera)
2nd	P.W. Read (Gilera)
3rd	P.J. Dunphy (Norton)
4th	M. Duff (Matchless)
5th	D. Ainsworth (Petty Norton)
6th	E.G. Driver (Kirby Matchless)

Race of the Year

The organisers for the Race of the Year at Mallory Park on Sunday 29 September 1963 billed it as World Champion Mike Hailwood 500cc MV versus Derek Minter 500cc Gilera, with a strong supporting cast including Jim Redman, John Hartle, Phil Read and many more.

But behind the scenes Derek's fitness had not been quite as good as press and public alike believed at the time. For a start he had badly bruised his shoulder when he came off the Gilera at Scarborough – and this was still painful for some time afterwards. But an amazing after-effect from his Scarborough prang occurred while Derek was in bed one night. He was awakened by a twinge from his spine with an audible click. And after suffering a niggling pain, which had dogged him since he had injured his spine in May, this was suddenly gone and his back felt 'absolutely normal.'

Additionally, in the first British short circuit clash between the 500cc four-cylinder MV Agusta and Derek's Gilera, as *Motor Cycle News* pointed out in its 2 October 1963 issue, the MV 'clearly demonstrated the mechanical and navigational superiority of the Gallarate world beater. While Hailwood flicked his big MV round with apparent ease, Minter really struggled as his Gilera stepped out on every bend.' And Phil Read's Gilera, in fourth place, a lap adrift, finished the race on three cylinders – again highlighting reliability problems.

Race of the Year, Mallory Park – 40 laps – 54 miles
1st   S.M.B Hailwood (MV Agusta)
2nd   D.W. Minter (Gilera)
3rd   A. Shepherd (Matchless)
4th   P.W. Read (Gilera)
5th   J. Redman (Honda)
6th   J. Cooper (Norton)
Note: fourth onwards only completed 39 laps.

As it turned out, Mallory Park was Derek's last ride on the Gilera – at least as a member of the Scuderia Duke team.

Even before the end of October 1963 questions were being asked about the future of the team. Charlie Rous commented: 'One I do not think will race [as regards Scuderia Duke] again is Derek Minter.'

Mallory Park 'Race of the Year', 29 September 1963. Derek is on his way to runners'-up spot behind Mike Hailwood (MV Agusta).

Of course, Derek's year had been a bad one. And as Charlie Rous also said: 'Minter certainly didn't get back into his old groove.' Of course the reasons for this have already been outlined – the crash, then missing the major part of the season, going to tracks he was unfamiliar with (examples being Dundrod, the Sachsenring and Scarborough – even Mallory Park which Derek had never liked) and the fact that the team did not have full factory backing; finally, the machines had had no development from 1957 and were prone to breaking down.

So one can only dream of what might have been, if Gilera's had been a proper works effort.

Duke's views

In his autobiography *In Pursuit of Perfection* (Osprey, 1988) Geoff Duke wrote: 'Of course, it is easy to be wise after the event. Derek, with the prospect of a great Grand Prix season ahead of him and the possibility of the 500cc world title, should perhaps have been more restrained and settled. But he hated to be beaten, particularly at Brands, and in the heat of battle it is sometimes difficult to think logically.' But of course, had the right backing and funding been in place, Derek would not have been racing his own bikes at Brands...

But perhaps most telling is another extract form the Duke book:

To say that I was shattered when I heard the news [of his Brands crash] would be an understatement. I had pinned my faith in Minter who, at the peak of his racing career, was the only rider capable of beating Mike Hailwood. I had a gut feeling there and then that any plan for a victorious return by Gilera had been dealt a mortal blow.

But most important to Derek's own story, is the undoubted fact that on that spring day at Brands Hatch in May 1963 he had suffered a setback from which he would never quite regain the level he had achieved in the months leading up to the accident.

Even in retrospect, the time with the Scuderia Duke Gilera team had not been a good one, yet Derek's experience of racing the Arcore fire engines had left its mark to such an extent that for the rest of his racing career – and for years thereafter – he always held the Italian factory and its motorcycles in high regard.

Chapter 8

Cotton

First news that Derek was forming a new partnership – with the old-established Gloucester firm of Cotton – emerged in early October 1962, when it was announced that he would be riding a two-fifty Cotton in trials during the coming winter months. At the same time he said that he had also agreed to race one of the firm's new two-fifty production racers in 1963.

Motor Cycle News revealed that 'arrangements were made for Minter to have a trials Cotton following a telephone call to the Gloucester factory last Thursday [4 October].'

Derek, who had been using a Norman in trials (to 'keep fit' as he described his dirt bike activities) for several years, made his first appearance as a Cotton rider at the Williams Trial near Detling, Kent, on Saturday 27 October 1962, organised by the Rochester club. Derek ended the event conceding 92 marks, against the winner, Murray Brush, with a deficit of five marks.

Debut of the Telstar

At the end of October came official confirmation that both Cotton and Greeves were to launch their Formula Junior racers at the London Earls Court Show.

These two newcomers were the first two-fifty road racers to be marketed by any British manufacturer since World War Two. Both, as launched, used Villiers engines, but different types. The Greeves Silverstone used a 36A, while the Cotton Telstar was equipped with one of the newly released Starmaker units (designed by Bernard Hooper). Technical details concerning the Starmaker engine and the motorcycle that Derek was to use – and the development – are contained within a separate boxed section in this chapter.

Shortly after Derek had agreed to race the new Cotton, came first hints that he might be riding four-cylinder 350 and 500cc Gilera machines in a tie-up involving former World Champion and Gilera works rider Geoff Duke. The full story of this venture is fully explained in chapter seven, but suffice to say it was to have a considerable impact upon what Derek could do with Cotton in 1963. In fact, due to his Gilera commitment and a major crash at Brands Hatch in May that year, Derek was to have only four races for the Gloucester firm in 1963.

Testing at Brands

With lap times around 63 seconds (70mph), Derek was out at Brands Hatch in mid-March for the first track test of his 250cc Cotton racer. Derek told Charlie Rous of *Motor Cycle News* that he was very pleased with the machine, saying: 'It steers very well and the brakes are very good. I was particularly pleased with the Starmaker engine and the revs indicated it was doing about 112mph.'

Derek said he would be testing the machine at Brands again on Wednesday 27 March, and if the final tests were satisfactory he would be racing the newcomer at Mallory Park on Sunday 31 March and Brands Hatch on good Friday, 12 April, in company with his own three-fifty Petty-tuned Norton and the works five-hundred Gilera.

An excellent debut

As the front-page story in *MCN* dated 3 April 1963 said:

> what a cracking debut for the 250 Cotton. One could hardly expect more, not even Derek Minter or the Cotton factory, than second place to Mike Hailwood on a Desmo Ducati twin. But for consolation Derek scored the fastest 250 lap of the day at 81.82mph. Racing the Starmaker Cotton for the first time, he tore through the field after a bad start to chase Mike Hailwood on John Surtees' Desmo Ducati across the line.

And as development work on the machine continued, improvement could obviously be expected. Derek told Charlie Rous at Mallory that a big improvement

Derek's Cotton debut came at the Mallory Park season-opener on 31 March 1963, when he finished second to Mike Hailwood and set the fastest lap.

would come when the gearbox internal ratios were finally sorted out. Bottom gear of the close ratios of the four-speed box fitted to the bike at Mallory Park was, Derek said 'much too high and caused me quite a "delay" coming out of the hairpin.' With the ratio lowered, Derek considered, it would be 'much better.'

250cc Mallory Park – 15 laps – 19.5 miles
1st   S.M.B. Hailwood (JSD)
2nd   D.W. Minter (Cotton)
3rd   R. Good (Ariel)
4th   C. Vincent (Aermacchi)
5th   R. Bryans (Benelli)
6th   B. Clark (Aermacchi)

At Brands Hatch on Good Friday Derek looked like winning every race he entered. And with Mike Hailwood out after crashing his AJS at high speed when chasing the "Mint" in the 350cc event, there was no Hailwood to challenge him in the 250cc race, where for three laps Derek held a substantial lead on the Cotton, until the spark plug failed. This let Brian Clark, on Bill Webster's Aermacchi, who had been chasing our hero hard, into the leading berth – and Brian went on to a comfortable victory.

It was not until some four weeks later that Derek next rode the Gloucester-built two-stroke. Back at Brands Hatch on Sunday 12 May the bike kept going to get revenge over Brian Clark. As *MCN* said in its report of the meeting: 'fifth at the end of the first lap, Derek Minter threaded his Cotton through very nicely to record the first win for the Gloucester marque in the 250 race at 79.24mph, with the fastest lap of 81.39mph.'

A measure of the Cotton's pace can be seen from its finishing some 18 seconds ahead of Brian Clark's Aermacchi, and as *MCN* said: 'Clark wasn't dawdling!' as the latter had all his work cut out trying to keep ahead of Terry Grotefeld and Chris Vincent on similar Italian machines. Fifth place went to Brands regular Alan Pavey (NSU), after a long dice with John Cooper on the new DMW Hornet (like Derek's Cotton, powered by a Villiers Starmaker engine).

250cc Brands Hatch – 8 laps – 21.2 miles
1st   D.W. Minter (Cotton)
2nd   B. Clark (Aermacchi)
3rd   T. Grotefeld (Aermacchi)
4th   C. Vincent (Aermacchi)
5th   A. Pavey (NSU)
6th   J. Cooper (DMW)

Cotton Telstar

Located in Gloucester, the Cotton firm began motorcycle production in 1919. In the mid-1950s the company was taken over by Pat Onions and Monty Denley. From then on the firm mainly used Villiers two-stroke engines. Back in the immediate aftermath of the Great War, Cotton had considerable success in road racing, winning the 1923 Junior and 1926 Lightweight TTs.

But it was not until the autumn of 1962, that Cotton launched the Telstar – the first of Britain's new generation 'Formula Junior' specification racers to be publicly announced. The machine arrived in concert with the introduction of the Villiers Starmaker engine (the latter designed by Bernard Hooper). Like Greeves (through Reg Everett), the Cotton Telstar had come about via a privateer (Peter Vallis), using a racerised scrambler during the 1962 season. Although the Wolverhampton-based Villiers works had its own dynamometer, it was Cotton who primarily race developed the new Starmaker engine. This began in late 1962 and the Cotton staff included Fluff Brown, who years later went on to run the FB-AJS organisation in Andover.

But it was the signing of Derek Minter in time for the 1963 season that really set Cotton on their way. With its Telstar, at the very first national of the year, Derek finished an impressive runner-up to Mike Hailwood (riding a twin-cylinder Desmo Ducati). However, the remainder of that summer was spent on development, both squeezing out more power and improving reliability. In truth, these early Starmaker engines were what can be described as 'fragile.'

Minter's works development bike received a number of important modifications, including remote contact breakers, a single Amal GP carb (the original Starmaker had featured twin Monoblocs) and a more rigid cylinder liner. But the most important of these changes came in June 1964 with the arrival (for the works machines only) of a six-speed close ratio gearbox (the customer bikes were always four-speed 'boxes). This was vital in making use of the ever-narrowing powerband of Minter's rapidly developing factory power unit. The only other Cotton with this gearbox (designed by John Favill at the beginning of 1964) was the equally competitive privately-backed machine ridden by the up-and-coming Bill Ivy. Minter's

1964 250 c.c. A.C.U. ROAD RACING STAR WON BY

DEREK MINTER
riding a

also 250 c.c. BRANDS HATCH SHIELD

This actual machine will be on view at STAND NO. 54 at next month's EARLS COURT SHOW

Send for details of all models to

E. COTTON (MOTOR CYCLES) LTD.
VULCAN WORKS, QUAY STREET, GLOUCESTER
Telephone Gloucester 22303

Derek Minter had a successful four-year relationship with the Gloucester Cotton factory, including winning the 1964 250cc ACU Star (British) Championship series.

(and Ivy's) engines progressed from the original 25bhp at 6,500rpm to 31.2bhp at 7,800rpm. This was more or less the power available when Derek Minter rode his Telstar to victory in the 1964 250cc ACU Star (British Championship) title. However, it was not the engine alone which took the Championship – but also the skill of a top line pilot combined with excellent handling characteristics provided by the lightweight (230lb) machine.

Having already been manufacturing motorcycles for the previous four decades and more, Cotton obviously knew a thing or two when it came to making them handle. The Telstar frame consisted of a full duplex layout, manufactured from seamless 'A' grade cold drawn steel tubing. The top rail and swinging arm were constructed of 1⅛in x 14swg with the cradle and subframe made from ⅞in x 14swg. Actually, the Cotton factory produced little else apart from the frame and swinging arm, utilising Armstrong leading-link front forks and rear shock absorbers (later Girling units were used at the rear) to provide the machine's suspension. The initial machines were equipped with the infamous 6in single leading shoe British Hub Company's CD full-width alloy brake assembly. Unfortunately this assembly was known for its lack of efficiency and was soon dumped in favour of a superior 7½in twin leading shoe device, which British Hub had produced to quell the many complaints arising from the earlier stopper. Unlike machines from other factories who produced rival British two-fifties of the era such as DMW, Greeves and Royal Enfield, the Telstar was fitted with 19in wheels front and rear throughout its entire production life. This, if one considers modern trends, should have been a disadvantage. However, it does not appear to have hampered Derek Minter who, along with the other supported rider Bill Ivy, claimed many a victory aboard these Gloucester flyers.

Derek seen here at Brands Hatch in winning form riding his works Telstar with six-speed box, 15 August 1965.

When tested by *Motor Cycling* in its 21 November 1965 issue, works rider Minter and *Motor Cycling* staffman Bruce Main-Smith rode one of the latest four-speed production bikes. Staged over the 1.6-mile Silverstone Club circuit, the best flying lap put on by Derek was 1 minute 16.67 seconds, a speed of 75.9mph; while the best speed through the trap, again by the King of Brands, was 102.27mph.

A distinctive feature of the Telstar was its Mitchenhall Brothers (Avon) fibreglass ware. On its launch in late 1962, the Telstar was equipped with a 2.5 gallon jelly-mould continental-style tank and a rather awkward looking single-piece fairing. However, with the Mark 2's appearance in 1964 the fuel tank, seat and fairing came in for a change and the Cotton now looked far more conventional with its maroon-coloured fibreglass styled in the conventional British racer mode. The majority of Telstar production occurred during 1964–65 and by the time of its demise in 1967 over 60 examples had been produced. They have found their way to various corners of the globe, with Australia at present holding the honour of the highest known example – machine number 66.

Once Derek Minter left at the end of 1966, Cotton's fortunes deteriorated rapidly, as by then the Japanese bike, in the shape of Yamaha's TD series, was beginning its surge to the top as the clubman's mount, in the process making all the singles, including the Cotton, obsolete almost overnight. The only area where Cotton could still compete after this was in the production racing class. And it achieved considerable success with the Conquest, which was essentially a Telstar with lights. There were class victories at venues throughout Great Britain with riders such as Minter, Peter Inchley and Reg Everett. The highlights without doubt were class wins at the prestigious 500-mile races at Castle Combe in 1965 (Minter and Inchley – they also finished third overall) and Inchley/Everett at Brands Hatch the following year.

But of course, as detailed in chapter seven, 12 May 1963 was also the day when Derek suffered the serious accident in which he was badly injured and Dave Downer died, while battling for the lead in the main race of the day, the 1000cc solo event. This crash was to mean that Derek did not appear in a race until the British Championship meeting held at Oulton Park in early August; thus putting him out of action for a large chunk of the season. In fact, as far as his Cotton effort was concerned, his one and only race for the remainder of 1963 came at Brands Hatch on 13 October.

Motor Cycle News considered that 'the 10-lap 250 race was possibly the best seen at Brands Hatch this season.' For even though there was a Honda production racer in this race – and it won in the hands of Tommy Robb – it was no runaway affair. Far from it, in fact. Phil Read chased Tommy all the way on a Syd Lawton Aermacchi and was a mere second in arrears at the finish, which went to the Honda rider at 82.72mph. Behind this duo Brian Clark (Aermacchi) came out on top of a three-way battle between himself, Tom Phillips (Greeves) and Derek on the Cotton.

250cc Brands Hatch – 10 laps – 26.5 miles

1st	T. Robb (Honda)
2nd	P.W. Read (Aermacchi)
3rd	B. Clark (Aermacchi)
4th	T. Phillips (Greeves)
5th	D.W. Minter (Cotton)
6th	C. Doble (Greeves)

Technical developments

By the end of 1963, the Villiers company had engaged Peter Inchley in the development of the Starmaker engine – and, said *Motor Cycle News* in its 18 December issue, this was 'showing quite a lot of progress.' Charlie Rous went on to say: 'I wouldn't suggest for one moment that Peter alone is responsible for the work, but he was at Brands Hatch last week with a Cotton Telstar fitted with an engine he has been working on and was getting it around quite nicely.' The differences included the substitution of one large Amal GP racing carburettor in place of the previously employed twin Monobloc instruments, plus a modified ignition system.

Derek rode this particular machine at Brands on the same day and commented that it was 'far more powerful than my machine.' He estimated it to be 'at least 5mph faster.'

Certainly development by both Inchley and other members of the Villiers technical team (including a new six-speed gearbox) made a considerable difference to Derek's machine, and at the season opener at Mallory Park on

Snetterton National Road Races, 4 September 1964. Derek is seen here on the grid before the 250cc race with his works Cotton (11). Also on the grid are Terry Pallister (38) and Peter Darvill (14) (also Cottons); plus John Blanchard (Aermacchi, 7), J. Fincham (FNS, 29), Martl Drixl (Aermacchi, 39) and Reg Everett (Yamaha, 9).

22 March 1964 he lapped at precisely the same speed as Alan Shepherd, the winner, on a works MZ 250 twin. Unfortunately for Derek, his race ended when the carburettor came adrift.

Although Derek had many more outings on the Cotton in 1964 than he had in 1963 (20 in total, compared to four in 1963), the year was one of development rather than race winning. In fact, Derek only gained two victories on the single-cylinder two-stroke: Castle Combe on 18 April (including a record lap) and Snetterton on 6 September (where he set the fastest lap). However, together with the Mallory Park

Derek riding his Cotton trials bike (modified with Triumph Cub front end), winter 1964–65.

meeting referred to above, he suffered several retirements, notably in the Isle of Man TT. Usually these retirements were engine related. Overall development of the Starmaker engine was further assisted by Inchley's own racer. But, unlike Minter's machine, this employed the chassis, suspension and cycle parts from a Spanish Bultaco TSS.

The one really big news story of 1964 concerning the Minter/Cotton story was Derek's Championship-winning performance in the ACU's 250cc Star series on the Gloucester machine.

A new year, a new start

With the arrival of 1965 came a new year and a new start. And the fruits of the previous two years' development work.

Cotton's Pat Onions acknowledged the help which the firm had received from Villiers and, when interviewed in January 1965, he said: 'Villiers have given a lot of attention to the motor.' And 'for our part, we have meticulously looked after the cycle details.' As an example Pat Onions went on to explain:

> The wheels come out before each meeting to check the bearings and the brakes. The grease in the standard wheel bearings has been removed; instead, three drops of R (Castrol R racing oil) are put into each. The brakes are cleaned out with the air line. It is surprising how much dust collects during a race. I always check over wheel alignment, and gearbox and primary chain case oil levels, as a matter of course before each meeting. Chains must be in exact adjustment. Derek uses standard springs. They have been carefully paired on Girling's matching machine at Tyseley to make sure that both respond in the same way to impacts.

Pat Onions also revealed that Derek was 'fastidious about all controls working freely' and he did not 'like the sudden-death, all-on-at-once type of super-quick-action twistgrip. Additionally, the brake pedal 'must be set high – and if it isn't he'll not leave the paddock until it has been made just so.' The purpose of this was quite straightforward – cornering clearance.

Other details of the Cotton's preparation included tyre pressure of 24/26psi front and rear. They started the engine on a Lodge RL49 to warm up the Starmaker engine. For the race 'we use 50, 51 or even the allegedly-unobtainable 52, depending on the conditions.' The main jet of the GP carburettor was normally a five-twenty. And 'surprisingly' this was 'right' for both Snetterton's long and flat straight and for Brands' twisting undulations. Only weather conditions forced a change, and then rarely by more than 10cc.

Lydden Hill circuit

Another happening at the beginning of 1965 was an invitation from *Motor Cycling* for Derek to give Britain's newest racing circuit, Lydden Hill, the once-over. And after some 50 laps on the Cotton and his own three-fifty Norton, Derek, who only lived nearby at Blean, pronounced that course 'A-OK.'

Also at the test session was Sittingbourne businessman Bill Cheeson, advisor to the circuit owner, William Mark Holdings Ltd.

Lydden, already well known for grass-track events organised by the Astra club, was also a former scrambles circuit; the newly tarmacked road-racing circuit measured 1,240 yards in length.

After lapping in both directions, Derek opted for a clockwise circuit. That way he said it 'would be faster, safer for the riders and more interesting for the spectators.' So that the way it was, and still is today.

Minter sidecar man

In February 1965 Derek borrowed Chris Vincent's 654cc BSA A65 sidecar outfit and at Silverstone – after only eight laps – was circulating at over 86mph (the lap record for chairs at that time being just over 90mph) – and the circuit was damp and cold.

Chris Vincent commented afterwards: 'I think that in a short circuit race he'd finish very well up.' Derek's passenger for the day was Englishman John Robinson, who normally rode with the Swiss star, Fritz Scheidegger.

Derek's own reaction to his three-wheel outing was: 'It was marvellous. Vincent's outfit really shook me – I took my solo line on the corners and never had any trouble. It was easy – but I doubt if I could do it on anyone else's outfit.'

When interviewed in 2007, Derek commented: 'Nothing further happened, because I realised of course, it was only because of the superb quality of Vincent's machine – plus the expertise of my passenger [John Robinson] – that

February 1965. Derek borrowed Chris Vincent's BSA A65 sidecar outfit and put in a number of impressive laps around Silverstone. John Robinson (normally Fritz Scheidegger) is in the chair.

it had seemed comparatively 'easy' to me. Without these two aspects, I'm sure I would have achieved nothing much.'

The Mallory opener

At the Mallory Park season opener, on Sunday 10 March 1965, Derek suffered starting problems with his Petty-tuned Nortons (see chapter nine) and his sole victory that day came aboard the Cotton.

And as *Motor Cycling* commented:

> As luck – or good programme planning – would have it, those great rivals John Cooper and Derek Minter clashed in the very first race of the day – in fact of the season – heat one for the 250cc event. Out on his new mount, the Reg Orpin-entered 'works' Greeves, Cooper flashed ahead from the start, Minter also got away well, and, on the second lap, he nosed ahead and stayed there to win by a few lengths.

> Again in the final Cooper made a quick getaway. But Derek's Cotton had 'the edge' (*Motor Cycling*) and Minter steamed into the lead. The crowd had expected a battle royal. But the clutch of Cooper's machine failed at the hairpin and Derek was left to win, easing up.

250cc final, Mallory Park – 8 laps – 10.8 miles

1st   D.W. Minter (Cotton)

2nd   D.F. Degens (Aermacchi)

3rd   D.A. Simmonds (Honda)

4th	W.D. Ivy (Cotton)
5th	R.J. Everett (Yamaha)
6th	R.F. Pladdys (Honda)

Next, at Brands Hatch on Sunday 24 March, Derek scored another victory on the Cotton, so it was two rides, two wins. But this winning run came to an abrupt end at Snetterton a week later, on 31 March, when he retired on the second lap of the 250cc race with his Cotton 'making expensive motor noises' (*Motor Cycling*).

Then, after finishing fourth at Brands Hatch on Good Friday 19 April and third at Snetterton on Easter Sunday, the following day, Easter Monday, Derek scored victory number three for 1965 on the Cotton at Oulton Park.

With Phil Read and Mike Duff and their works Yamahas on the line, no one gave much for the chances of the other competitors in the 250cc race at Oulton. But as *Motor Cycling* said: 'The Japanese "hares" soon fell by the wayside – Duff on the second lap when his gearchange lever broke and Phil three laps later when he "dropped it" at the Hairpin.' This left Bill Ivy (Cotton), Gordon Keith (Royal Enfield) and Derek battling at the front – which our man won.

250cc Oulton Park – 19 laps – 51.3 miles

1st	D.W. Minter (Cotton)
2nd	W.D. Ivy (Cotton)
3rd	D.F. Degens (Aermacchi)
4th	E. Cowan (Greeves)
5th	R.W. Good (Ariel)
6th	D.L. Croxford (NSU)

Then came a win in his heat – and third in the final at Castle Combe on 4 May, followed by another victory at Brands Hatch on 12 May. Then, just before the Isle of Man TT, Derek finished third on the Cotton at Mallory Park behind the winning Bill Ivy (his Cotton, entered by Frank Higley, now sporting telescopic front forks and Oldani front brake) and Reg Everett's very fast Ted Broad-entered Yamaha TD1B. Actually, as was often the case during his racing career, Derek suffered a poor start in this race and this made things difficult.

250cc Mallory Park – 10 laps – 13.5 miles

1st	W.D. Ivy (Cotton)
2nd	R.J. Everett (Yamaha)

3rd   D.W. Minter (Cotton)
4th   D.F. Degens (Aermacchi)
5th   P. Inchley (Villiers Special)
6th   R.F. Pladdys (Honda)

The Lightweight TT

On Monday afternoon, 14 June 1965, 76 riders were ready to push their machines out on the Glencrutchery Road to line up for the start of the six-lap 226.4-mile 250cc Lightweight TT. The entry had been cut by 30 non-starters. Even so, this was easily the biggest field ever to line up for a quarter-litre race around the punishing 37.73-mile Mountain course. The question was, how many would finish, and would Derek and his Cotton be among them? The previous year, out of a field of 64, only 19 took the chequered flag.

As a measure of the Cotton's improving reliability Derek brought the bike home in a very respectable ninth position – out of 25 finishers. The race was won by Jim Redman riding a six-cylinder Honda. And the same rider also set the fastest lap (a record) at 100.09mph. But earlier Phil Read (Yamaha) – who was eventually to retire – became the first man in history to break the 100mph lap on a two-fifty.

250cc Lightweight TT – 6 laps – 226.4 miles
1st   J.A. Redman (Honda)
2nd   M.A. Duff (Yamaha)
3rd   F.G. Perris (Suzuki)
4th   T. Provini (Benelli)
5th   F. Stastny (CZ)
6th   D. Williams (FB Mondial)
7th   G. Milani (Aermacchi)
8th   B.P. Setchell (Aermacchi)
9th   D.W. Minter (Cotton)
10th   J. Findlay (DMW)
11th   D. Krumpholz (MZ)
12th   C.R. Conn (Cotton)

Long distance success

Next came victory on 13 July at Castle Combe, before returning to the Wiltshire course a couple of weeks later for the 500-mile race; the first year it had not been held at Thruxton.

Although a Syd Lawton-prepared machine won the marathon for the fourth time (Dave Degens and Barry Lawton – 649cc Triumph Bonneville),

Derek, walking with a stick following an earlier accident, with co-rider Peter Inchley and Cotton director Pat Onions at the prize presentations following their amazing third place overall in the 500-mile endurance race at Castle Combe, 27 July 1965.

the real news, as the headline in *Motor Cycling* read in its 31 July 1965 edition, 'Lawton's Fourth Year – But – 250 Steals 500-Mile Limelight.' The report continued: 'The day's sensation was the performance of a works 250 Cotton Conquest. Derek Minter and Peter Inchley rode it into third place overall – the best 250 performance ever in this event.'

What most race-goers did not realise was that Derek was in considerable pain. He had a torn cartilage in his left knee, and was hobbling along with the aid of a walking stick!

The event had been switched from Thruxton because of that course's poor surface. And, as the author well remembers, having ridden from Norfolk to spectate on my Southwell Triton, pouring rain swamped the Castle Combe circuit for the first half hour of racing, but things improved later.

By the end of the third hour, the Minter/Inchley Cotton was three laps up on the next two-fifty, the works Montesa ridden by the Spanish pairing of Jose Busquets and Carlos Rocamura. And it was the Montesa riders who remained Derek and Peter's main challengers for class honours throughout.

No fewer than 20 entries retired for various reasons, the majority with engine troubles such as seizures, big-ends, broken con-rods and dropped valves. Just studying the first 10 finishers tells the story – it was not a good day for the large capacity bikes.

500-mile race, Castle Combe – 27 July 1965 – Overall Classification

1st	D. Degens / B. Lawton (649cc Triumph)	272 laps
2nd	A. Smith / N. Ling (654cc BSA)	262 laps
3rd	D.W. Minter / P. Inchley (247cc Cotton)	259 laps
4th	J. Busquets / C. Rocamura (175cc Montesa)	257 laps
5th	W. Purnell / D. Cooper (649cc Triumph)	254 laps
6th	B. Davis / W. Scott (247cc Honda)	246 laps
7th	G. Keith / J. Rudge (248cc Royal Enfield)	246 laps
8th	C. Lodge / E. Webb (649cc Triumph)	244 laps
9th	W. Smith / P. Williams (745cc Matchless)	243 laps
10th	E. Sirera / J. Carne (249cc Montesa)	241 laps

Derek finished third at Snetterton on 28 July, when still hobbling around he was forced to start from the back of the grid with a pusher in the 250cc final.

Pressing the Yamahas at Silverstone

Another outstanding Cotton performance came at Silverstone, when the BMCRC held its annual International Hutchinson 100 meeting on Saturday 17 August 1965. With the likes of Phil Read and Mike Duff (Yamahas) and Derek Woodman (MZ), the various single-cylinder machinery, including Derek's Cotton, looked to have no chance. However, on a wet track it was the Cotton man who kept the Yamahas in sight, after Woodman had been slowed by gearbox gremlins. But then, on lap 11 of the 15 lap race distance, an ignition wire broke on Derek's machine, leaving Percy Tait (Royal Enfield) to take the glory of a rostrum position in third.

The following day, 18 August, the South African Martin Watson caused something of a stir when he led Derek and Dave Degens (Aermacchi) a 'merry dance' (*Motor Cycling*) in the early stages of the 250cc race. But eventually Derek took over at the front, with Degens second and Watson third at the finish.

But Derek was relegated to fourth behind Dave Simmonds (Honda), Inchley and Watson at Mallory Park on Sunday 25 August.

It was Watson who finished in front of Derek again when the two riders clashed again eight days later at the ACU International British Championships at Oulton Park on Bank Holiday Monday, 2 September. As Phil Read's Yamaha had broken a big-end after seven laps, his teammate Mike Duff took over the lead and won from Peter Inchley (Villiers Special), Watson (Bultaco) and Derek. But, later that day (see chapter nine), Derek rode one of his greatest races, when he just failed to beat Bill Ivy (Matchless) in the 500cc

Derek leading on the first lap of the 250cc final at Brands Hatch. Other riders include Ron Pladdys (62), Bill Ivy (9), Dave Simmonds (64) and Barry Lawton (37).

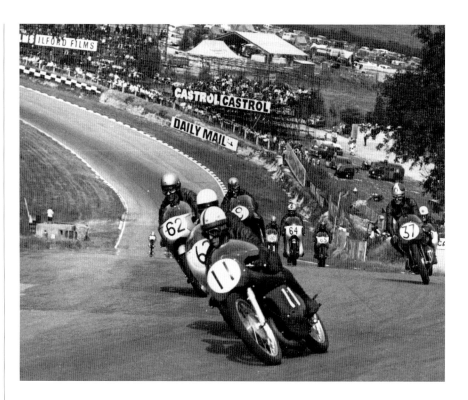

Championship race, after being left on the line, last away, on his larger Petty-tuned Norton.

To round off his Cotton rides in 1965, Derek finished third at Castle Combe on 7 September and runner-up to Reg Everett (Yamaha) at Brands

Cotton-mounted Derek at Brands Hatch in 1964, leading Tommy Robb (Yamaha, 90) Ron Pladdys (Honda, 92), Bill Ivy (Cotton) and Percy Tait (Royal Enfield).

Hatch on 22 September. But as *Motor Cycling* said: 'Veteran Derek Minter shook his critics when he slammed back to top form' beating many of the riders who had been the top men that season.

250cc Brands Hatch – 8 laps – 21.2 miles

1st	R.J. Everett (Yamaha)
2nd	D.W. Minter (Cotton)
3rd	D.A. Simmonds (Honda)
4th	M. Carney (Bultaco)
5th	M. Watson (Bultaco)
6th	P.G. Inchley (Villiers Special)

Derek had also been due to race the Cotton (together with his 350 Norton) at the Japanese GP at Suzuka on 23–24 October 1965, but a high-speed crash at Mallory Park on his five-hundred Norton (see chapter nine) was to rule him out of the trip, which had been organised by Chester dealer Bill Smith.

During the 1965 season, the Cotton's engine had become far more reliable but there were now newer, faster bikes; particularly, if one discounts the factory efforts from the likes of Yamaha, Honda and MZ, the fast developing Yamaha TD1 series.

Changes for 1966

As detailed in chapter nine, the big news concerning Derek's plans for 1966 centred around exactly what machinery he would be riding in the 350 and 500cc classes – would it be AMC racers from either Tom Kirby or Colin Seeley, or his own Petty-tuned Nortons? In the end he chose to go with Seeley. But behind the scenes, he also continued his association with Cotton.

The two main changes, compared with 1965, were the use of an experimental cylinder barrel, of the type developed by Peter Inchley, and improved porting. It is worth noting that by now Derek had returned to the Armstrong forks, after having occasionally tried the Norton type.

Derek got his Cotton season off to a slow start with third at Mallory Park (6 March), sixth at Brands Hatch (13 March) and third at Snetterton (20 March). But his fortunes improved over the Easter weekend, with three excellent results at Brands Hatch, Snetterton and Oulton Park.

First, at Brands on Easter Friday, 8 April, he began with a win, *Motor Cycle News* enthusiastically saying: 'Cotton-mounted, Minter led the 250 event from start to finish. Fight as they did, Peter Inchley (Villiers), John Blanchard (Bultaco) and Dave Degens (Aermacchi) could not get near him.'

Winning on the works
Cotton at Brands Hatch,
8 April 1966.

250cc Brands Hatch – 10 laps – 26.5 miles

1st	D.W. Minter (Cotton)
2nd	D. Degens (Aermacchi)
3rd	P. Inchley (Villiers Special)
4th	D. Simmonds (Honda)
5th	M. Carney (Bultaco)
6th	M. Watson (Bultaco)

The Snetterton Skid Pan

Sunday 10 April 1966 will forever be known as 'The Snetterton Skid Pan' meeting, when the infamous newly-created Russells Corner took out so many riders in the 350cc race (including Honda-mounted Mike Hailwood!) that the race had to be stopped when only four laps had been completed. Derek had the good sense to tour back to the paddock after viewing the carnage! (See chapter nine).

In the lightweight events, Tommy Robb, with a brace of new water-cooled Bultacos, took the honours, while Derek won a private battle with Peter Inchley for the runner-up spot.

Peter Inchley with the works development Villiers Special was one of Derek's main challengers in the hotly contested 250cc class. He is seen here at Snetterton on Easter Sunday, 10 April 1966.

250cc Snetterton – 6 laps – 16.3 miles

1st   T.H. Robb (Bultaco)
2nd   D.W. Minter (Cotton)
3rd   P. Inchley (Villiers Special)
4th   D. Simmonds (Honda)
5th   V.D. Chatterton (Yamaha)
6th   T. Phillips (Ducati)

In great form at Oulton

Derek enjoyed a great day at Oulton Park on Easter Monday, 11 April, with victory (over John Cooper) in the 500cc race, runner-up to Mike Hailwood (Honda four) in the 350cc and an equally impressive runner-up spot to Derek Woodman (MZ) in the 250cc class. Even though Woodman's bike was probably at least 20mph quicker for most of the race distance, Derek held the lead. And it was a relatively long race (over 50 miles). So how did he manage this? *Motor Cycle News* has the answer: 'he kept Woodman in second place with the most incredible tactics around the many corners.' But as *MCN* pointed out 'there is no substitute for power' – and Woodman showed this on the last corner of the race, by nipping past to take a well-planned win ahead of a rider who just did not have the horsepower to deal with the situation. However, the pace of these two was such that they came home together by less than a second, more than a minute ahead of the rest – at 82.40mph.

In retrospect this was probably Derek's greatest-ever Cotton performance. But he had had to ride the wheels off his bike. Just think about it: the Cotton produced around 30 bhp – the latest twin-cylinder water-cooled MZ doubled this figure.

250cc Oulton Park – 19 laps – 52.5 miles
1st   D. Woodman (MZ)
2nd   D.W. Minter (Cotton)
3rd   T. Burgess (Greeves)
4th   D. Simmonds (Honda)
5th   B. Warburton (Yamaha)
6th   C. Ward (DMW)

No luck in Italy

Then it was off to Italy to race in a couple of meetings. Originally the plan was to ride a works two-fifty Moto Morini, which the organisers of the international Shell Gold Cup meeting thought they could persuade the Bologna company to release. This machine was not available, but a spare five-hundred Gilera was made available after Derek had seen off Remo Venturi on another Gilera during practice on his five-hundred Seeley G50 (see chapter nine).

And as Derek had been 'none too sure of the Morini ride' and had taken his Cotton, he turned out on the Gloucester model for a star-studded 250cc race staged over 16 laps, 49.8 miles in length. With two of the leading contenders for the world title clashing for the first time that season in the shape of Jim Redman (Honda) and Phil Read (Yamaha), plus a host of other works stars including Tarquinio Provini (Benelli) and Bill Ivy (Yamaha), it was perhaps quite amazing that at the end of the first lap Derek should be lying a magnificent third, behind Read and Derek Woodman (MZ). By mid-race, having dropped to seventh, Derek retired. But it still has to be an excellent showing.

A week later, at Cesenatico, Derek pitted the Cotton against the same set of stars. And although he was destined for another retirement when the Villiers big-end failed when ninth, the two riders directly in front of him were none other than Jim Redman (Honda four) and Bill Ivy (Yamaha twin).

Then, at Castle Combe on Saturday 30 April, Derek suffered more disappointment with the Cotton when, after winning his 250cc heat, the machine seized in the final on the fourth lap when in the lead. The eventual winner was Rod Gould (Aermacchi).

Action at Snetterton and Brands

Then came the Whitsun holiday weekend. First, at Snetterton on Sunday 29 May, Derek had what he described as an 'odd day.' He did not qualify for the

500cc final, having lost his primary chain as he shoved off in the heat. Earlier, in the 350 final, he retired with a puncture in his rear tyre.

So, as he told Peter Howdle of *Motor Cycle News*: 'now I'll have to try and murder the 250 race.' And that is exactly what he did. Peter Inchley led for several laps, with Reg Everett on his tail and Derek a few yards behind. Then Derek got into top gear and 'ousted them' (*MCN*). But Everett and Inchley fought back. Unfortunately Reg than dropped his Ted Broad Yamaha at Riches Corner; Inchley could not avoid him and went down in a heap. This left Derek well ahead of the rest of the field and he went on to score a comfortable victory. Derek also set the fastest lap at 88.53mph.

250cc Snetterton – 6 laps – 16.3 miles
1st	D.W. Minter	(Cotton)
2nd	V.D. Chatterton	(Yamaha)
3rd	R. Pladdys	(Yamaha)
4th	M. Taylor	(Yamaha)
5th	D. Degens	(Aermacchi)
6th	T. Grotefeld	(Yamaha)

The Continental Circus came to Brands Hatch on Monday 30 May 1966. And a huge crowd watched the World Champions and local specialists battle it out. But, strangely, the only improvement in record lap speeds came when Phil Read took his works Yamaha twin round the 2.65-mile Kent GP course at 87.36mph, 0.8 of a second faster than Derek's Honda record, established in 1962 (see chapter five).

And so to the race itself. The big question at the start of the 250 event was could Jim Redman (Honda twin) provide any sort of challenge to the Yamahas of Phil Read and new teammate Bill Ivy? The answer was no, and it was a Yamaha-only duel between Ivy and Read. Bill got the verdict, Phil the lap record. Behind these two came the quick-starting Tommy Robb (Bultaco). Then, with only inches separating them, Derek's Cotton got the better of Redman. This was also the last time that Derek and Jim were to meet in a race, because Redman was to retire shortly afterwards following a serious accident on the works Honda four in a rain-swept 500cc Belgian Grand Prix at the beginning of July.

250cc Brands Hatch – 10 laps – 26.5 miles
1st	W. Ivy	(Yamaha)
2nd	P.W. Read	(Yamaha)
3rd	T. Robb	(Bultaco)

4th   D.W. Minter (Cotton)
5th   J. Redman (Honda)
6th   R. Pladdys (Yamaha)

Crashes and more crashes

At Mallory Park, on Sunday 19 June, Derek had more than his fair share of troubles. First he was flung off his 500 Seeley in practice and also off the Cotton in his 250cc heat. He suffered a badly bruised left heel in the latter incident and did not race again that day.

But he still told *MCN's* Robin Miller that he was a 'happy man.' Why? Well, Derek put his troubles down to his testing of a 500 Gilera at Monza the previous week, saying 'the front brake needs a very firm application. But the Seeley [he called it a Matchless] and Cotton front brakes are both feather light, and I'm sure the reason I came off both times was because unconsciously I applied the brakes too firmly.'

Derek had been down to once again partner Peter Inchley on the Cotton Conquest in the 500-mile endurance race (on 26 June), which had been

Racing the JW4 at Castle Combe in summer 1966. Derek admits he much preferred two wheels.

switched once again, this time from Castle Combe to Brands Hatch. But his Mallory Park crashes ruled him out, and Reg Everett took his place (finishing seventh overall).

On Saturday 9 July, Derek (in his first meeting since the Mallory crashes) rode a Seeley for the last time (in the 500cc race) and after setting the fastest lap of the 250cc race, Derek christened his new dark green leathers by dropping the Cotton at Camp Corner while challenging Reg Everett's Yamaha for the lead. This had come after his machine had broken its clutch cable and partly seized in his heat – but he still managed to qualify for the final!

Also during mid-July Derek revealed that he had been unable to get an entry for the Hutchinson 100 at Brands Hatch on 14 August with the Cotton and complained: 'I am the only one keeping the British flag flying at the moment and yet I get turned down.' Robin Miller of *Motor Cycle News* commented: 'I for one, would certainly like to see Derek in the 250 race just to keep the works men on their toes.'

Derek was deeply involved with the development of the Johnnie Walker Formula 4 racing car powered by the Villiers Starmaker 250cc engine.

Trying his hand at speedway

Also in July 1966, Derek tried his hand at speedway. Going along to the Hackney stadium in East London, he borrowed Malcolm Brown's machine and on a rain-soaked track acquitted himself well. But when questioned by the *MCN* speedway correspondent Peter Arnold, Derek denied that he was going to take it up, saying: 'Too dangerous, there's no brakes on the wretched things.'

In August, after racing his Nortons at the Hutchinson 100 at Brands Hatch (the circuit ran in the opposite direction to normal for the first time), Derek flew to Italy to test the 500 Gilera that he was due to ride in the Senior TT. The annual Isle of Man races had been postponed from their usual June date because of the National Seaman's Strike. Instead the TT was staged in late August.

A sad end to Derek's season

Derek's TT hopes were dashed in the final practice session on the Saturday evening when he crashed his five-hundred Gilera four-cylinder racer at Brandish Corner and broke his arm.

The injuries also included facial cuts and a slight concussion – and combined this meant that he was to miss the remainder of the season.

Not only was Derek unable to race again in 1966, but in effect, his Gilera TT practice crash also brought down the curtain on his four-year long Cotton

In July 1966 Derek even tried speedway, at the Hackney Wick Stadium in east London.

career. Although, as charted in chapter nine, he was to continue riding his Nortons for another season, Derek decided to quit the 250cc.

The following are Derek's own views of his period with the Gloucester firm:

No, Cottons did not 'pull the plug', but we felt there were no further developments in hand from Villiers!

I thoroughly enjoyed my time with Cottons and got on very well with all the people in the factory. I remember at one stage, I took a Norton frame down there, laid it on the floor (with the Cotton frame on top) and from this they were able to establish the 'head angle' needed for the 'tele' front forks on the Cotton (when Norton Roadholder forks were used).

The Cotton was an easy bike to ride and the period with them was happy, due largely to the presence of Pat Onions. We built up a strong friendship, which lasted until Patrick sadly died in 2000.

The Armstrong front forks were alright for trials and scrambling, but not for road-racing, as you go round corners much quicker! They were unable 'to ride the bumps' as well as the 'tele' forks.

Chapter 9

Finale

During 1963, Derek's Norton (and Cotton) rides were kept to only a small number – due to a combination of his Scuderia Gilera involvement (see chapter seven) and a career changing crash at Brands Hatch in May that year.

A bright beginning

But it had all begun so brightly with a series of wins, fastest laps and record laps, not just on the Gilera but on his own Nortons and to a lesser extent the new Cotton Telstar over-the-counter racer on which Derek had made his debut at Mallory Park at the end of March (see chapter eight).

And prior to the meeting at Brands Hatch where the accident referred to above had occurred, Derek had begun the season in absolutely brilliant form, only retirements stopping him from a clean sweep, except on his debut ride on the Cotton at Mallory Park when he had finished runner-up to Mike Hailwood. His Norton victories came at Mallory Park (31 March, 350 and 500cc), Brands Hatch (12 April, 350cc) and Oulton Park (15 April, 350cc).

Brands Hatch, 12 May 1963

The day had begun brilliantly, with Derek winning the 250cc race on his Cotton, then finishing runner-up to Phil Read (Norton) on his smaller Norton, and then winning the 10-lap 500cc Redex Trophy race on his 499cc model.

500cc Redex Trophy, Brands Hatch – 10 laps – 26.5 miles

1st	D.W. Minter (Norton)
2nd	P.W. Read (Norton)
3rd	D. Downer (Norton)
4th	D.F. Degens (Norton)
5th	G.A. Jenkins (Norton)
6th	J. Dunphy (Norton)

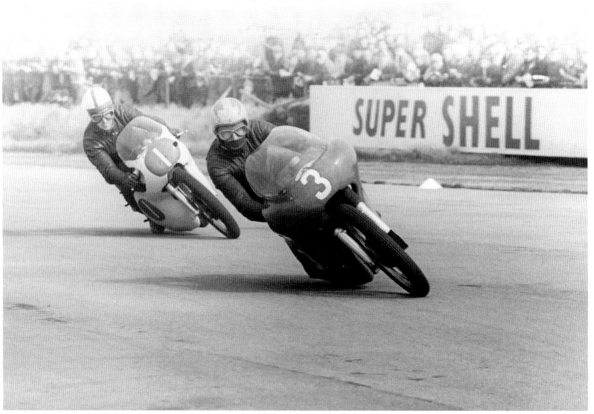

At the beginning of 1963 Derek had a wide range of machinery to chose from: 250cc Cotton, 250/500cc Gileras and his own Ray Petty-tuned Nortons. He is seen here on the smaller Norton following Mike Duff (AJS) at Silverstone on 6 April; he was later forced to retire with a split exhaust pipe.

The crash

For everyone who was there to witness it, the Solo 1000cc race, over 15 laps of the full 2.65-mile Grand Prix circuit, was, as Charlie Rous told readers in *Motor Cycle News* on Wednesday 15 May 1963 'the most terrific race I have ever seen.' Unfortunately, it also ended with the two main combatants badly injured (Derek) and dead (Dave Downer).

These two riders, in company with Phil Read, had simply stormed away from the rest of the field in what was the final event of the day. Read initially led, but with Downer and Derek hard on his heels. As Charlie Rous explained: 'Downer then exerted the full potential of Paul Dunstall's incredibly fast 650 Norton and went ahead – but nothing separated the three riders. And although he led the race at the end of each subsequent lap by virtue of the Norton twin's fantastic acceleration, the lead changed constantly.' For 10 laps this 'near-indescribable no-holds-barred' battle raged until Read dropped out and this, with the race reaching its closing stages, seemed to 'spur Minter and Downer' into even greater efforts as they lapped the circuit literally neck and neck. For although the time keepers only credited Derek with lapping at this figure, there was little doubt that Downer had achieved similar figures.

Charlie Rous picks up the story: 'with Downer constantly blasting past Minter's 500 Manx Norton to lead the race at the conclusion of each lap, Minter's only hope of victory was to shake the 650 rider off on the corners. As they rocketed around on the final circuit, Minter took the lead at Westfield Bend and was in front when they arrived at Dingle Dell. As Derek braked hard for the corner, Downer – who was still very close behind – was unable to avoid a crash.

The after-effects of the accident

At first the press, and certainly members of the general public, did not appreciate just how serious Derek's injuries were. Charlie Rous wondered: 'Will Derek Minter miss the TT? Even though the TT practising begins in just over a couple of weeks time I fancy he will be there to ride for Gileras.'

Even a week later no one outside the medical staff at Dartford Hospital realised the full extent of his injuries. Later, in the 5 June 1963 issue of *MCN*, there was a photograph of Derek in bed at his Blean home with two of his Siamese cats for company.

By then Derek's injuries were now known to be more serious than was at first thought. He had two fractured vertebrae in his spine and a broken left shoulder blade. He also had eight stitches in his left knee and a badly gashed head. Doctors didn't think he would be fully fit for 'four to five months.'

Castle Combe in Wiltshire was always a happy hunting ground for Derek. This photograph from 1963 shows Welsh star Selwyn Griffiths leading the field.

Meanwhile, Phil Read, who had so seriously challenged the Minter-Hartle duo at Silverstone (see chapter seven), had been signed up as an official Scuderia Duke Gilera rider. And this was no temporary signing, as team manager Geoff Duke commented: 'If Minter makes a wonder recovery and comes back this season, then I'll have three Gilera riders.'

As for Phil himself, he said: 'I am very, very pleased, although I am sorry that I should have got this chance because of an injury to Derek.'

And, as detailed in chapter seven, although Derek did make a quicker recovery than his medical team had envisaged, and rode Gilera machines in the British Championship meeting at Oulton Park (5 August), the Ulster GP (10 August), the East German GP (18 August) and the Italian GP at Monza (15 September), Derek's first outing on a Norton was not until 21 September at Scarborough.

Back on his Nortons

Derek had got back on his Ray Petty-tuned 350 and 500cc Nortons on Saturday 31 August, when he put in around 70 laps of the Brands Hatch short circuit. Afterwards Derek commented: 'I was pretty pleased with myself. I was lapping within one second of my best times on both machines, and I'm looking forward to riding at Brands in the meeting there on 22 September, when I hope to be on the 500 Gilera and 350 Norton.'

Actually, Scarborough was very much a bitter-sweet experience for Derek. After winning his heat on the Gilera in the 500cc class, he crashed at the first bend on the first lap of the final and retired (see chapter seven). In the 350cc category race, with his Norton, he worked up from fifth on lap two to finish third, setting the fastest lap of the race, his 12th, at 66.33mph.

Oulton Park and Brands Hatch

Next, with both his Nortons (after an exclusively Gilera meeting at Mallory Park on 29 September), Derek had four races at Oulton Park on Saturday 12 October – winning both the 350 and 500cc heats – and finished runner-up to Phil Read in the finals. He also had the satisfaction of setting the fastest lap of the day on his biggest Norton at 88.91mph.

Then came the final meeting of 1963 at Brands Hatch on Sunday 13 October, with victory (and fastest lap) in the main race of the day, for 1000cc machines; when on his 499cc Manx Norton Derek won from Denis Ainsworth and Joe Dunphy (both Norton mounted). But in the 350 and 500cc events our man was beaten by Phil Read (Lancefield Nortons).

1000cc Brands Hatch – 15 laps – 39 miles

1st	D.W. Minter (Norton)	
2nd	D. Ainsworth (Norton)	
3rd	P.J. Dunphy (Norton)	
4th	D.F. Degens (Matchless)	
5th	R.E. Butcher (Norton)	
6th	M. Duff (Matchless)	

And so the 1963 season ended. One which had promised so much, but in the end delivered very little. It was also the beginning of Derek's 'finale' in the racing world, although no one realised it at the time. And, certainly, there were very many successes and victorious days to come. But somehow Derek would not quite be able to capture the spirit of absolute invincibility which he had shown in 1962 and for the first part of 1963.

The 'back-to-front' Norton
Then in November 1963 came the first details of the newly created 'back-to-front' three-fifty Norton, which Ray Petty had created especially for Derek. Ray commented: 'Whether it will work or not I haven't the faintest idea, but I've got a few theories about this thing.' Mr Petty also considered the project offered the possibility of being more suitable for short circuit work than the conventional Manx production model, the bike being owned by Petty's friend John Viccars. The full story of this interesting technical development is detailed in a special boxed section within this chapter.

Plans for 1964
With no sign of works machinery in the offing (see chapter seven), Derek's plans for 1964 centred around his Nortons, plus the Cotton ride (see chapter eight).

Amazingly, as he entered the new year, Derek could count no fewer than eight Nortons. These were his own stable of four, plus the 1962 pair belonging to his entrants, Hallet's of Canterbury (which were still brand new and unraced) and now two more from John Viccars (the back-to-front machine, plus a conventional machine). Ray Petty had also arranged to supply a couple of spare engines, should they be needed.

Patchy form
Except for a one-off ride on the newly released Honda 125cc double-overhead camshaft twin cylinder CR93 production racer at Oulton Park on Easter Monday, 30 March, Derek's early meetings of the 1964 season were exclusively on Nortons (350 and 500cc) and Cotton (250cc).

Ray Petty's reverse head
350 Norton, summer 1965.

Petty Back-to-Front Norton

Originally rumoured in late 1962, the famous Ray Petty back-to-front three-fifty Manx Norton was first fired up in November 1963 and tested at Brands Hatch shortly afterwards. The engine was originally built (as a standard Manx) in 1957, and before the conversion was last used as a conventional Manx single by Frank Perris. The conversion began in the closed season of 1962–63. The frame and suspension for the one-off machine (owned by John Viccars) were purchased new in 1963.

It was Ray's idea to locate the exhaust port at the rear and the carburettor at the front, while retaining the bevel-drive to the double overhead camshafts on the offside (right) of the engine. Ray Petty viewed the following as the 'hoped-for objects' of the exercise:

- straight exhaust pipe giving an easier exit for the outgoing gases
- opportunity to employ pipe lengths from the ultra short 15in to the normal 30in
- superior cooling – as Petty said: 'There is not some 18 inches of red-hot pipe to heat the cooling air before it reaches the cylinder head and barrel'
- a more natural positioning of the cams in their box.

The difficulties that he encountered were as follows:

- the need to resite the spark plug (the cylinder head was tried with no less than three positions (threads) although only a single plug was used to fire the engine)
- poor angle of entry of the carburettor inlet tract because the bellmouth was badly placed in relation to the nearside (left) top frame tube
- getting the engine to run hot enough.

The back-to-front engine also proved extremely difficult to carburate. And did not, noticeably, respond even to what Petty described as 'gross'

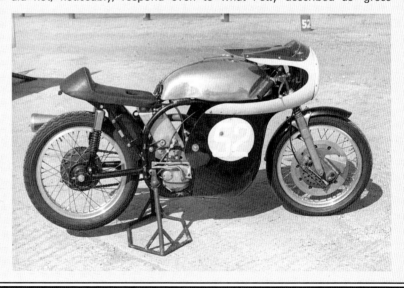

Photograph showing the layout of the reverse head engine.

variations in jet sizes, nor much to lower fuel levels. For example, when it was tested at Silverstone by Derek Minter and Bruce Main-Smith for a *Motor Cycling* Racer Test in 1965, it was then using a 250 main jet – described as 'outrageously small', but still refused to give the piston a 'good colour'. The compression ratio at that time had been set at 11:1, though as the test revealed 'the engine is clearly detonation proof up to much higher values.' The engine used coil valve springs, specially made to Ray Petty's specification. And it was said that they stood up well to the additional rpm of which the unit was capable. But when first built in 1962–63 it still had conventional Manx-type hairpins. As Bruce Main-Smith revealed: 'Main characteristics of the motor was its curious carburation.' Ray tried small jets and big jets, lowering the float level, and ringing changes on the exhaust. This was its biggest problem throughout its development.

In racing, Derek Minter found it was entirely possible to rev the motor to 9,000 – way above a conventional three-fifty Norton. Of course, in theory at least, the biggest advantage of the reverse head was a direct supply of cold air to the carburettor and that the carburettor body temperature was drastically reduced. The cooled charge was denser, hence more potent. Amazingly, except for the details outlined above, the operation was relatively painless. Probably the main modification was a new hole in the cylinder head casing for the camshaft vertical tube. And, of course, the inlet and exhaust cams had to be reversed and timing reset ·to match. The float chamber was now on the centre line of the machine, where it suffered least from directional changes. There is no doubt that the bike's development was held up considerably by the regular tuning commitment which Ray Petty had to undertake – his riders' successes simply bringing in ever more work.

The rest of the bike, except for features such as the hi-level megaphone found on the nearside (left) and a Ray Petty speciality, the large cooling-cum-rigidity disc on the front brake hub, was essentially standard Manx Norton. Twin spark ignition (two plugs) was tried initially, before reverting, as explained earlier, to a single plug system. The bike's first race competitively came at the final meeting at Brands Hatch on 11 October 1964 (see the main text), finishing in third. After the Brands meeting the piston crown was machined as it was slightly hitting the head. A 14mm plug blank was made and fitted (going from twin to single spark ignition as already explained). The flywheels were replaced with standard production Manx components, while more finning was removed from both the head and barrel, the oil pipes were modified and, again as already outlined, coil valve springs replaced the original hairpins. Finally, the inlet cam was retimed.

Settings at Mallory Park on 29 October 1965 were as follows:

- main jet 280
- rpm achieved 8,400
- gearing 18 x 46 (wet track).

There is no known record of what happened to this machine after Ray Petty abandoned the project when the Yamaha invasion began in the late 1960s. It surfaced at the Stafford Classic Bike show in October 1998. Derek Minter paraded it at Snetterton during 1999. Now owned by Adrian Sellars, it has been carefully restored by Gerry Brown and is displayed and run from time to time. It was judged 'Best at Show' at the prestigious Louis Vuitton Classic at the Hurlingham club in May 2002.

While Derek's larger displacement Norton was flying, with victories at Mallory Park (22 March), Brands Hatch (27 March) and Snetterton (29 March), his performances on the three-fifty were far from satisfactory. After the meeting at Brands Hatch, where Derek could do no better than finish ninth, Ray Petty diagnosed magneto trouble. The assembly was changed and at the same time the decision was taken to fit a twin spark unit. However, this proved to be even worse. There was no opportunity to test the machine before Snetterton, where the engine seized during the qualifying heat, due, said Ray, to being over-advanced and running with too weak a jet size.

A successful TT
With fourth in the Junior (350cc) on 10 June and second in the Senior (500cc) on 12 June, Derek was one of the stars of the 1964 Isle of Man TT races. And if he had not been slowed by a broken valve spring on his smaller Norton, he could well have repeated his magnificent Senior result, when he came home runner-up to Mike Hailwood's four-cylinder works MV.

350cc Junior TT – 6 laps – 226.4 miles

1st	J. Redman (Honda)
2nd	P.W. Read (AJS)
3rd	M.A. Duff (AJS)
4th	D.W. Minter (Norton)
5th	D. Woodman (AJS)
6th	J. Dunphy (AJS)
7th	P.J. Darvill (AJS)
8th	W.S. Mizen (AJS)
9th	E.G. Driver (AJS)
10th	C.R. Conn (Norton)
11th	B. Beale (Honda)
12th	F.J. Stevens (AJS)

500cc Senior TT – 6 laps – 226.4 miles

1st	S.M.B Hailwood (MV Agusta)
2nd	D.W. Minter (Norton)
3rd	F.R. Stevens (Matchless)
4th	D. Woodman (Matchless)

Derek seen at speed during the 1964 Senior TT on his Norton at Union Mills, on his way to a magnificent second to Mike Hailwood (MV Agusta).

Derek (Petty Norton) during his wonderful ride to second place in the 1964 Senior TT, with a race average speed of 98.47mph.

5th	G. Jenkins (Norton)
6th	W. McCosh (Matchless)
7th	B. Setchell (Norton)
8th	C. Ward (Norton)
9th	J. Cooper (Norton)
10th	D. Lee (Matchless)
11th	P. Bettison (Norton)
12th	A. Harris (Matchless)

Mike Hailwood on his way to victory during the 1964 Senior TT on his works four-cylinder MV Agusta.

John Cooper (Mooneyes –
due to his helmet decor) in
action at Oliver's Mount,
Scarborough, 30 June
1964.

John Cooper

Nicknamed 'Mooneyes' due to the 'eye' motifs on his 'pudding basin' red-painted crash helmet when battling every weekend during the summer months against men such as Derek Minter on the British short circuits aboard a pair of Manx Nortons during the mid-1960s, John Cooper had been born in Derby during 1938, just prior to the outbreak of World War Two a few months later.

His first racing motorcycle was a 197cc Villiers-powered James two-stroke, which he rode during the mid-1950s at local circuits including Alton Towers. Progressing from club level to national and finally international, his first victory at the latter level came at Oliver's Mount, Scarborough during 1961. At this time, at least in the 350 and 500cc classes, British short circuit racing meant big four-stroke singles such as the AJS 7R, Matchless G50 and of course the Manx Norton. And John's choice for many years, like Derek Minter, was a pair of Nortons.

In 1966 Cooper became double (350 and 500cc) British Champion, the last honours the Derby star would win on his Petty-tuned Nortons. Although he rode (like Minter) a pair of Seeleys for a while in the 350 and 500cc categories, it was to be in the 250cc sector where he was to score his next major success, winning the 1968 British title on a Japanese TD1C twin-cylinder two-stroke machine. This led John and Colin Seeley to develop the Yamsel machine. This was essentially one of the new TR2 three-fifty Yamaha engines mounted in one of Seeley's excellent chassis. This combination was to prove an instant success, with John winning countless races on this bike, including the big money Race of the Year event at Mallory Park in September 1970.

Then, after being loaned a works three-cylinder BSA 750 for the 1971 Easter Match Race series (held annually over the holiday weekend at venues including Brands Hatch, Mallory Park and Oulton Park between teams from Great Britain and the United States), Cooper managed to secure full factory backing from the Birmingham company. At last John Cooper had machinery to realise his true potential, and with it was to come the most successful period of his racing career.

Who will ever forget that dramatic day in September 1971, when the Derby man beat Italian star Giacomo Agostini (MV Agusta) in one of the greatest motorcycle races of all time at Mallory Park's Race of the Year? John followed this up with another victory over the Italian World Champion at Brands Hatch later that year. He then travelled to North America for the first time, where he won the prestigious 250-mile Ontario Classic in California, with its massive pay cheque. Then it was back home to a hero's welcome, which culminated with readers of *Motor Cycle News* voting John 'Man of the Year' by a clear margin. Sticking with BSA in 1972, Cooper won the *Motor Cycle News* Superbike Championship title, but at the end of that year, and with the entire BSA Group on the verge of financial collapse, he signed for Norton. But after crashing at Brands Hatch at the start of the 1973 season and breaking a leg, John called it a day, hanging up his leathers after almost 20 years in the sport.

Although John was tempted to consider a comeback, he never did. However, he retained an interest in bikes and helped several riders, including Heron Suzuki teamster John Newbold, while building up a garage business in his native town of Derby. Later still, with the arrival of the classic scene, John Cooper was to be seen parading, but not racing, his Seeley G50 at events such as the Post TT at Mallory Park.

But then, at the Post TT at Mallory Park on Sunday 14 June, it was back to the problems which Derek had experienced in the first half of the 1964 season, with a fifth in the 350cc final after fighting his way through the field after an atrocious start and a retirement in the 500cc.

A change of fortune

Then came a change in fortune, beginning at Brands Hatch on Sunday 21 June, when after finishing runner-up on the Cotton in the 250cc race, Derek won all three races entered on his Nortons. Not only this, but he also set the fastest lap in each for good measure. And as *Motor Cycle News* pointed out:

Whatever the dictates of world classic [GP] racing, with classes up to 250cc taking pride of place, nothing will replace the lusty 500s as the prime-movers in British home races – as Derek Minter and John Cooper showed with their cut-and-thrust dicing at Brands Hatch on Sunday.

But Cooper was to come out second best in all three classes when the two came together. And as *MCN* said: 'It seemed impossible that Minter would even catch Cooper in the 10-lap 350 race.' Cooper shot away from the line like a dart while Minter pushed off in midfield and was third the first time around. But Derek was not having anybody challenge him for his long-held 'Brands Crown'. Cooper had not been quite as slick as Dave Degens (AJS) off the mark, but took Degens as they went into Druids Hill hairpin. Minter, meanwhile, was gaining fast and after streaming past Degens, who held third place to the finish, took Cooper at Clearways.

350cc Brands Hatch – 10 laps – 26.5 miles
1st   D.W. Minter (Norton)
2nd   J. Cooper (Norton)
3rd   D.F. Degens (AJS)
4th   R.E. Butcher (Norton)
5th   W.D. Ivy (AJS)
6th   M. Duff (AJS)

Frustration in Holland

The Dutch TT at Assen on 27 June followed, but it was to prove a frustrating journey. Out of three starts Derek twice retired, and his only placing was sixth in the 350cc race. As detailed in chapter eight, his 250 Cotton was really flying while it lasted, but the big-end went on the fourth lap. His breakdown in the five-hundred race must have been even more frustrating. A broken brake shoe spring in his Oldani front brake caused it to lock on. And even in the three-fifty race he finished with a broken inlet valve spring on his Norton.

Mallory boycott

Derek, together with many other top riders, decided to boycott the national meeting at Mallory Park scheduled for 12 July. A drastic reduction in starting money was the reason. Some riders had been informed that, owing to financial restrictions, no start money could be offered to them. Whereas what *MCN* referred to as 'Star riders such as Minter' could now expect only £10, although 'they normally ask for 10 or more times that figure' (*MCN*). The decision to axe starting money stemmed from the Brands Hatch race circuit group management who now owned the Leicestershire circuit.

The management felt that, because the meeting took place the day after the European Car Grand Prix at Brands, attendance at Mallory would be affected.

This meant that after the Dutch TT, Derek did not race for an entire month.

Back to winning ways

Upon Derek's return to British soil his luck changed for the better.

First at Castle Combe he dominated the larger classes, winning both heats and finals in the 350 and 500cc races. After setting a fastest lap in the smaller class, he established a new record for the Wiltshire circuit on his 499cc Petty-tuned Norton at 91.25mph.

The following day, Sunday 26 July, Derek was repeating his Castle Combe form at Snetterton in Norfolk. The *Motor Cycle News* headline read: 'Minter Still the Master at Snetterton.' It went on to say: 'John Cooper "King of Mallory" had to be content with second best at Snetterton on Sunday, when "King of Brands", Derek Minter, beat him in both 350 and 500cc finals on the "neutral" Norfolk circuit.'

Another journalistic report summed up Minter's dominance nicely:

Derek was in complete control of the larger capacity race, sitting in Cooper's slipstream for most of its length. Then, just as the two were nearing the end of the penultimate lap, Minter, on his Ray Petty-tuned Norton, casually pulled out of the "vacuum" and shot by right out of the copybook. Cooper could do nothing about it and eventually finished 150 yards down on the winner.

Derek also set the fastest lap at 93.27mph.

350cc Snetterton – 10 laps – 27.1 miles

1st	D.W. Minter (Norton)
2nd	J. Cooper (Norton)
3rd	D. Williams (MW Special)
4th	R. Butcher (Norton)
5th	D. Degens (AJS)
6th	W.D. Ivy (Norton)

500cc Snetterton – 10 laps – 27.1 miles

1st	D.W. Minter (Norton)
2nd	J. Cooper (Norton)
3rd	C.R. Conn (Norton)
4th	R.E. Butcher (Norton)
5th	J.C. Simmonds (Norton)
6th	D. Croxford (Matchless)

500cc British champion for a third year running

On Bank Holiday Monday, 3 August 1964, Derek created history by winning the 500cc British Championship title for the third year running. And he simply dominated the race, winning with ease. But no fewer than seven riders battled it out in a tremendous scrap for second place, which was eventually won by Derek Woodman (Matchless).

500cc British Championship, Oulton Park – 25 laps – 69 miles

1st	D.W. Minter (Norton)

2nd   D. Woodman (Matchless)

3rd   M.A. Duff (Matchless)

4th   G. Marsovzky (Matchless)

5th   D.F. Shorey (Norton)

6th   P. Bettison (Norton)

Derek retired earlier in the 350cc race when his Norton holed a piston.

Master at Brands

Although he did not break any records, Derek was in unbeatable form at Brands Hatch on Sunday 16 August 1964, winning the 250, 350 and 500cc races with ease. And it was not a case of no opposition, with many other stars present. After victory in the 250cc event on his Cotton (beating Reg Everett on Ted Broad's Yamaha in the process), Derek 'hoovered' up the opposition in the bigger classes in impressive style. Press reports showed Derek achieving his victories with the handicap of typically poor beginnings:

> Paddy Driver, on his Tom Kirby 7R, built up a commanding lead while Minter, who was slow off the mark, was very much in the mid-field as they went out of sight round South Bank Bend. But Derek's progress during that opening lap on the 2.65-mile course was meteoric, for when Driver came back into view at Clearways the first time round the Canterbury ace was right on his tail! And that's where he chose to remain for the first eight laps until he made his move to pull ahead and win at 83.01mph (*Motor Cycling*).

350cc Brands Hatch – 10 laps – 26.5 miles

1st   D.W. Minter (Norton)

2nd   E.G. Driver (AJS)

3rd   C.R. Conn (Norton)

4th   M. Duff (AJS)

5th   R.E. Butcher (Norton)

6th   R. Pickrell (Norton)

500cc Brands Hatch – 10 laps – 26.5 miles

1st   D.W. Minter (Norton)

2nd   E.G. Driver (Matchless)

3rd   D. Degens (Dunstall Domiracer)

4th   P.J. Dunphy (Norton)

5th   J. Smith (Norton)

6th   M. Duff (Matchless)

Another clean sweep at Snetterton

After Brands came Snetterton on 6 September – and another clean sweep for Derek. After winning the 250cc race on the Cotton, he was able to adopt a touring-type stance (sitting out of his fairing) right on the tail of his main competition (John Cooper) in both the 350 and 500cc finals. To be fair, Cooper was 'far from his best' (*MCN*) but nonetheless having Derek win as he pleased must have been morale-sapping for John. And, in fact, the Derbyshire rider faded badly in the later 500cc final and could only finish fourth.

350cc Snetterton – 10 laps – 27.1 miles

1st	D.W. Minter (Norton)
2nd	J.H. Cooper (Norton)
3rd	A. Peck (Norton)
4th	W.D. Ivy (AJS)
5th	C.R. Conn (Norton)
6th	R. Watmore (AJS)

500cc Snetterton – 10 laps – 27.1 miles

1st	D.W. Minter (Norton)
2nd	C.R. Conn (Norton)
3rd	R. Watmore (Matchless)
4th	J.H. Cooper (Norton)
5th	J.C. Simmonds (Norton)
6th	P.J. Dunphy (Norton)

Unbeatable on his 500cc Norton at Brands

With his 500cc Nortons, Derek was in unbeatable form at Brands Hatch on Sunday 20 September 1964, winning the 500cc Redex Trophy (sixth round) with ease – a competition he had already clinched for the season – and he just as easily won the 1000cc Alan Trow challenge Trophy Race. But Derek could only finish third in the 350cc Fred Neville Trophy Race, behind John Cooper (Norton) and Paddy Driver (AJS).

500cc Redex Trophy, Brands Hatch – 10 laps – 26.5 miles

1st	D.W. Minter (Norton)
2nd	P.J. Dunphy (Norton)
3rd	E.G. Driver (Matchless)
4th	J.H. Cooper (Norton)
5th	W.D. Ivy (Monard)
6th	G.A. Jenkins (Norton)

1000cc Alan Trow Trophy, Brands Hatch – 10 laps – 26.5 miles

1st   D.W. Minter (499cc Norton)
2nd   D.F. Degens (647cc Norton)
3rd   J. Cooper (499cc Norton)
4th   E.G. Driver (496cc Matchless)
5th   D.L. Croxford (496cc Matchless)
6th   C.R. Conn (499cc Norton)

Back-to-front testing

Development of the Ray Petty 'back-to-front' Norton had continued and it was hoped to have the machine finally race-ready at Brands in early October. But before that Derek was in action at Mallory Park, at the annual Race of the Year meeting on 27 September. He finished third in the main race, held over 40 laps (54 miles), with only Mike Hailwood (MV) and John Cooper (Norton) in front. But otherwise it was not one of Derek's better weekends that year, with fourth in the 350cc class and sixth in the 500cc event.

Winning the Bob McIntyre Memorial Trophy

But Derek was back to his best a week later at Oulton Park on Sunday 3 October, when in winning the 500cc event his progress was described by *Motor Cycle News* as 'simply outstanding', and once clear of the field he raced away alone. His victory also brought him the Bob McIntyre Memorial Trophy, and also the fastest lap at 87.80mph.

500cc Bob McIntyre Memorial Trophy, Oulton Park – 8 laps – 22 miles

1st   D.W. Minter (Norton)
2nd   J.H. Cooper (Norton)
3rd   W.D. Ivy (Monard)
4th   D. Croxford (Matchless)
5th   P.J. Dunphy (Norton)
6th   J. Evans (Norton)

A double ACU Star

It took the entire season to decide the winner of the 1964 ACU Star series. The climax came at the season's last meeting, at Brands Hatch on Sunday 11 October, when by winning the 500cc race Derek clinched the Senior Star from John Cooper. With 10 wins each to their credit, Minter had to win this race. If he had finished anywhere else the Star would have gone to Cooper – even though, in this grand finale, he retired. John had already won the 350 Star.

Derek also took the 250 Star with his Villiers Starmaker-powered Cotton (see chapter eight) by six points from Tom Phillips (Greeves).

Besides the Star contest, there were also points to be awarded for a substantial bundle of bonus prize money – the October Brands meeting also determining the circuit's 1964 champions in each capacity class. Derek scored a hat-trick in the 250, 350 and 500cc categories with his Cotton and Ray Petty-prepared Nortons.

Finally, as expected, Derek had his first race on the Ray Petty 'back-to-front' model in the 350cc event, but after his usual slow start could not make up enough ground to get past the winner John Cooper (Norton), or the runner-up Mike Duff (AJS), so had to be content with third position at the flag.

And so the 1964 season came to an end. And after all the disappointments of 1963, it was good to see Derek have a successful season, in which besides a host of victories he also won the 500cc British title for a record-breaking third term, finished runner-up in the Senior TT and won the 250 and 500cc ACU Star Championships.

These results also prompted renewed interest from the East German MZ factory for Derek to race their two-stroke machines in the 1965 TT. However, even though both Derek and MZ were contracted to Castrol (this having been the stumbling block in the past), he declined an offer in November 1964, commenting: 'I intend to concentrate on riding Ray Petty's Nortons in world classics in which I feel I have a better chance of being well placed.'

But a month later, in mid-December, Derek flew to Italy to discuss with Gilera the possibility of racing one of their 500cc fours again in the following year's GPs. If the talks were satisfactory, Derek hoped to be able to test-ride a bike at Monza.

Into 1965

In mid-February 1965, Derek gave Ray Petty's 350cc Norton with reversed cylinder head an extensive test at the Silverstone circuit. Ray said he was 'working hard to iron out the few snags that the first outing revealed' and that both he and Derek were pleased with the results. 'It accelerates like a rocket' commented Derek.

Derek's first outing in anger came at Mallory Park, on Sunday 10 March, but it was John 'Moon Eyes' Cooper who celebrated the start of the 1965 season with what *Motor Cycling* described as a 'brilliant double' on his Beart-prepared 350 and 500cc Nortons. As for Derek, he was 'plagued by his now notorious inability to start a "Manx" Norton quickly' and never 'looked like catching Cooper in either class.' Derek's only consolation was winning his heat and the final on the latest Cotton (see chapter eight).

And our hero's start to the season did not get any better at Brands Hatch on 24 March, as Mick Woollett's *MCN* headline in the race report read 'Minter's D-Day', going on to explain: 'King Minter slid gallantly from his throne on Sunday – beaten twice by the same man, Dave Degens. No neck-and-neck-all-the-way stuff either. The invader came from sixth to zoom past, pipping the Mint right where it hurt – on the finishing line. For Derek it was D-Day.'

However, Woollett's headline hid the fact that actually Derek beat Degens as much as Degens had beaten him – with two victories in the 250cc (Cotton) and 500cc (Norton).

500cc Brands Hatch – 10 laps – 26.5 miles

1st	D.W. Minter (Norton)
2nd	D.F. Degens (Dunstall Domiracer)
3rd	P.J. Dunphy (Norton)
4th	D.L. Croxford (Matchless)
5th	L.P. Young (Matchless)
6th	G.A. Jenkins (Norton)

A week later, at Snetterton on Sunday 31 March, Derek carried off the main race of the day, the East Anglian Trophy, in the 500cc event. But it was Dan Shorey (Norton) who was his main challenger that day, finishing runner-up to Derek in the 500cc and winning the 350cc. The anticipated three-cornered Cooper-Degens-Minter 500cc battle did not materialise, Degens suffering mechanical trouble and Cooper simply unable to get up front to mix it in the Minter–Shorey duels.

350cc Snetterton – 10 laps – 27.1 miles

1st	D.F. Shorey (Norton)
2nd	J.H. Cooper (Norton)
3rd	D.W. Minter (Norton)
4th	W.D. Ivy (Norton)
5th	R.G. Gould (Norton)
6th	D.L. Croxford (AJS)

500cc Snetterton – 10 laps – 27.1 miles

1st	D.W. Minter (Norton)
2nd	D.F. Shorey (Norton)
3rd	P.J. Dunphy (Norton)
4th	J.H. Cooper (Norton)

5th   W.D. Ivy (Monard)

6th   S. Graham (Matchless)

'King Derek Rules Brands'

So spat the massive double page headline in *Motor Cycling* dated 24 April 1965. The article went on to say: 'At last it's official! Derek Minter is the "King of Brands" – and he holds the title for a year after winning the feature race of Good Friday's "King of Brands" meeting.'

Easter Friday, 19 April 1965, was a great occasion for Derek. Riding his Nortons in front of a tremendous crowd – estimated to have been well over 50,000 strong – he completely outclassed the opposition to win all three of the big races: the 350cc, 500cc and the all-important unlimited "King of Brands" event.

And with the fastest lap of the day at precisely 88mph, as *Motor Cycling* said: 'It was a very happy Minter who received his crown – a replica of Henry VIII's – from pop singer Lulu.'

When one realises the opposition Derek faced that day in the shape of

Leading Phil Read (354cc works Yamaha) on his Petty Norton on his way to victory in the 350cc race, Brands Hatch, 19 April 1965.

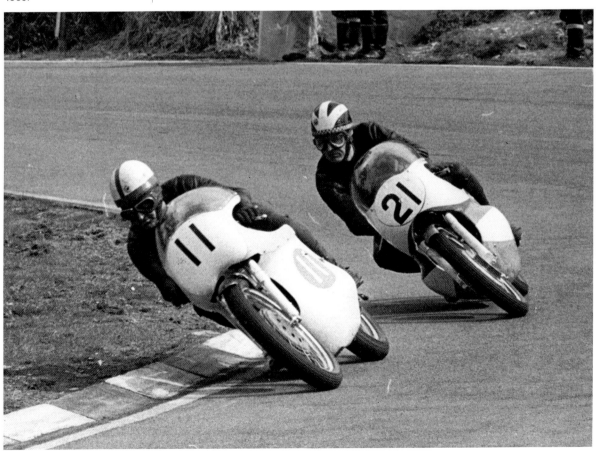

Mike Hailwood, Phil Read, Bill Ivy, John Cooper and many, many more, his were real victories, not easy ones.

1000cc "King of Brands", Brands Hatch – 10 laps – 26.5 miles

1st	D.W. Minter (Norton)
2nd	P.W. Read (Yamaha)
3rd	P.J. Dunphy (Norton)
4th	E.G. Driver (Norton)
5th	D.L. Croxford (Matchless)
6th	J.H. Cooper (Norton)

With popstar Lulu, after winning the 'King of Brands' title, 19 April 1965.

Derek and Lulu doing a lap of honour at Brands in a Triumph Spitfire sports car.

Two days later, on Easter Sunday, 21 April, in cold, blustery conditions, Derek finished third (350cc) and fourth (500cc) at the international Snetterton Race of Aces meeting.

350cc Snetterton – 10 laps – 27.1 miles
1st   P.W. Read (Yamaha)
2nd   D.F. Shorey (Norton)

At the rear of his Ford Thames van, Snetterton, Easter Sunday, 21 April 1965.

3rd   D.W. Minter (Norton)
4th   J.H. Cooper (Norton)
5th   D.L. Croxford (AJS)
6th   S.M.B. Hailwood (AJS)

On Easter Monday, 22 April, Derek was favourite to win the 19-lap, 51.3-mile 500cc race at Oulton Park. And Derek led for 15 laps until, with his boots soaked in oil, he began missing gears and John Cooper managed to get past to win.

But riding his three-fifty Norton, Derek wreaked his revenge in the final race of the day. After an 11-lap duel with Dan Shorey (Norton), the 'Mint' pulled away to victory, while Cooper could finish no higher than sixth.

Peter Williams

Although John Cooper was out with flu, Derek still had considerable opposition at Castle Combe on Saturday 4 May, from riders such as Rod Gould, Dave Degens and a youngster named Peter Williams. And although well-known now, Peter, 20 years of age and the son of former AMC chief race engineer Jack Williams, was not familiar to race-goers at the time. In fact Williams led the 500cc final for five laps. And even though Derek then got past, Peter pressed him right to the flag and was beaten by only a couple of lengths. Derek had earlier beaten Rod Gould in the 350cc final after winning both his heats, making it five wins, counting his heat victory in the 250cc class on the Cotton.

Peter Williams, son of AMC race designer and engineer Jack Williams, burst on to the race scene at Castle Combe in 1965 (seen here on the Arter Matchless in 1967).

500cc Castle Combe – 10 laps – 18.5 miles

1st   D.W. Minter (Norton)
2nd   P. Williams (Norton)
3rd   D.L. Croxford (Matchless)
4th   S. Griffiths (Matchless)
5th   M. Uphill (Norton)
6th   D.F. Degens (Dunstall Domiracer)

Next came a series of meetings at Brands Hatch (12 May), Snetterton (19 May) and Mallory Park (26 May), before Derek left to race in the Isle of Man TT. But after finishing ninth on the Cotton in the Lightweight event (see

Joe Dunphy (seen here during the 1965 Senior TT) was one of several who attempted to challenge Derek's number-one spot on the British short circuits during the mid-1960s.

chapter eight) the remainder of the TT was a disaster, as he retired in both the Junior (engine) and Senior (magneto). And things did not improve when he crossed to continental Europe to compete in the Dutch TT at Assen on 29 June. He once again suffered engine failure on the three-fifty Norton, while in the 500cc race he experienced yet another retirement, this time when his front brake anchor-arm came loose.

Overnight to Brands

After competing at Assen on Saturday 29 June, Derek made the overnight 500-mile journey to Brands Hatch to compete at his local circuit the following day. With little or no sleep to refresh him, he still managed to put in some excellent performances. And with his best three-fifty Norton out of action after the Dutch, Derek rode one of Tom Arter's AJS 7R models – not only winning at Brands, but setting the fastest lap at 85.79mph on the unfamiliar machine. Then, after finishing runner-up in the 500cc race to Bill Ivy (who he had beaten in the 350cc event), Derek took part in the newly introduced 20-lap Brands Relay Race. Derek's team (comprising himself on his five-hundred Norton, plus Ron Chandler's 350cc AJS, Barry Lawton's 250cc Aermacchi and Rod Scivyer's 125cc Honda) finished third in the contest. Derek also had the satisfaction of setting the fastest lap at 88.83mph.

Third in Belgium

Then came one of Derek's finest performances of the mid-1960s, when he finished a truly magnificent third in the 500cc Belgian Grand Prix held over the 8.8-mile Spa Francorchamps circuit in the heavily wooded eastern area of the country, near the German border.

With a near 100,000 crowd, although Mike Hailwood and teammate Giacomo Agostini scored a one–two for the MV Agusta factory, it was the 'series of tremendous struggles' among the Norton and Matchless-mounted men which kept the spectators on their toes. And it was Derek who came out on top of this 131.5-mile battle. Oh what Derek would have given for a Gilera four that day!

500cc Belgian GP – 15 laps – 131.41 miles
1st	S.M.B. Hailwood (MV Agusta)
2nd	G. Agostini (MV Agusta)
3rd	D.W. Minter (Norton)
4th	E.G. Driver (Matchless)
5th	F.J. Stevens (Matchless)
6th	G. Marsovzky (Matchless)

7th	C.R. Conn (Norton)
8th	I. Burne (Norton)
9th	J.J. Ahearn (Norton)
10th	D.F. Shorey (Norton)
11th	S. Graham (Matchless)
12th	J. Findlay (McIntyre Matchless)

Castle Combe action

With Derek slowed by carburettor trouble – after setting a new outright Castle Combe lap record of 91.76mph on his five-hundred Norton – Ray Watmore (Matchless) scored a surprise victory in the Wessex Centre's Avon Trophy race at Castle Combe on Saturday 13 July 1965. But Derek still had three wins to his credit, in 250, 350 and 500cc supporting events, on a Cotton and his Nortons respectively.

As detailed in chapter eight, Derek (together with co-rider Peter Inchley) was back at the Combe a couple of weeks later, causing a sensation by finishing third overall in the 500-mile endurance race on a 250cc Cotton Conquest – beaten only by a couple of six-fifties!

A busy weekend

Then came a busy weekend, when Derek took in the Hutchinson 100 meeting at Silverstone on Saturday 17 August, followed by Brands Hatch the following day. His only finish at Silverstone was a third in the 350cc event (behind Mike Hailwood and John Cooper), but he retired in both the 250cc and 500cc races (the latter with a broken oil pipe). But interestingly, in *Motor Cycling's* electronic speed trap (over 176 yards) he recorded 132.4mph – an identical figure to that of Phil Read on the works 254cc Yamaha twin. And before his retirement Derek had challenged Hailwood (MV) for the lead in the 500cc outing.

At Brands Derek won the 250cc (Cotton) and 350cc (Norton) races, while finishing runner-up to Bill Ivy (Kirby Metisse) in the 500cc class.

One of his greatest races

As the 4 September 1965 issue of *Motor Cycling* described: 'Derek Minter (Norton) rode one of the greatest races of his career at the ACU's international British Championships at Oulton Park on Monday – but just failed to beat Bill Ivy (Matchless) in the 500cc title race.' The report continued: 'Minter, winner of the 500cc title for the past four [actually this should have read three] years, was hopelessly left at the start when his Norton refused to run cleanly. As he sat astride the "Manx", juggling the throttle, the

Bill Ivy (Kirby Metisse), who won the Mallory Park 500cc race on 6 March 1966.

entire field left him behind.' But in typical fighting fashion, Derek roared through the field to catch the leader, Ivy, and just failed to score an incredible victory.

500cc British Championships, Oulton Park – 19 laps – 51 miles

1st	W.D. Ivy	(Kirby Metisse)
2nd	D.W. Minter	(Norton)
3rd	G.A. Jenkins	(Norton)
4th	D.F. Shorey	(Norton)
5th	R. Watmore	(Norton)
6th	J.H. Cooper	(Norton)

End of season meetings

Thereafter came a succession of end of season meetings at Castle Combe (7 September), Snetterton (8 September) and Brands Hatch (22 September), before 1965 came to a dramatic end when Derek crashed at around 90mph attempting to make up ground in the 500cc final at Mallory Park on Sunday 29 September.

This incident also meant that he was ruled out for the remainder of the meeting – including the lucrative Race of the Year event.

Derek had been due to travel to Japan for that country's Grand Prix at Suzuka over the 23–24 October. But a painful hand injury as a result of his

Mallory crash put him out for the remainder of the season. So he took the opportunity to go into hospital – for a cartilage operation on his knee!

A change of machinery

By mid-November Derek was out of hospital and his injured hand was healing well. And at the same time came the first rumours that Derek would be racing AMC machinery in 1966, in the shape of a three-fifty AJS and five-hundred Matchless. Mick Woollett got things right when he wrote the following in *Motor Cycling*, dated 13 November 1965: 'The sponsor, well known in his own right, is relatively new to the game as an entrant.' But in *Motor Cycling* of 27 November Mick Woollett said:

> It now seems almost certain that Derek Minter will be Norton mounted again in 1966. Plans that I hinted at two weeks ago which would have meant the 'Mint' switching to AJS and Matchless mounts are apparently falling through, and Ray Petty – the man who has prepared Derek's Nortons for the past two seasons – is already scheming up very special 350cc (not the reverse head machine) for Minter to race next year.

Minter and Seeley

By the end of November the AMC idea seemed back on track, when Derek tested a G50 Matchless belonging to Colin Seeley at Brands Hatch. Unfortunately snow started to fall after he'd covered only a few laps, and Derek was forced to pack things in for the day. Afterwards he said: 'It was my first ride since I came off at Mallory Park in September, and it was good to get back in the saddle.'

On Sunday 15 December, Derek rode his Cotton trials model in the North Kent Trials combined event – his first competitive outing on a motorcycle since his Mallory Park crash in September. Asked how he got on, Derek replied: 'shocking – but my injured hand stood up to the hammering well except that the vibration from the engine on the road sections irritated it.' He went on to say that he intended riding in as many trials as he could to strengthen his hand and make sure that he would be in tip-top form when the 1966 season started. But he had already decided to remain with the Cotton works in the 250cc class. And in fact he spent a few days at the factory in Gloucester just before Christmas – working on his trials bike and discussing his racing plans. But, as regards his other plans, those were to 'remain secret for the time being.'

A dilemma

Except for his intention of riding for Cotton, Derek had 'not fixed up anything' when 1966 began. In fact, as he told Charlie Rous of *Motor Cycle*

Seeley

Derek Minter was the first works-supported rider following the Seeley buy-out of the AMC race shop, with Derek riding under the Seeley banner from the beginning of the 1966 season on 350 and 500cc Seeley machines. Colin Seeley had been born on 2 January 1936 at Crayford, Kent. From his early childhood, motorcycles were very much a way of life in the Seeley household. Colin learned to ride his father Percy's HRD Vincent V-twin sidecar outfit at 14 in 1950, the young Seeley passing his driving test to ride a bike a couple of years later, in 1952.

As proof of just how keen Colin was to enter the motorcycle trade, at 15 years of age he gave up an engineering career to join Dartford dealers Schwieso Brothers as a mechanic. Harold and Les Schwieso had been leading grass-track riders at their local Brands Hatch circuit in pre-war days. In 1954, at 18 years of age, Colin opened his first motorcycle business venture, a repair shop in Belvedere, Kent. Two years later he went one step further, opening his first showroom with agencies from AJS and Matchless. Thus began Seeley's long association with the AMC (Associated Motor Cycles) works in Plumstead Road, Woolwich, south-east London. Other brands soon followed, including at various times Francis-Barnett, Ariel, Velocette, Greeves and NSU, plus sidecars from Busmar, Canterbury, Watsonian and Wessex.

'Colin Seeley' as a sporting name began to appear in many dirt bike programmes during 1957. His first competition iron was a Triumph T100C Trophy, with which he took part in scrambling, sprinting, hill climbs and grass-track events. With the words 'Colin Seeley – The Rider Agent' emblazoned on his company's pick-up truck, he then turned to a Greeves two-stroke, riding at Canada Heights near Swanley, Kent, at that venue's inaugural meeting. In 1961 he rode his first Matchless G50-engined machine fitted with a Canterbury racing sidecar, and finished a brilliant

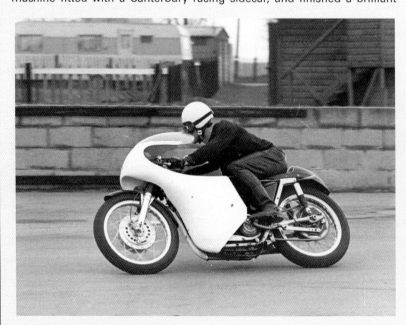

Colin Seeley testing the original G50 Matchless-engined prototype Seeley racer, January 1966.

Colin Seeley (left) and co-director Wally Rawlings.

sixth in his first Isle of Man TT, averaging 77.93mph for the four-lap 150.92-mile race. This proved a major turning point in his life, as he recalled to the author, saying 'What a proud moment for me, my passenger Wally Rawlings and the AMC factory.' Two more TT replicas were to follow on the Matchless, with third and sixth places in 1962 and 1963 respectively.

Colin Seeley's racing career then moved up a gear with the purchase of a BMW Rennsport outfit, and a leap on to the world stage. Seeley and Rawlings finished third overall in the 1964 World Championship series, their best placing being victory in the Dutch TT at Assen, and runner-up (behind World Champion, Max Deubel). Another third place in the Championship table came in 1966, with runner-up position in France, together with third places in both Belgium and West Germany. On the commercial front Colin came to an agreement with AMC – who announced that after 1965 the factory would no longer produce any more racers – to fit the AJS 7R and Matchless G50 engines into frames of his own design and manufacture. And so the era of the Seeley racing motorcycle was born.

The first of the new breed was raced by Derek Minter after extensive testing, including Colin himself taking to the saddle. What happened during that first year (1966) is detailed elsewhere in this chapter. But although Derek ultimately made the switch back to his more familiar Norton machines, it is still a fact that our hero was the man who first put the new Seeley solo racers in the public eye. With AMC itself hitting the financial rocks that same year – and the subsequent decision to stop production of 7R/G50 engines, Colin decided to purchase all the remaining components and production rights from the London firm. In addition, the deal also involved gaining the Norton side of the business, this later being sold on to John Tickle in 1969. Based at Forge Works, Stapley Road, Belvedere, Colin Seeley Racing Developments soon built up an enviable reputation among racers, not only in Britain, but also all around the world, for its high standard of workmanship.

After Derek Minter, the next rider to receive official Seeley backing was John Blanchard, followed in 1967 by John Cooper. By the end of that year, at the annual Earls Court Show, the Mark 2 Seeley chassis was launched. In Colin's own words, the frame had been: 'Lightened, tidied up and made much neater in appearance.' Mark 2 machines were built and sold from the beginning of 1968 until late 1969. The Mark 3 arrived during mid-1969, with production overlapping between Marks 2 and 3, depending upon customer preference. The main difference was the deletion on the latter of the frame's front down-tubes. Amazingly, the revised assembly offered just as good handling, while weight (of the main frame) was reduced by some 25 percent. The Mark 3 also coincided with the decision by Colin and co-director Wally Rawlings to drop the AJS 7R engine in favour of the newly released Japanese Yamaha TR2 engine for the 350cc class, with the resultant bike being called the Yamsel.

Although the G50 Matchless-based Seeley engine continued in production into the 1970s, as the new decade dawned it was to come under increasing pressure. And so came a host of new engined Seeley racers. These included the Dr Gordon Blair QUB (Queens University Belfast) 500 single cylinder two-stroke (1970), the Suzuki T500 Daytona (1972) and various big twins of 750cc from Norton, Triumph (plus the triple) and Weslake. Later still came a succession of Honda powered bikes, including a 200cc ohc single trials plus various across-the-frame four-cylinder models for fast roadwork, in 750, 900 and 1000cc engine sizes. By the time the last Seeley G50 was built (autumn 1972), the design had reached the Mark 4 stage.

The Seeley manufacturing business finally ceased during the late 1970s. But this was certainly not the end of the man behind the name. With his vast experience, his talents at first played a vital role in the Brabham F1 car team. Later still he became a team manager for, among others, the Duckham Oils/Crighton Norton Rotary race team.

News: 'Never in all my racing career as a professional rider have I been so unsettled about the future.' He had offers to race AJS and Matchless machines from both Tom Kirby and Colin Seeley. But his dilemma was – would they prove superior to his own Ray Petty Nortons?

But then, in *Motor Cycle News* dated 12 January 1966, there was a news story (and front page photograph) of a possible Minter-Seeley tie-up for the year. The picture showed Derek rushing the new Seeley Matchless around the outside of an unfamiliarly-mounted Colin Seeley having a ride on Minter's Norton at Brands Hatch the previous Saturday.

Track conditions at Brands were not good, the surface being slippery in places, particularly at Druids Hill hairpin. But afterwards Derek commented:

The Matchless was much easier to ride than my Norton. The power comes in much smoother and lower down, whereas the Norton comes in at higher revs with a much fiercer punch. What amazed me most of all was that although the Matchless felt quite docile, I don't think it was any slower than the Norton. Even allowing for the slippery track on Saturday and that the G50 was fitted with a five-speed gearbox, whereas the Norton had only a four, I do feel I have underestimated the G50 in the past. In addition to the performance of the G50, another feature which delighted me was the easy starting.

In addition Derek said: 'I couldn't fault the handling at all and the new front brake made by Edwin Robinson is superior to either a Norton or an Oldani. I think I could win on that bike.'

Signing for Seeley

'So where does Minter go from here?' asked Charlie Rous. And although he did test one of Tom Kirby's Matchless G50 machines, he eventually decided to plump for the Seeley, the official announcement being made in mid-January.

When signing, Derek said his decision to team up with the Erith dealer and sidecar racer was determined more by personal agreement than by a comparison of machines.

The next month or so saw Derek's Seeley connection making front page news. During his extensive testing with his new mount, Derek also circulated the full 2.65-mile GP Brands Hatch circuit in reverse direction – as it was

Brands Hatch, 13 March 1966. Derek lines up in the assembly area with the new Seeley 350cc model. Others in the frame include: Ron Chandler, Peter Williams, Bill Ivy and John Cooper.

On the start line prior to the 350cc action at Brands Hatch on 13 March 1966, with Rex Butcher, Rod Gould, Tom Phillips, Ron Chandler and Peter Williams, among others.

planned for that year's international Hutchinson 100 meeting. Derek's view was that it would provide 'more exciting but safer racing.'

Going Veedol

At the end of February 1966 it was announced that Veedol, the international oil company owned by Paul Getty, then reputed to be the richest man in the world, was to support the Seeley effort, including Derek.

The new association did not get off to a winning start (except for a heat victory in the 350cc class) when Derek, on Seeley machinery, made his debut at Mallory Park on Sunday 6 March. The new pairing came away with a third in the 500cc final (behind Bill Ivy on the new Kirby Rickman Metisse G50 machine and Dave Degens on Ivy's old Kirby Matchless). In the 350cc final Derek retired the smaller AJS-powered Seeley with a loose exhaust header pipe.

Back to top form at Brands

A week later, at Brands Hatch on 13 March, Derek, showing all his old style, took his shining metallic gold-finished Seeley (nicknamed 'Goldfinger' after the James Bond film) to a magnificent victory in the 500cc Redex Trophy race, despite a split megaphone – with Mallory victor Bill Ivy back in fifth. And there was little doubt that Derek would have repeated this performance in the subsequent 1000cc race, except that a hurriedly fitted 7R mega

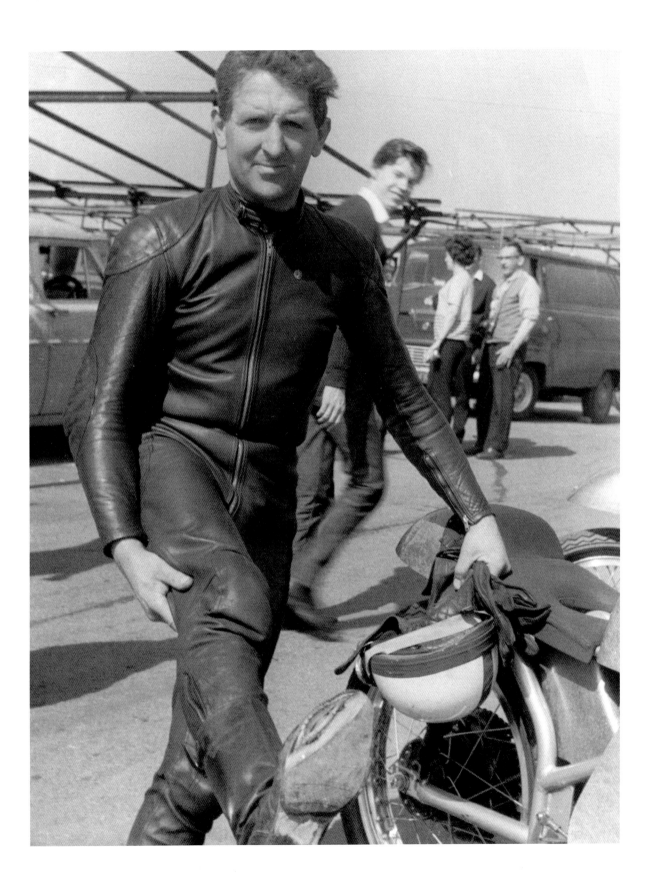

knocked the edge off performance on the G50 engine. But in the 350cc event – after being first away, which in itself was almost a first for Derek – he could finish no higher than eighth.

500cc Redex Trophy, Brands Hatch – 12 laps – 31.8 miles
1st   D.W. Minter (Seeley)
2nd   G.A. Jenkins (Dunstall Domiracer)
3rd   J.H. Cooper (Norton)
4th   D.F. Degens (Matchless)
5th   W.D. Ivy (Matchless Metisse)
6th   R.E. Butcher (Norton)

Mixed fortunes

Then came a series of meetings where Derek experienced mixed fortunes on his new Seeley machines, at Brands Hatch, Snetterton and Oulton Park over the Easter weekend, 8, 10 and 11 April respectively, with his only victory coming at Oulton in the 500cc race. *Motor Cycle News* reported: 'It's Goldfinger Minter. Derek Minter scored his first international win on his "Goldfinger" 500cc Seeley-Matchless, at Oulton Park on Monday.' Derek also finished runner-up to Mike Hailwood on a works four-cylinder Honda in the 350cc race on the AJS 7R Seeley.

Opposite: After winning the 500cc race on the bigger Seeley at Brands on 13 March 1966, Derek shows the cameraman just how hard he had ridden that day!

A week later, at Snetterton on 20 March 1966, Derek took the Seeley AJS to heat and final victories in the 350cc class at the Norfolk circuit.

Derek thunders the Seeley
Matchless over the line at
Snetterton to take a 500cc
heat victory. Later Derek
was beaten by rival John
Cooper into runner-up
spot in the final.

To cap an excellent days racing in front of 40,000 spectators, Derek also
finished runner-up to Derek Woodman on a factory MZ twin in the 250cc
event on his Cotton (see chapter eight).

500cc Oulton Park – 19 laps – 52.5 miles
1st   D.W. Minter (Seeley-Matchless)
2nd   J.H. Cooper (Norton)

Derek's Seeley 350 in the
Brands Hatch paddock,
Good Friday, 1966.

3rd   G. Jenkins (Dunstall Domiracer)
4th   M. Uphill (Norton)
5th   W.D. Ivy (Matchless-Metisse)
6th   S. Graham (Matchless)

On Good Friday, 8 April 1966, Derek raced this experimental 646cc Matchless CSR-engined machine in the 1000cc race. However, he was forced to retire due to grounding problems.

An Italian journey

Then Derek journeyed to Italy, where he rode the AJS Seeley at Imola (17 April) finishing sixth, and a week later at Cesenatico (24 April). But the big news was his return to the Gilera squad, finishing runner-up to Giacomo Agostini (MV Agusta) at Imola, although retired on the Italian four at Cesenatico with magneto trouble.

Then came meetings at Castle Combe (30 April) and Brands Hatch (1 May) before Derek went abroad once more, this time to Hockenheim for the West German Grand Prix on 22 May. But it was largely a wasted trip – he finished eighth (two laps down) on the winner Mike Hailwood (Honda) in the 350cc race, while Derek was forced to retire in the 500cc race with a leaking fuel tank on his bigger Seeley.

Derek at Monza in the summer of 1966 with the modified seven-speed 500cc Gilera four. The man holding the machine is works mechanic Luigi Columbo. It was not a happy return as Derek crashed heavily during TT practice, putting himself out of action for the remainder of the season.

Crunch time

But the real crunch time for Derek's Seeley connection came over the weekend of 29–30 May, when he suffered a mixture of niggling problems and poor results at Snetterton and Brands Hatch respectively.

His Snetterton problems were highlighted by the *Motor Cycle News* report: 'Derek Minter had an odd day. He didn't qualify for the 500cc final, having lost his primary chain as he shoved off for a heat. Earlier, in the 350 final, he retired with a flat back tyre.'

While at Brands, Derek could manage no higher than fourth on his three-fifty and fifth in the five-hundred.

Then followed a period where Derek was testing the Gilera in Italy and trying various cars (a Johnnie Walker Villiers Starmaker 250cc Formula 4 and a Ron Harris Lotus). But at Mallory Park on 19 June, he was flung off the five-hundred Seeley in practice and then fell from his Cotton in the two-fifty heat. At the time Derek put these crashes down to 'testing a Gilera four at Monza', due to the Gilera needing a very 'firm' application to the front brake, whereas both the Seeley and Cotton were 'feather light.'

The effects of these crashes (including a badly bruised heel) put Derek out of action until Castle Combe on 9 July.

'The old firm is back in business'

'The old firm is back in business.' So said *Motor Cycle News* in its 13 July 1966 issue. This came in response to Derek taking his Norton 'from under the dust sheets' and winning the 350cc final at the Wiltshire circuit – his first outing since crashing twice at Mallory Park the previous month. And after finishing runner-up to Peter Williams (Arter Matchless) in the 500cc final, it seemed very likely that Derek would be going back to Norton machinery in the bigger classes.

On Monday 11 July Colin Seeley was quoted as saying: 'I have left Derek to make the decision but it is probably the best for everyone. The bikes have had teething troubles but no more than any other machine, the Metisse for instance.' And soon afterwards Derek and Colin split, but remained on good terms, John Blanchard taking over the Seeley bikes.

Although Derek was subsequently to renew his association with Ray Petty, *Motor Cycle News* reported: 'Minter is under contract to Veedol and it is only the business of oil contracts that prevent him rejoining his old ally, Steve Lancefield, whose Nortons are standing idle for want of a rider.' When questioned by the author over this statement Derek's reply was: 'No, the reason was because when I left Steve, there were bad feelings between the two of us.'

Minter-Petty

The Derek Minter – Ray Petty partnership was resumed on 16 July, with Derek due to take his three-fifty engine over to the tuner's premises at Cove, near Farnborough in Hampshire, the following week.

His first race on the Petty-tuned Nortons was due to be at the Hutchinson 100 at Brands Hatch on 14 August. Just prior to this, Derek's entry for the Senior TT was confirmed to be on a Gilera. It was said that he was due to fly to Italy to collect the machine after the Hutchinson 100 meeting. It was also reported that Derek would have two machines, plus mechanic Luigi Columbo, in the Isle of Man.

Certainly, as regards his return to Ray Petty and Nortons, the Hutchinson 100 meeting was something of a non-event – thanks to a practice crash and subsequent injury sustained when he dropped the Cotton while practising for the 250cc race (see chapter eight). This was subsequently to cause his retirement from the 500cc event. However, he did have the satisfaction of finishing runner-up behind Mike Hailwood (Honda four) in the 350cc race – and beating his replacement on the Seeley, John Blanchard.

350cc Hutchinson 100, Brands Hatch – 20 laps – 53 miles

1st   S.M.B. Hailwood (Honda four)
2nd   D.W. Minter (Petty Norton)
3rd   J. Blanchard (Seeley AJS)
4th   D.F. Degens (Lawton Aermacchi)
5th   D.F. Shorey (Norton)
6th   K.L. Carruthers (Norton)

TT troubles

1966 was the year of the infamous Seaman's Strike; which meant that for the first time in history the TT dates were switched from early June to late August.

Derek's number one Gilera was fitted with a seven-speed gearbox, but his practice bike and spare motor had five-speed 'boxes. And Derek was staying at Geoff Duke's Arragan hotel.

However, Derek's hopes of TT success were dashed when he crashed in the final practice session on Saturday evening, 27 August, when out on the seven-speed race model Gilera at Brandish corner, breaking his left wrist. He was taken to Nobles Hospital, Douglas. His injuries, which also included facial cuts and slight concussion, ruled him out of not only the TT, but also racing at Monza on 10 September, when he had been due to race the Gilera again in the 500cc Italian Grand Prix.

Derek had spent the entire TT practice week trying to sort out the Gilera handling. During the final practice, he passed Giacomo Agostini (three-fifty MV) before he crashed on a wet road. The previous evening Derek did a lap on a three-fifty four-cylinder Benelli. It had been offered to him after Tarquinio Provini had crashed – and Derek did a lap of just over 90mph – but on Saturday morning, following a phone call to Italy, the Benelli bikes and personnel were flown back to Italy.

Even as late as mid-November Derek's wrist was still causing problems. And he was due to go back into the Kent and Canterbury Hospital for treatment to solve the problem. But by the end of November 1966, despite a session of manipulation under anaesthetic, Derek still found he was unable to bend the wrist broken in the Isle of Man spill on the Gilera. He was due to make a return visit to his specialist at the beginning of December.

At this stage there was press speculation about whether Derek would be racing bikes in 1967. There was talk of him getting behind the wheel of a Johnnie Walker Formula 4 car as a works driver.

When questioned about the truth of this matter by the author, this is what Derek said: 'From what I remember, I only competed in one race meeting at

Castle Combe in the Formula 4 car, finishing, I believe, in the first six. However, I never felt really comfortable in the car world and was much more in control on two wheels.'

1967 begins

As 1967 began, Derek was more confident that he would be back on bikes for the new season.

His left wrist, badly broken in the previous year's TT practice crash on the Gilera, was at last responding to treatment after daily exercise. Derek also said he was to visit the Gilera factory in Italy in the hope of arranging a ride for 1967. He said: 'If Gilera are agreeable, I will concentrate entirely on the world classics and quit home racing.' He continued: 'I am convinced it is still capable of winning. It is definitely fast enough. It is the steering and handling that need to be improved.'

In 2007, Derek explained these remarks when he told the author: 'I made these comments, because I was so desperate to persuade Gilera to return to racing! However, they refused.'

Back in the saddle

Derek finally got his first outing on a racing bike since his TT practice crash on Thursday 22 January 1967. Naturally enough it came at Brands Hatch, the circuit owners arranging a special test session for him alone. Riding his five-hundred Norton, Derek did a dozen laps of the short circuit and, despite damp patches and some mud on the course where alterations were being made to Paddock Hill bend, he was soon lapping at around the minute mark. After the test, he said: 'I enjoyed it. It was my first time out on a bike for five months and I was taking it steady, but I soon got back in the groove. My wrist was a bit tired afterwards but I'm confident that I'll be completely fit by the time the season starts – and that's only six weeks away now.'

At this stage he still hoped to be riding for Cotton (but this did not happen due to the Manganese Bronze take-over of Villiers and subsequent refusal by the former to supply the latter with engines). But he had not visited Gilera and was pessimistic about the chances of the company racing again (which proved well-founded).

By mid-February Derek had returned to Brands Hatch and put in around 40 additional laps (again on his bigger Norton), commenting: 'At first I was a bit doubtful about my ability to make a comeback after a five-month lay-off, but everything clicked and I really enjoyed myself. I'm a lot happier now and for the first time this winter, I'm looking forward to the season.'

The season gets under way

The British short circuit racing season got under way at Mallory Park (not one of Derek's favourites) on Sunday 8 March. And although he retired his smaller Norton in its heat with faulty carburation, he won his 500cc heat and came third in the final, which for someone in effect making a comeback was pretty good.

Then came a whole host of meetings, both in Britain and Italy: Snetterton (15 March), Modena (22 March), Brands Hatch (27 March), Oulton Park (29 March), Riccione (5 April), Cervia (12 April), Cesenatico (19 April), Imola (25 April), Rimini (17 May), Mallory Park (31 May), Brands Hatch (1 June) and Mallory Park (18 June).

Derek's best results came at Oulton Park, with *Motor Cycling's* headline reading: 'Minter's Top Form At Oulton' going on to say: 'Derek Minter regained his best form to win the 500cc race, the major event of Easter Monday's "Daily Express" sponsored international "Race of the North".' It continued: 'Riding his Ray Petty-tuned Norton, Derek fought a great duel with "Master of Mallory" John Cooper (Norton) until the Derby man crashed on lap 16. Earlier, on his smaller Norton, Minter had beaten Cooper (Norton) by a few yards to take second place in the 350cc race – won, as expected, by Mike Hailwood on the works four cylinder Honda.'

350cc Oulton Park – 19 laps – 52.5 miles

1st	S.M.B. Hailwood (Honda)	
2nd	D.W. Minter (Norton)	
3rd	J.H. Cooper (Norton)	
4th	P.J. Williams (Paton)	
5th	D.F. Shorey (Norton)	
6th	J. Hartle (AJS)	

500cc Oulton Park – 19 laps – 52.5 miles

1st	D.W. Minter (Norton)	
2nd	P.J. Williams (Arter Matchless)	
3rd	S. Spencer (Norton)	
4th	G.A. Jenkins (Dunstall Domiracer)	
5th	B.J. Randle (Norton)	
6th	M. Uphill (Norton)	

The Dutch and Belgian

The Dutch TT at Assen on Saturday 27 June and the Belgian Grand Prix over the Spa Francorchamps circuit on Sunday 5 July were to be Derek's final races

Derek (14) closely following John Cooper during the 350cc Dutch TT at Assen, Saturday 27 June 1967.

500cc Dutch TT action, 27 June 1967. Derek leads a group of riders including Fred Stevens (Paton 21).

counting towards World Championship points. And, with a couple of sixth places on his five-hundred Norton, he went out in some style. Other highlights in the second half of the 1967 season came with victory at Snetterton in the 500cc event on 30 July, a couple of seconds at Oulton Park on 28 August in the 350cc and Les Graham Trophy 500cc races, plus a victory (and fastest lap) at Brands Hatch in the Redex Trophy 500cc event on 3 September.

Glory at Snetterton and Brands

Strangely, Derek's final two meetings garnered his best results. Headlines such as 'Magnificent Mint' and 'Top of the Tree' were typical of the press reaction to Derek's performances at Snetterton on Sunday 15 October 1967. In *Motor Cycling* David Dixon began his report of the meeting: 'Retire while at the top of the ladder, while the fans remember you as a great force in racing. That's Derek Minter's plan. And on Sunday at Snetterton he gave another example of short-circuiteering at its most scintillating – Minter on his very best form.'

Derek at Snetterton on 15 October 1967, on his way to victory in the 500cc final. Here he leads Dave Croxford (3), John Cooper (4) and Ron Chandler.

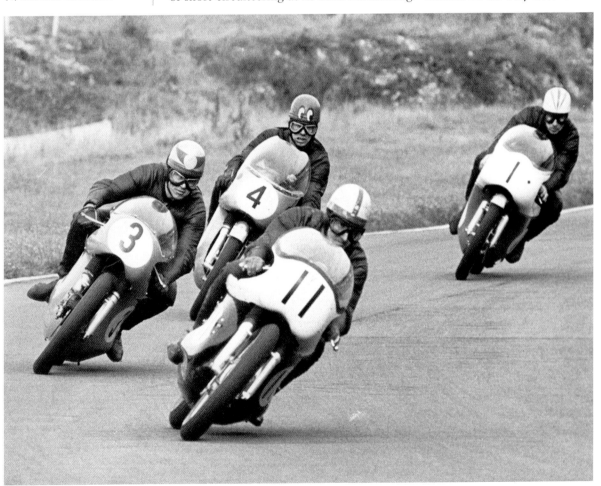

Not only did he win both his heat and final in the 500cc class, but Derek also broke the lap record for the Norfolk circuit by going round in 1m 46s, a speed of 92.04mph.

500cc Snetterton – 7 laps – 18.97 miles
1st   D.W. Minter (Norton)
2nd   R.S. Chandler (Seeley Matchless)
3rd   A.J. Barnett (Matchless Metisse)
4th   R.G. Gould (Norton)
5th   P.J. Dunphy (Norton)
6th   D.F. Shorey (Norton)

Then came what was billed as 'The end of an Era', which referred to Derek's last meeting at Brands Hatch – or anywhere else for that matter. And this is what *Motor Cycling* said:

> It was the end of an era. Minter and Brands – like Jack and Jill or fish and chips. The two seemed inseparable until last Sunday, the day it had to end. It is 14 years since Derek's first race, and that was at Brands on a 499cc BSA Gold Star. He finished his final outing on Sunday in a blaze of glory, with sparkling wins in the 350 and 1000cc events. As near as dammit he notched a third win, for he was only two lengths behind Dan Shorey (Norton) in the 500cc final.

Derek's successes that day inspired a tremendous roar in each of his races from thousands of his loyal supporters in the vast crowd. Even the weather played its part – dry and sunny on this autumn day over 40 years ago.

Brands Hatch, 22 October 1967. Derek is seen taking his 500 Norton to victory for a final time.

Derek also won the 1000cc race on this six-fifty Curtis Domiracer twin at Brands on 22 October 1967.

350cc Brands Hatch – 8 laps – 21.2 miles

1st	D.W. Minter	(Norton)
2nd	D.F. Shorey	(Norton)
3rd	D.L. Croxford	(AJS)
4th	R.E. Butcher	(Norton)
5th	G.A. Jenkins	(Norton)
6th	V.D. Chatterton	(Kawasaki)

1000cc Brands Hatch – 8 laps – 21.2 miles

1st	D.W. Minter	(647cc Curtis Norton)
2nd	J.H. Cooper	(496cc Seeley Matchless)
3rd	R. Pickrell	(745cc Dunstall Domiracer)
4th	D.F. Degens	(649cc Dresda Metisse)
5th	D.L. Croxford	(496cc Matchless)
6th	R.S. Chandler	(496cc Seeley Matchless)

By way of showing his appreciation for their support and help over the years, Derek had a crate of champagne delivered to the starting area at Brands for all the officials and marshals. As one said: 'I came to see the racing, but never thought I'd end up at a champagne party.' But it was a nice gesture from the man who had earned the title 'King' at the famous Kentish circuit.

Would he really retire?

But would Derek really retire from a sport and a profession he had so vividly

made his mark upon over so many years? It must be said that he came close to continuing. But in the end he decided now was the time to pack it in.

However, Derek did have one more race at Brands Hatch. This came on 14 May 1968, when he and Reg Everett shared the riding on Walthamstow Ducati specialist Vic Camp's 340cc Ducati Sebring in the 500-mile endurance race for sports machines. The pairing eventually finished fourth in the 500cc class. But this time Derek had retired for real.

However, as detailed in chapter 10, Derek did make a return to parading racing machines, but this time in classic events aboard the Summerfield Nortons. It was a pretty special partnership as the Summerfield brothers had taken over from where Ray Petty had left off. But as for as Derek Minter the professional road racer, it was, truly, the end of an era.

As a way of showing his appreciation for the support and help he had received from the marshals and officials at Brands Hatch, at his farewell meeting in October 1967 Derek had a crate of champagne delivered to the starting area. Here he pours out the bubbly.

Chapter 10

A Place in History

Derek Minter, above everyone else, except possibly Bob McIntyre, was my own personal motorcycle racing hero when as a teenager I first began to take an interest in the sport during the late 1950s and early 1960s. Yes, of course there were other brilliant riders of the era, including Duke, Surtees and Hailwood, but Derek was the one I noticed. On my visits to Brands Hatch, Snetterton, Silverstone and Oulton Park, Derek was the man who stood out. A major reason for this was that he almost always seemed to get an awful start, but would claw his way up through the field, and often as not cross the finishing line at the end of the race as the winner.

In those far off days, Derek was very much on one side of the fence and myself on the other. But more recently, having got to know him well, I have found exactly what Murray Walker described in 1965 as 'an infectiously cheerful enthusiast.' Murray also got it spot on when he went on to say: 'He is essentially an individualist, frank, outspoken and a fighter every inch of the way.'

To Derek, racing motorcycles really was a way of life, a profession and his living, to which he dedicated himself whole-heartedly and single-mindedly. It was something Derek loved doing and it was always far more than simply a job.

Unlike many of today's star riders, fame never changed him. He remained, as he is today, a man of rural Kent. Someone who was brought up to certain values and has followed this way throughout his life.

Like Bob McIntyre, Derek was not best suited to being a works rider. There were various reasons. This is what World Champion Bill Lomas said of him in December 1966:

> I have tremendous respect for Derek and I think that had a factory really taken him in hand many years ago he would have been one of the great greats. Instead, Derek has been guided by fancy and chance and he has not made the most of himself. But Derek is Derek – a great character and a man who likes to look after his interests himself.

On numerous occasions he proved himself – a few examples being his exploits in the early days when, mounted on the BSA Gold Star, he managed to see off almost everyone, his epic victory on a Norton against John Surtees on a works MV at Brands Hatch in 1957, his 100mph lap on a Norton in the 1960 Senior TT (the first ever by a rider on a single), his 1962 250cc TT win on a Honda four and his numerous British Championship titles.

In retrospect, Derek probably needed a manager. But knowing Derek, I do not think this would have worked, as he really is his own man. And in the author's view Derek would have been better off in the Honda team in 1963, rather than the Scuderia Duke Gilera squad. The latter was frankly a second-rate effort because Gilera would not put any funds into it. But unfortunately, as explained elsewhere, Derek fell out of favour with the Japanese firm.

Certainly, had not the Brands Hatch accident occurred in May 1963, one can only speculate about what Derek might have gone on to achieve. But the accident happened, and Derek's career was from then set on a different course.

So it would be truthful to say that Derek Minter is today seen as a British legend, rather than a world star. And at that most British of all the short circuits, Brands Hatch, Derek really was the King, with a capital 'K'. Brands was Derek's natural racing home, but he also shone at many other circuits, notably the Isle of Man, Oulton Park, Snetterton, Silverstone and Castle Combe. He was also very safety conscious and did not like Mallory Park, refusing to ride there for several years.

Without doubt Derek's most serious on-track fault was his poor starting. I feel sure that today's clutch starts would have meant that Derek would have been much less likely to have had to make up so much lost ground almost every time he raced. But this also showed what a great rider he was – once he got going. Few other men could have made up so much lost time! He even attempted to get over this glitch in his performance by practising – but to little avail.

Derek never achieved his ultimate dream, that of winning the Senior TT in the Isle of Man, but to his countless fans this did not matter, he was still *Derek Minter – King of Brands*. And at his final meeting there (if one discounts his one-off ride with Reg Everett on a Ducati in the 1968 500-mile Production race), Derek rode through a white wall of programmes waved in the air by the masses of spectators after victory on

Ken Hayward (photographed by the author at Mallory Park in June 2007) was named by *Motor Cycle News* in November 1973 as Derek Minter's biggest fan.

Derek and his second wife Jenny in 1971 with their children Michelle, then three months, and Leanne, 16½ months.

the Curtis Domiracer in the 1000cc event; the last of that final day's meeting in October 1967.

Derek was 35 when he stopped racing.

For many years Derek had an army of faithful fans, one of whom was his future second wife, Jenny, who recalls:

> In the early days, it was very much a case of hero worship. I would travel from my home in Wembley with my brother Chris and a group of motorcycling friends, to Brands Hatch to watch the racing. After every meeting I, along with many more of Derek's fans, would head for the paddock clutching a programme or a much-prized photograph, on which we hoped to get Derek's autograph.

In November 1964, when Derek was guest of honour on the Brands Hatch stand at the London Earls Court Show, Derek and Jenny began a friendship which culminated in their marriage on 22 March 1968, and the birth of two lovely daughters, Leanne and Michelle. Leanne and her husband Ian presented Derek and Jenny with a granddaughter, Honor, while Michelle and husband Conrad also added to the family with their children, Lara and Callum.

Back in 1965, Derek had set up a haulage business, which was a success until his enforced retirement in June 1999 following a crash and resulting serious injury to his left leg when parading at the Isle of Man TT.

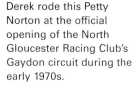

Derek rode this Petty Norton at the official opening of the North Gloucester Racing Club's Gaydon circuit during the early 1970s.

The Summerfield team at Snetterton in the mid-1990s, left to right: Jerry (28), Roger (27), Derek (51), the late Ivor Brame (a great friend and supporter) mounted on 27 and finally Mike (28).

Summerfield Racing

As Jerry Summerfield told the author recently: 'It all started by accident.' This was in relation to how the three Summerfield brothers, Roger, Mike and Jerry, got into the sport of classic racing; and subsequently their involvement with not only the legendary Manx Norton, but also having Derek Minter as one of their riders.

So what sparked off this series of events? Well, it had all begun when the brothers answered an advertisement in a magazine during 1983, which had been placed by Dave Duxbury of north London, the latter offering for sale a Manx constructed from various component parts.

Jerry continued: 'The bike was alright as a showpiece, but less so as a competitive machine.' Originally the bike was displayed statically in the foyer of the family firm, Summerfield Engineering. But when Jerry decided to use it in anger at a Classic Club meeting at Mallory Park, the big-end promptly seized. And it was this which led the Summerfields to the door of ace Norton tuner Ray Petty. Not only did Ray sort the engine out, but the Summerfields were later able to repay his help by machining a batch of crankcases Ray had cast. Later still a batch of Manx cylinder heads were produced, the first of the latter appearing in 1987. By this time Ray Petty was an ill man, and he died later that same year. Ray's second wife, Jayne, subsequently followed instructions left by her late husband that the Summerfields were to carry on the 'manufacture of his parts.' And the wide use of the Petty name by the Summerfield organisation since that time is a fitting tribute to this fact.

Although the brothers now trade under the Summerfield Racing Ltd name (since 2004), while Summerfield Engineering Ltd is now run by Roger's three sons, the quality of both Racing and the Engineering arms is equally first class, as witnessed by the author himself. Both are based at substantial factory premises in Somercotes near Derby. The Racing company not only manufacture complete Norton engine units, but also the PGT gearbox (based on the Austrian Schafleitner 'box later used by Colin Seeley up to the mid-1970s, when design was taken over by Ray Petty).

In 1989, Mike Summerfield, together with Bernie Allen, visited the Norton works in Shenstone to obtain official permission to use the name. When Doug Hele, the man responsible for the development of the original Manx design in its final years, saw what they were offering, he gave their joint efforts his blessing. Since then the Summerfield operation has supplied engines, gearboxes and spare parts all over the world.

Although Mike has never competed, both Roger and Jerry have won many races on their own products, including six National Championships and 13 Club Championships. The two brothers, in earlier years and before their Norton involvement, were both active motocross competitors. Roger campaigned several machines, beginning in 1957 with a Francis-Barnett two-stroke, followed by an ex-works (David Tye) BSA Gold Star, a 500 unit Triumph and a Cheney B50. Jerry used a Metisse with a BSA unit B44 motor, followed by a 580cc CCM. Even earlier, father Peter had owned several motorcycles including a McEvoy, a Norton International and a fore-and-aft Douglas flat twin.

As for Summerfield Engineering, this was formed in 1967. Roger had previously worked for himself, Jerry was an industrial chemist and Mike worked at Rolls-Royce in Derby. It is best described as one of the few remaining specialist engineering companies that once dominated the East Midlands area. And because of this, the company's services are much in demand for its quality work, much of it being exported. Of course, this is a background which has been ideal in their Norton involvement over the past two decades.

Besides Derek Minter (whose Summerfield career is described elsewhere in this chapter), many other well-known riders have straddled Summerfield Nortons, including John Surtees, Jack Ahearn, Frank Perris, Tommy Robb and Rudi Thalhammer, plus Steve Ruth, Bill Swallow, Colin Breeze and Nick Jefferies. Their current racing star is Lea Gourlay with three national and three club Championships in 2005–06.

Jerry Summerfield, photographed by the author, c.2002.

With the birth of classic racing, Derek, like many other star riders of the past, came out of retirement and was often to be seen aboard Norton bikes; latterly the property of the Summerfield brothers (see separate boxed section within this chapter).

On 11 April 1993, Derek was introduced to Mike and Jerry Summerfield at Mallory Park (VMCC Meeting) by Andy Walker and was asked if he would consider riding their 500cc Manx Norton in the parade. It should be noted that since retiring from professional racing Derek had always been very cautious about accepting offers of machinery to ride in various events. Derek readily agreed as the Summerfields already enjoyed an excellent reputation and were literally leading the field in classic motorcycle racing, in which both Jerry and Roger Summerfield had actively participated for many years. Thus

With John Surtees at Brands Hatch, Surtees Day, 1981.

began one of the happiest periods of Derek's life. For the following 7½ years, Derek, along with the Summerfield team, attended many classic racing motorcycle events throughout the country, parading the Summerfield Manx Nortons.

The Summerfield team at Knockhill, 22–23 June 1996. Derek is on the number 15 machine.

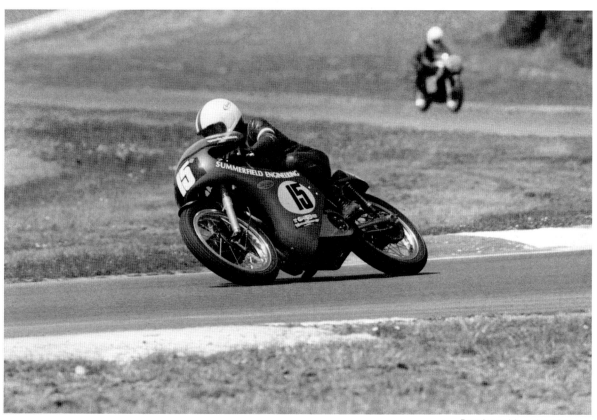

Derek pushing the 500cc Summerfield Norton hard at Knockhill, 22 June 1996.

Cresting the famous 'Mountain' at Cadwell Park on the Summerfield Norton, 1997.

Opposite: During the early 1990s Derek joined the Summerfield Classic Racing Team. It was to prove an enjoyable experience for all concerned.

Posing for the camera with the Summerfield race transporter in the background.

Unfortunately, on 15 October 2000, in the last meeting of the season at Darley Moor, Derbyshire, this 'Indian Summer' of his career suddenly came to an abrupt end, when Derek fell from the Summerfield Norton, having suffered a massive brain haemorrhage.

He was rushed to Derby Royal Infirmary and then quickly transferred to the Queens Medical Centre in Nottingham. Here they realised the severity of his injury. At this point he could easily have died, but his life was undoubtedly saved by leading neurosurgeon Mr D. Hope. Even so, Derek was critically ill and remained in intensive care for seven days. It was a total of three weeks before Derek was allowed to return to his home in Kent, some 200 miles away. During this time Jenny stayed in a nearby hotel to be at her husband's bedside. In 2007, Jenny commented:

The Minter family pictured in June 2007. Back row, left to right: Michelle and Conrad Earll, Ian and Leanne Woollams. Front: Honor Woollams, Jenny Minter, Lara Earll, Callum Earll and Derek.

Derek and Jenny photographed by the author at Cadwell Park, August 2007.

Derek and Dick Leather with the latter's BSA Gold Star, October 2007.

I personally will never forget Mike Summerfield's generosity when he insisted on settling the rather sizeable hotel bill for me and my family, and refused to let me contribute anything! Although Derek and I had always felt like part of a big family with Mike, Jerry and Roger Summerfield, together with the rest of the team, it is only in times of crisis that you really appreciate how helpful and caring friends can be.

Everything considered, Derek has made a pretty good recovery – but has to take life somewhat steadier than his previous hectic lifestyle. He can still be seen as a spectator at certain CRMC race meetings during the summer months – and he is still the real *King of Brands*.

Appendices

Derek Minter Motorcycle Road Racing Results

RL + Record Lap; FL = Fastest Lap.

Note: Derek Minter began racing on a newly-purchased BSA BB34 Gold Star 500 at Brands Hatch in the spring of 1953. No complete record exists of his results until the beginning of 1956. But his entire racing up to that time was on the same BSA, and his early career is charted in the main text, together with all the prominent results.

1956

Position	Class	Machine	Circuit	Date
Retired (faulty plug lead)	200cc	MV Agusta 172cc	Brands Hatch	30 March
2	1000cc	BSA 499cc	Brands Hatch	30 March
Retired (broken rocker arm)	200cc	MV Agusta 172cc	Crystal Palace	2 April
3	500cc (heat)	BSA	Crystal Palace	2 April
6	500cc (final)	BSA	Crystal Palace	2 April
4	125cc	MV Agusta	Snetterton	8 April
Retired (did not start, van broke down)	500cc	BSA	Snetterton	8 April
4	125cc	MV Agusta	Silverstone	14 April
Retired (misfiring, faulty plug)	1000cc	BSA 499cc	Silverstone	14 April
2	200cc	MV Agusta 172cc	Brands Hatch	22 April
5	1000cc	BSA 499cc	Brands Hatch	22 April
Retired (crash in practice)	250cc	MV Agusta	North West 200	11/12 May
Retired (not allowed to ride by Ron Harris)	250cc	MV Agusta 203cc	Brands Hatch	24 June
2	500cc Team Race	BSA	Brands Hatch	24 June
2	500cc Scratch Race	BSA	Brands Hatch	24 June
1	125cc	MV Agusta	Castle Combe	14 July
Retired (broken rocker arm in practice)	250cc	MV Agusta 172cc	Castle Combe	14 July
Retired (water in electrics)	500cc	BSA	Castle Combe	14 July
2	125cc	MV Agusta	Aintree	28 July
Retired (bent pushrod, broken rocker)	1000cc	BSA 499cc	Aintree	28 July
4	125cc	MV Agusta	Snetterton	5 August
8	250cc	MV Agusta 172cc	Snetterton	5 August

Position	Class	Machine	Circuit	Date
6	500cc (heat)	BSA	Snetterton	5 August
Retired (stopped, misfiring)	500cc (final)	BSA	Snetterton	5 August
2	125cc British Ch'ship	MV Agusta	Thruxton	6 August
6	500cc (heat) British Championship	BSA	Thruxton	6 August
Retired (faulty spark plug)	500cc (heat) British Championship	BSA	Thruxton	6 August
6	1000cc	BSA 499cc	Brands Hatch	26 August
10	500cc	BSA	Cadwell Park	16 September
10	500cc (heat)	BSA	Silverstone	22 September
23	500cc (final)	BSA	Silverstone	22 September
Retired (broken timing shaft)	Invitation	BSA	Brands Hatch	23 September
3	350cc (heat)	AJS	Brands Hatch	7 October
5	350cc (final)	AJS	Brands Hatch	7 October
2	1000cc (heat)	Matchless G45 498cc	Brands Hatch	7 October
3	1000cc (final)	Matchless G45 498cc	Brands Hatch	7 October

1957

Position	Class	Machine	Circuit	Date
Retired (plug trouble)	350cc	Norton	Brands Hatch	19 April
Retired (plug trouble)	500cc	Norton	Brands Hatch	19 April
4	350cc (heat)	Norton	Crystal Palace	22 April
6	350cc (final)	Norton	Crystal Palace	22 April
7	1000cc (heat)	Norton 499cc	Crystal Palace	22 April
5	1000cc (final)	Norton 499cc	Crystal Palace	22 April
9	Handicap	Norton	Crystal Palace	22 April
5	350cc	Norton	Castle Combe	27 April
3	500cc	Norton	Castle Combe	27 April
2	350cc	Norton	Brands Hatch	12 May
1	350cc	Norton	Brands Hatch	12 May
1	350cc	Norton	Brands Hatch	12 May
1	500cc	Norton	Brands Hatch	12 May
1	500cc	Norton	Brands Hatch	12 May
1	500cc (final)	Norton	Brands Hatch	12 May
14	350cc Junior TT	Norton	Isle of Man	3 June
16	500cc Senior TT	Norton	Isle of Man	7 June
2	350cc (heat)	Norton	Brands Hatch	10 June
1	350cc (final)	Norton	Brands Hatch	10 June

Position	Class	Machine	Circuit	Date
1	350cc Invitation	Norton	Brands Hatch	10 June
1	1000cc (heat)	Norton 499cc	Brands Hatch	10 June
1	1000cc (final)	Norton 499cc	Brands Hatch	10 June
1	1000cc Invitation	Norton 499cc	Brands Hatch	10 June
7	350cc Dutch TT	Norton	Assen	29 June
9	500cc Dutch TT	Norton	Assen	29 June
16	350cc Belgian GP	Norton	Spa Francorchamps	7 July
3	500cc Belgian GP	Norton	Spa Francorchamps	7 July
4	350cc (heat)	Norton	Castle Combe	13 July
2	350cc (final)	Norton	Castle Combe	13 July
1	500cc (heat)	Norton	Castle Combe	13 July
3	500cc (final)	Norton	Castle Combe	13 July
2	350cc (heat)	Norton	Snetterton	14 July
Retired (crash, when leading)	350cc (final)	Norton	Snetterton	14 July
2	500cc (heat)	Norton	Snetterton	14 July
4	500cc (final)	Norton	Snetterton	14 July
1	350cc	Norton	Brands Hatch	21 July
1	1000cc	Norton 499cc	Brands Hatch	21 July
6	350cc (heat)	Norton	Thruxton	5 August
6	350cc (final)	Norton	Thruxton	5 August
3	500cc (heat)	Norton	Thruxton	5 August
4	500cc (final)	Norton	Thruxton	5 August
2	350cc (heat)	Norton	Crystal Palace	17 August
2	350cc (final)	Norton	Crystal Palace	17 August
2	500cc (heat)	Norton	Crystal Palace	17 August
4	500cc (final)	Norton	Crystal Palace	17 August
Retired (oil leak)	250cc	REG	Brands Hatch	8 September
1	350cc (heat)	Norton	Brands Hatch	8 September
1	350cc (final)	Norton	Brands Hatch	8 September
1	500cc (heat)	Norton	Brands Hatch	8 September
1	500cc (final)	Norton	Brands Hatch	8 September
1	350cc Invitation	Norton	Brands Hatch	8 September
1	500cc Invitation	Norton	Brands Hatch	8 September
2	350cc (heat)	Norton	Snetterton	22 September
Retired (rear tyre flat, when lying in third place)	350cc (final)	Norton	Snetterton	22 September
1	500cc (heat)	Norton	Snetterton	22 September
1	500cc (final)	Norton	Snetterton	22 September FL
1	350cc	Norton	Aintree	28 September

Position	Class	Machine	Circuit	Date
2	500cc	Norton 348cc	Aintree	28 September
3	Handicap	REG 248cc	Aintree	28 September
4	250cc	REG	Brands Hatch	13 October
1	350cc Eynsford Trophy	Norton	Brands Hatch	13 October
2	1000cc Slazenger Trophy	Norton 499cc	Brands Hatch	13 October
Retired (crash)	1000cc Darenth Trophy	Norton 499cc	Brands Hatch	13 October

1958

Position	Class	Machine	Circuit	Date
1	250cc	REG	Brands Hatch	4 April RL
1	350cc	Norton	Brands Hatch	4 April
1	1000cc	Norton 499cc	Brands Hatch	4 April
1	1000cc	Norton 499cc	Brands Hatch	4 April FL
4	250cc	REG	Snetterton	6 April
1	350cc	Norton	Snetterton	6 April
Retired (gearbox after winning heat)	500cc	Norton	Snetterton	6 April
Retired	250cc	REG	Crystal Place	7 April
1	350cc	Norton	Crystal Palace	7 April FL
1	1000cc	Norton 499cc	Crystal Palace	7 April
2	250cc	REG	Silverstone	19 April
6	350cc	Norton	Silverstone	19 April
5	500cc	Norton	Silverstone	19 April
2	250cc	REG	Castle Combe	26 April
1	350cc	Norton	Castle Combe	26 April
1	500cc	Norton	Castle Combe	26 April FL
Retired (crash in final after new lap record in heat)	250cc	REG	Brands Hatch	4 May
2	350cc	Norton	Brands Hatch	4 May
2	1000cc	Norton 499cc	Brands Hatch	4 May
3	250cc	REG	Aintree	10 May
8	350cc (heat)	Norton	Aintree	10 May
4	350cc (final)	Norton	Aintree	10 May
4	500cc (heat)	Norton	Aintree	10 May
Retired (water in electrics)	500cc (final)	Norton	Aintree	10 May
Retired (misfiring)	250cc Lightweight TT	REG	Isle of Man	4 June
9	350cc Junior TT	Norton	Isle of Man	2 June
4	500cc Senior TT	Norton	Isle of Man	6 June

Position	Class	Machine	Circuit	Date
2	350cc	Norton	Snetterton	15 June FL
1	500cc	Norton	Snetterton	15 June FL
4	350cc Dutch TT	Norton	Assen	28 June
3	500cc Dutch TT	Norton	Assen	28 June
4	350cc Belgian GP	Norton	Spa Francorchamps	6 July
Retired	500cc Belgian GP	Norton	Spa Francorchamps	6 July
2	350cc	Norton	Castle Combe	12 July
1	500cc	Norton	Castle Combe	12 July FL
1	250cc (heat)	REG	Brands Hatch	13 July
1	350cc	Norton	Brands Hatch	13 July
1	1000cc	Norton 499cc	Brands Hatch	13 July
4	250cc British Ch'ship	REG	Thruxton	4 August RL
1	350cc British Ch'ship	Norton	Thruxton	4 August RL
1	500cc British Ch'ship	Norton	Thruxton	4 August RL
6	350cc Ulster GP	Norton	Dundrod	9 August
4	500cc Ulster GP	Norton	Dundrod	9 August
Retired (engine trouble)	250cc	REG	Brands Hatch	24 August
1	350cc	Norton	Brands Hatch	24 August
1	1000cc	Norton 499cc	Brands Hatch	24 August
2	350cc	Norton	Silverstone	13 September
2	500cc	Norton	Silverstone	13 September
1	250cc	REG	Brands Hatch	21 September FL
1	350cc	Norton	Brands Hatch	21 September FL
1	500cc	Norton	Brands Hatch	21 September FL
1	Mockford Trophy	Norton 499cc	Brands Hatch	21 September RL
3	350cc	Norton	Aintree	26 September
3	500cc	Norton	Aintree	26 September
4	Aintree Century Handicap	Norton 499cc	Aintree	26 September
Retired (engine blew up in practice)	250cc	REG	Brands Hatch	12 October
2	350cc	Norton	Brands Hatch	12 October
1	1000cc Race 1	Norton 499cc	Brands Hatch	12 October FL
1	1000cc Race 2	Norton 499cc	Brands Hatch	12 October FL

350 and 500cc British Champion

1959

Position	Class	Machine	Circuit	Date
3	250cc	REG	Brands Hatch	27 March

Position	Class	Machine	Circuit	Date
Retired (crash)	350cc	Norton	Brands Hatch	27 March
1	1000cc Race 1	Norton 499cc	Brands Hatch	27 March
2	1000cc Race 2	Norton 499cc	Brands Hatch	27 March
4	250cc	REG	Oulton Park	30 March
2	350cc	Norton	Oulton Park	30 March
2	500cc	Norton	Oulton Park	30 March
3	250cc	REG	Silverstone	18 April
Retired (crash)	350cc	Norton	Silverstone	18 April
6	500cc	Norton	Silverstone	18 April
3	200cc	EMC 125cc	Brands Hatch	19 April
2	250cc	REG	Brands Hatch	19 April
Did not start (bike damaged)	350cc	Norton	Brands Hatch	19 April
1	1000cc Race 1	Norton 499cc	Brands Hatch	19 April FL
1	1000cc Race 2	Norton 499cc	Brands Hatch	19 April FL
2	125cc	EMC	Castle Combe	25 April
1	350cc	Norton	Castle Combe	25 April FL
1	500cc	Norton	Castle Combe	25 April FL
Retired (crash)	250cc	REG	Oulton Park	16 May
3	350cc	Norton	Oulton Park	16 May
1	Les Graham Trophy	Norton 499cc	Oulton Park	16 May RL
2	250cc	REG	Blandford	18 May FL
1	350cc (heat)	Norton	Blandford	18 May FL
2	350cc (final)	Norton	Blandford	18 May RL
1	500cc	Norton	Blandford	18 May RL
Retired (engine)	250cc Lightweight TT	REG	Isle of Man	3 June
8	350cc Junior TT	Norton	Isle of Man	1 June
Retired (clutch)	500cc Senior TT	Norton	Isle of Man	5 June
5	125cc Dutch TT	MZ	Assen	27 June
3	250cc Dutch TT	Morini	Assen	27 June
No start	350cc Dutch TT	Norton	Assen	27 June
Retired (engine)	500cc Dutch TT	Norton	Assen	27 June
4	125cc Belgian GP	MZ	Spa Francorchamps	5 July
10	350cc Belgian GP	Norton	Spa Francorchamps	5 July
10	500cc Belgian GP	Norton	Spa Francorchamps	5 July
4	125cc	EMC	Castle Combe	11 July
2	250cc	REG	Castle Combe	11 July
1	350cc	Norton	Castle Combe	11 July FL
No start	500cc	Norton	Castle Combe	11 July
2	Handicap	REG 249cc	Castle Combe	11 July

Position	Class	Machine	Circuit	Date
3	250cc	REG	Snetterton	19 July
1	350cc	Norton	Snetterton	19 July FL
1	500cc	Norton	Snetterton	19 July FL
Retired (crash, sustained concussion)	250cc	REG	Oulton Park	3 August
6	250cc	REG	Silverstone	22 August
5	350cc	Norton	Silverstone	22 August
2	1000cc	Norton	Silverstone	22 August FL
1	350cc	Norton	Brands Hatch	23 August FL
1	1000cc	Norton 499cc	Brands Hatch	23 August FL
4	125cc Italian GP	MZ	Monza	6 September
4	250cc Italian GP	Morini	Monza	6 September
Retired (engine would not start)	250cc	REG	Brands Hatch	20 September
1	350cc	Norton	Brands Hatch	20 September FL
1	1000cc	Norton 499cc	Brands Hatch	20 September FL
2	350cc	Norton	Aintree	26 September
2	500cc	Norton	Aintree	26 September
Not allowed to start	350cc Aintree Century	Norton	Aintree	26 September
16	125cc	EMC	Biggin Hill	4 October
9	250cc	EMC 125cc	Biggin Hill	4 October
2	200cc	EMC 124cc	Brands Hatch	11 October
1	350cc	Norton	Brands Hatch	11 October FL
1	Invitation	Norton 499cc	Brands Hatch	11 October FL

1960

Position	Class	Machine	Circuit	Date
1	350cc	Norton	Brands Hatch	15 April RL
1	500cc	Norton	Brands Hatch	15 April RL
1	1000cc	Norton 499cc	Brands Hatch	15 April RL
1	350cc (heat)	Norton	Snetterton	17 April
1	350cc (final)	Norton	Snetterton	17 April RL
1	500cc (heat)	Norton	Snetterton	17 April
1	500cc (final)	Norton	Snetterton	17 April RL
2	350cc	Norton	Oulton Park	18 April RL
1	500cc	Norton	Oulton Park	18 April RL
1	350cc (heat)	Norton	Castle Combe	23 April
2	350cc (final)	Norton	Castle Combe	23 April

Position	Class	Machine	Circuit	Date
1	500cc (heat)	Norton	Castle Combe	23 April
1	500cc (final)	Norton	Castle Combe	23 April FL
Retired (engine)	350cc	Norton	North West 200	14 May
1	500cc	Norton	North West 200	14 May FL
Non-starter (no bike)	350cc	Norton	Brands Hatch	15 May
1	500cc Race 1	Norton	Brands Hatch	15 May FL
1	500cc Race 2	Norton	Brands Hatch	15 May FL
1	350cc	Norton	Silverstone	27 May RL
2	500cc	Norton	Silverstone	27 May
Retired (seized engine)	250cc Lightweight TT	Bianchi	Isle of Man	13 June
4	350cc Junior TT	Norton	Isle of Man	15 June
Retired (split oil tank)	500cc Senior TT	Norton	Isle of Man	17 June (first 100mph single lap)
Retired (crash)	350cc	Norton	Brands Hatch	10 July (first meeting on 2.65-mile circuit)
2	350cc	Norton	Brands Hatch	21 August
1	500cc	Norton	Brands Hatch	21 August RL
1	1000cc	Norton 499cc	Brands Hatch	21 August RL
1	350cc (heat)	Norton	Snetterton	4 September
1	350cc (final)	Norton	Snetterton	4 September FL
1	500cc (heat)	Norton	Snetterton	4 September
1	500cc (final)	Norton	Snetterton	4 September
Retired (crash in practice)	Italian GP	Bianchi 248cc	Monza	11 September
5	350cc	Norton	Brands Hatch	9 October
4	1000cc	Norton 499cc	Brands Hatch	9 October

1961

Position	Class	Machine	Circuit	Date
4	350cc	Norton	Brands Hatch	31 March
1	1000cc Race 1	Norton 499cc	Brands Hatch	31 March FL
2	1000cc Race 2	Norton 499cc	Brands Hatch	31 March
2	350cc	Norton	Snetterton	2 April
1	500cc (heat)	Norton	Snetterton	2 April
1	500cc (final)	Norton	Snetterton	2 April FL
1	350cc	Norton	Oulton Park	3 April RL
1	500cc	Norton	Oulton Park	3 April RL
1	350cc	Norton	Silverstone	9 April FL
Retired (engine)	500cc	Norton	Silverstone	9 April RL

Position	Class	Machine	Circuit	Date
1	350cc	Norton	Brands Hatch	30 April RL
1	500cc	Norton	Brands Hatch	30 April RL
4	350cc	Norton	North West 200	6 May
Retired (crash)	500cc	Norton	North West 200	6 May
1	350cc (heat)	Norton	Thruxton	23 May
1	350cc (final)	Norton	Thruxton	23 May RL
1	500cc (heat)	Norton	Thruxton	23 May
1	500cc (final)	Norton	Thruxton	23 May RL
4	350cc Junior TT	Norton	Isle of Man	14 June
30	500cc Senior TT	Norton	Isle of Man	16 June
3	350cc	Works development Norton	Brands Hatch	9 July
1	500cc	Standard Norton	Brands Hatch	9 July FL
1	1000cc	Standard Norton 499cc	Brands Hatch	9 July FL
1	350cc (heat)	Norton	Castle Combe	16 July
1	350cc (final)	Norton	Castle Combe	16 July FL
1	500cc (heat)	Norton	Castle Combe	15 July
2	500cc (final)	Norton	Castle Combe	15 July FL
Retired (contact breakers)	350cc (heat)	Norton	Snetterton	31 July
1	500cc (heat)	Norton	Snetterton	31 July
1	500cc (final)	Norton	Snetterton	31 July FL
Retired (seized engine)	350cc	Norton	Oulton Park	8 August RL
1	500cc	Norton	Oulton Park	8 August
Retired (crash)	350cc	Norton	Brands Hatch	21 August
2	500cc	Norton	Brands Hatch	21 August
1	350cc (heat)	Norton	Snetterton	4 September
1	350cc (final)	Norton	Snetterton	4 September FL
Retired	500cc (heat)	Norton	Snetterton	4 September
1	350cc	Norton	Brands Hatch	18 September
1	1000cc Race 1	Norton 499cc	Brands Hatch	18 September
1	1000cc Race 2	Norton 597cc Domiracer	Brands Hatch	18 September
1	125cc	EMC	Aintree	1 October FL
5	350cc	Norton	Aintree	1 October
4	500cc	Norton	Aintree	1 October
1	150cc	EMC 124cc	Oulton Park	8 October RL
Retired (ignition)	350cc	Norton	Oulton Park	8 October FL
4	500cc	Norton Dominator	Oulton Park	8 October
1	125cc	EMC	Brands Hatch	9 October RL
1	350cc	Norton	Brands Hatch	9 October FL
1	500cc	Norton	Brands Hatch	9 October FL

Position	Class	Machine	Circuit	Date
2	1000cc	Norton 597cc	Brands Hatch	9 October

1962

Position	Class	Machine	Circuit	Date
1	350cc (heat)	Petty Norton	Mallory Park	1 April
1	350cc (final)	Petty Norton	Mallory Park	1 April FL
1	500cc (heat)	Petty Norton	Mallory Park	1 April
3	500cc (final)	Petty Norton	Mallory Park	1 April FL
1	125cc	EMC	Silverstone	7 April
1	350cc	Norton	Silverstone	7 April FL
Retired (magneto)	500cc	Norton	Silverstone	7 April
2	125cc	EMC	Brands Hatch	20 April
1	250cc	Honda	Brands Hatch	20 April FL
2	350cc	Norton	Brands Hatch	20 April
1	500cc Redex Trophy	Norton	Brands Hatch	20 April FL
1	1000cc	Norton 499cc	Brands Hatch	20 April FL
3	350cc	Norton	Snetterton	22 April
4	500cc	Norton	Snetterton	22 April
Retired (radiator leak)	125cc	EMC	Oulton Park	23 April RL
1	250cc	Honda	Oulton Park	23 April RL
4	350cc	Norton	Oulton Park	23 April
3	500cc	Norton	Oulton Park	23 April
3	350cc	Norton	Mallory Park	29 April
3	500cc	Norton	Mallory Park	29 April
1	350cc (heat)	Norton	Castle Combe	5 May
1	350cc (final)	Norton	Castle Combe	5 May FL
1	500cc (heat)	Norton	Castle Combe	5 May
1	500cc (final)	Norton	Castle Combe	5 May FL
1	250cc	Bianchi 235cc	Brands Hatch	13 May FL
1	350cc	Norton	Brands Hatch	13 May FL
1	500cc Redex Trophy	Norton	Brands Hatch	13 May FL
1	1000cc	Norton 499cc	Brands Hatch	13 May FL
Retired (puncture)	1000km Production (shared with Joe Dunn)	Honda CB72 250cc	Silverstone	19 May
1	250cc	Honda	Snetterton	20 May RL
1	350cc (heat)	Norton	Snetterton	20 May
1	350cc (final)	Norton	Snetterton	20 May FL
1	500cc (heat)	Norton	Snetterton	20 May

Position	Class	Machine	Circuit	Date
1	500cc Molyslip Trophy	Norton	Snetterton	20 May FL
9	50cc TT	Honda	Isle of Man	8 June
4	125cc Ultra Lightweight TT	Honda	Isle of Man	6 June
1	250cc Lightweight TT	Honda	Isle of Man	4 June
Retired (oil leak)	350cc Junior TT	Norton	Isle of Man	6 June
Retired (crash)	500cc Senior TT	Norton	Isle of Man	8 June
1 class, 9 overall	Thruxton 500-mile Production (shared with Bill Smith)	Honda CB72 250cc	Thruxton	23 June
5	350cc Dutch TT	Norton	Assen	30 June
2	500cc Dutch TT	Norton	Assen	30 June
1	125cc	Honda	Brands Hatch	8 July RL
1	250cc	Honda	Brands Hatch	8 July RL
1	350cc	Norton	Brands Hatch	8 July FL
1	500cc	Norton	Brands Hatch	8 July FL
1	1000cc	Norton Domiracer 647cc	Brands Hatch	8 July FL
1	350cc (heat)	Norton	Castle Combe	21 July
1	350cc (final)	Norton	Castle Combe	21 July FL
2	500cc (heat)	Norton	Castle Combe	21 July
1	500cc (final)	Norton	Castle Combe	21 July RL
1	350cc (heat)	Norton	Snetterton	29 July
Retired (ignition)	350cc (final)	Norton	Snetterton	29 July FL
1	500cc (heat)	Norton	Snetterton	29 July
1	500cc (final)	Norton	Snetterton	29 July FL
1	250cc British Ch'ships	Honda	Oulton Park	6 August RL
1	350cc British Ch'ships	Norton	Oulton Park	6 August FL
1	500cc British Ch'ships	Norton	Oulton Park	6 August FL
Retired (crash)	125cc Ulster GP	EMC	Dundrod	11 August
1	250cc	John Surtees Ducati	Brands Hatch	23 September FL
1	350cc	Norton	Brands Hatch	23 September FL
1	500cc Redex Trophy	Norton	Brands Hatch	23 September RL
1	1000cc	Norton Domiracer 647cc	Brands Hatch	23 September FL
3	250cc	John Surtees Ducati	Aintree	29 September FL
1	350cc (heat)	Norton	Aintree	29 September
2	350cc (final)	Norton	Aintree	29 September FL
1	500cc (heat)	Norton	Aintree	29 September
1	500cc (final)	Norton	Aintree	29 September FL
1	Aintree Century	Norton 499cc	Aintree	29 September FL
1	250cc	Honda	Mallory Park	30 September RL

Position	Class	Machine	Circuit	Date
4	350cc	Norton	Mallory Park	30 September
1	500cc	Norton	Mallory Park	30 September
1	Race of the Year	Norton 499cc	Mallory Park	30 September
1	350cc	Norton	Oulton Park	6 October RL
1	500cc	Norton	Oulton Park	6 October FL
Retired (crash)	125cc	EMC	Brands Hatch	14 October
1	350cc	Norton	Brands Hatch	14 October FL

250, 350 and 500cc British Champion

1963

Position	Class	Machine	Circuit	Date
2	250cc	Cotton	Mallory Park	31 March FL
1	350cc	Norton	Mallory Park	31 March
1	500cc	Norton	Mallory Park	31 March
Retired (split exhaust pipe)	350cc	Norton	Silverstone	6 April
1	500cc	Gilera	Silverstone	6 April FL
Retired (spark plug)	250cc	Cotton	Brands Hatch	12 April
1	350cc	Norton	Brands Hatch	12 April FL
1	500cc	Gilera	Brands Hatch	12 April FL
1	1000cc	Gilera 499cc	Brands Hatch	12 April RL
1	350cc	Norton	Oulton Park	15 April RL
1	500cc	Gilera	Oulton Park	15 April RL
Retired (crash)	350cc	Gilera	Imola	24 April
1	500cc	Gilera	Imola	24 April FL
1	250cc	Cotton	Brands Hatch	12 May FL
2	350cc	Norton	Brands Hatch	12 May
1	500cc	Norton	Brands Hatch	12 May FL
Retired (crash)	1000cc	Norton 499cc	Brands Hatch	12 May FL
1	500cc British Ch'ship	Gilera	Oulton Park	5 August RL
1	Les Graham Memorial	Gilera 499cc	Oulton Park	5 August RL
3	500cc Ulster GP	Gilera	Dundrod	10 August
2	500cc East German GP	Gilera	Sachsenring	18 August
Retired	250cc Italian GP	Benelli	Monza	15 September
Retired	500cc Italian GP	Gilera	Monza	15 September
3	350cc	Norton	Scarborough	21 September
1	500cc (heat)	Gilera	Scarborough	21 September
Retired (crash)	500cc (final)	Gilera	Scarborough	21 September
1	500cc Redex Trophy	Gilera	Brands Hatch	22 September FL

Position	Class	Machine	Circuit	Date
1	1000cc	Gilera 499cc	Brands Hatch	22 September FL
1	350cc (heat)	Norton	Mallory Park	29 September
4	350cc (final)	Norton	Mallory Park	29 September
1	500cc (heat)	Gilera	Mallory Park	29 September
3	500cc (final)	Gilera	Mallory Park	29 September
2	Race of the Year	Gilera 499cc	Mallory Park	29 September
1	350cc (heat)	Norton	Oulton Park	5 October
2	350cc (final)	Norton	Oulton Park	5 October
1	500cc (heat)	Norton	Oulton Park	5 October
2	500cc (final)	Norton	Oulton Park	5 October FL
5	250cc	Cotton	Brands Hatch	13 October
2	350cc	Norton	Brands Hatch	13 October
2	500cc	Norton	Brands Hatch	13 October
1	1000cc	Norton 499cc	Brands Hatch	13 October FL

500cc British Champion

1964

Position	Class	Machine	Circuit	Date
Retired (loose carburettor)	250cc	Cotton	Mallory Park	22 March FL
1	350cc (heat)	Norton	Mallory Park	22 March
2	350cc (final)	Norton	Mallory Park	22 March Fl
1	500cc (heat)	Norton	Mallory Park	22 March
1	500cc (final)	Norton	Mallory Park	22 March FL
2	250cc	Cotton	Brands Hatch	27 March
9	350cc	Norton	Brands Hatch	27 March
1	500cc	Norton	Brands Hatch	27 March FL
1	1000cc	Norton 499cc	Brands Hatch	27 March FL
14	250cc	Cotton	Snetterton	29 March
Retired (seized in heat)	350cc	Norton	Snetterton	29 March
1	500cc	Norton	Snetterton	29 March
6	125cc	Honda	Oulton Park	30 March
Non-starter	350cc	Norton	Oulton Park	30 March
Retired (crash)	500cc	Norton	Oulton Park	30 March
6	250cc	Cotton	Silverstone	4 April
5	350cc	Norton	Silverstone	4 April
Retired (crash)	500cc	Norton	Silverstone	4 April
1	250cc	Cotton	Castle Combe	18 April RL
Retired (broken megaphone)	350cc	Norton	Castle Combe	18 April RL

Position	Class	Machine	Circuit	Date
Retired (partial engine seizure)	500cc (heat)	Norton	Castle Combe	18 April
Retired (crash)	250cc	Cotton	Brands Hatch	19 April
1	350cc	Norton	Brands Hatch	19 April FL
2	500cc	Norton	Brands Hatch	19 April
3	1000cc	Norton 499cc	Brands Hatch	19 April
2	250cc	Cotton	Snetterton	26 April FL
2	350cc	Norton	Snetterton	26 April
1	1000cc Senior Service Trophy	Norton 499cc	Snetterton	26 April FL
2	250cc	Cotton	Mallory Park	3 May FL
3	350cc	Norton	Mallory Park	3 May
1	500cc (heat)	Norton	Mallory Park	3 May
Retired (crash, machine caught fire)	500cc (final)	Norton	Mallory Park	3 May
3	250cc	Cotton	Snetterton	10 May
6	350cc	Norton	Snetterton	10 May
1	500cc (heat)	Norton	Snetterton	10 May
1	500cc (final)	Norton	Snetterton	10 May FL
Retired (engine)	250cc	Cotton	Brands Hatch	18 May
Retired (oil leak)	350cc	Norton	Brands Hatch	18 May
1	500cc	Norton	Brands Hatch	18 May FL
Retired	250cc Lightweight TT	Cotton	Isle of Man	8 June
4	350cc Junior TT	Norton	Isle of Man	10 June
2	500cc Senior TT	Norton	Isle of Man	12 June
Retired	250cc	Cotton	Mallory Park	14 June
5	350cc	Norton	Mallory Park	14 June
Retired (ignition)	500cc	Norton	Mallory Park	14 June
2	250cc	Cotton	Brands Hatch	21 June
1	350cc	Norton	Brands Hatch	21 June Fl
1	500cc	Norton	Brands Hatch	21 June FL
1	1000cc	Norton 499cc	Brands Hatch	21 June FL
6	350cc Dutch TT	Norton	Assen	27 June
Retired	500cc Dutch TT	Norton	Assen	27 June
Retired (engine)	250cc (heat)	Cotton	Castle Combe	25 July
1	350cc (heat)	Norton	Castle Combe	25 July
1	350cc (final)	Norton	Castle Combe	25 July FL
1	500cc (heat)	Norton	Castle Combe	25 July
1	500cc (final)	Norton	Castle Combe	25 July RL
Retired (broken piston ring)	250cc	Cotton	Snetterton	26 July

Position	Class	Machine	Circuit	Date
1	350cc (heat)	Norton	Snetterton	26 July
1	500cc (heat)	Norton	Snetterton	26 July
1	500cc (final)	Norton	Snetterton	26 July FL
5	250cc British Ch'ship	Cotton	Oulton Park	3 August
Retired (holed piston)	350cc British Ch'ship	Norton	Oulton Park	3 August
1	500cc British Ch'ship	Norton	Oulton Park	3 August
5	Les Graham Trophy	Norton 499cc	Oulton Park	3 August
1	250cc	Cotton	Brands Hatch	16 August FL
1	350cc	Norton	Brands Hatch	16 August FL
1	500cc	Norton	Brands Hatch	16 August FL
1	250cc	Cotton	Snetterton	6 September Fl
1	350cc (heat)	Norton	Snetterton	6 September
1	350cc (final)	Norton	Snetterton	6 September FL
1	500cc (heat)	Norton	Snetterton	6 September
1	500cc (final)	Norton	Snetterton	6 September FL
Retired (engine)	250cc	Cotton	Scarborough	19 September
3	350cc Fred Neville Trophy	Norton	Brands Hatch	20 September FL
1	500cc Redex Trophy	Norton	Brands Hatch	20 September FL
1	1000cc Alan Trow Trophy	Norton 499cc	Brands Hatch	20 September FL
4	350cc	Norton	Mallory Park	27 September
6	500cc	Norton	Mallory Park	27 September
3	Race of the Year	Norton 499cc	Mallory Park	27 September
3	250cc	Cotton	Oulton Park	3 October
1	350cc (heat)	Norton	Oulton Park	3 October
2	350cc (final)	Norton	Oulton Park	3 October FL
1	500cc (heat) Bob McIntyre Memorial	Norton	Oulton Park	3 October
1	500cc (final) Bob McIntyre Memorial	Norton	Oulton Park	3 October
4	250cc	Cotton	Brands Hatch	11 October
3	350cc	Norton	Brands Hatch	11 October
1	500cc	Norton	Brands Hatch	11 October
1	1000cc	Norton 499cc	Brands Hatch	11 October

500cc British Champion

250cc & 350cc ACU Star

1965

Position	Class	Machine	Circuit	Date
1	250cc (heat)	Cotton	Mallory Park	10 March FL

Position	Class	Machine	Circuit	Date
1	250cc (final)	Cotton	Mallory Park	10 March FL
4	350cc	Norton	Mallory Park	10 March
2	500cc	Norton	Mallory Park	10 March
1	250cc	Cotton	Brands Hatch	24 March FL
2	350cc	Norton	Brands Hatch	24 March
1	500cc	Norton	Brands Hatch	24 March FL
2	1000cc	Norton 499cc	Brands Hatch	24 March FL
Retired (engine)	250cc	Cotton	Snetterton	31 March
3	350cc	Norton	Snetterton	31 March FL
1	500cc East Anglian Trophy	Norton	Snetterton	31 March FL
4	250cc	Cotton	Brands Hatch	19 April
1	350cc	Norton	Brands Hatch	19 April
1	500cc	Norton	Brands Hatch	19 April FL
1	1000cc King of Brands	Norton 499cc	Brands Hatch	19 April FL
3	250cc	Cotton	Snetterton	21 April
1	350cc (heat)	Norton	Snetterton	21 April
3	350cc (final)	Norton	Snetterton	21 April
1	500cc (heat)	Norton	Snetterton	21 April
4	500cc (final)	Norton	Snetterton	21 April
1	250cc	Cotton	Oulton Park	22 April
1	350cc	Norton	Oulton Park	22 April FL
2	500cc	Norton	Oulton Park	22 April
1	250cc (heat)	Cotton	Castle Combe	4 May
3	250cc (final)	Cotton	Castle Combe	4 May
1	350cc (heat)	Norton	Castle Combe	4 May
1	350cc (final)	Norton	Castle Combe	4 May FL
1	500cc (heat)	Norton	Castle Combe	4 May
1	500cc (final)	Norton	Castle Combe	4 May FL
1	250cc	Cotton	Brands Hatch	12 May
1	350cc	Norton	Brands Hatch	12 May FL
6	500cc	Norton	Brands Hatch	12 May FL
1	1000cc	Norton 499cc	Brands Hatch	12 May FL
Retired (crash)	350cc (heat)	Norton	Snetterton	19 May
4	500cc	Norton	Snetterton	19 May
3	250cc	Cotton	Mallory Park	26 May
1	350cc (heat)	Norton	Mallory Park	26 May
1	350cc (final)	Norton	Mallory Park	26 May FL
1	500cc (heat)	Norton	Mallory Park	26 May
6	500cc (final)	Norton	Mallory Park	26 May

Position	Class	Machine	Circuit	Date
9	250cc Lightweight TT	Cotton	Isle of Man	17 June
Retired (engine)	350cc Junior TT	Norton	Isle of Man	19 June
Retired (magneto)	500cc Senior TT	Norton	Isle of Man	21 June
Retired (engine)	350cc Dutch TT	Norton	Assen	29 June
Retired (loose front brake anchor arm)	500cc Dutch TT	Norton	Assen	29 June
1	350cc	Arter AJS	Brands Hatch	30 June FL
2	500cc	Norton	Brands Hatch	30 June
3	Team Relay Race	Norton 499cc	Brands Hatch	30 June FL
3	500cc Belgian GP	Norton	Spa Francorchamps	7 July
1	250cc	Cotton	Castle Combe	13 July FL
1	350cc	Norton	Castle Combe	13 July FL
1	500cc	Norton	Castle Combe	13 July FL
4	Avon Trophy	Norton 499cc	Castle Combe	13 July FL
1 in class; 3 overall	500-mile Production (shared with Peter Inchley)	Cotton Conquest 250cc	Castle Combe	13 July FL
3	250cc	Cotton	Snetterton	28 July
Retired (broken ignition wire)	250cc	Cotton	Silverstone	17 August
3	350cc	Norton	Silverstone	17 August RL
Retired (broken oil pipe)	500cc	Norton	Silverstone	17 August
1	250cc	Cotton	Brands Hatch	18 August
1	350cc	Norton	Brands Hatch	18 August RL
2	500cc	Norton	Brands Hatch	18 August
4	250cc	Cotton	Mallory Park	25 August
4	250cc British Ch'ship	Cotton	Oulton Park	2 September
3	350cc British Ch'ship	Norton	Oulton Park	2 September
2	500cc British Ch'ship	Norton	Oulton Park	2 September
1	Les Graham Memorial	Norton 499cc	Oulton Park	2 September
3	250cc	Cotton	Castle Combe	7 September
1	350cc	Norton	Castle Combe	7 September FL
1	500c	Norton	Castle Combe	7 September FL
1	350cc (heat)	Norton	Snetterton	8 September
1	350cc (final)	Norton	Snetterton	8 September FL
4	500cc	Norton	Snetterton	8 September FL
2	250cc	Cotton	Brands Hatch	22 September
2	350cc	Norton	Brands Hatch	22 September
1	500cc	Norton	Brands Hatch	22 September
1	1000cc	Norton 499cc	Brands Hatch	22 September FL
Retired (crash)	500cc	Norton	Mallory Park	29 September

1966

Position	Class	Machine	Circuit	Date
3	250cc	Cotton	Mallory Park	6 March
1	350cc (heat)	Seeley	Mallory Park	6 March
Retired (loose exhaust)	350cc (final)	Seeley	Mallory Park	6 March
3	500cc	Seeley	Mallory Park	6 March
6	250cc	Cotton	Brands Hatch	13 March
8	350cc	Seeley	Brands Hatch	13 March
1	500cc	Seeley	Brands Hatch	13 March FL
4	1000cc	Seeley 496cc	Brands Hatch	13 March
3	250cc	Cotton	Snetterton	20 March
1	350cc (heat)	Seeley	Snetterton	20 March
1	350cc (final)	Seeley	Snetterton	20 March
1	500cc (heat)	Seeley	Snetterton	20 March
2	500cc (final)	Seeley	Snetterton	20 March
1	250cc	Cotton	Brands Hatch	8 April
6	350cc	Seeley	Brands Hatch	8 April
3	500cc	Seeley	Brands Hatch	8 April
3	1000cc	Seeley	Brands Hatch	8 April
Retired (grounding)	King of Brands	Seeley 646cc	Brands Hatch	8 April
2	250cc	Cotton	Snetterton	10 April
Race abandoned	350cc	Seeley	Snetterton	10 April
3	500cc (heat)	Seeley	Snetterton	10 April
Retired (poor start)	500cc (final)	Seeley	Snetterton	10 April
2	250cc	Cotton	Oulton Park	11 April
2	350cc	Seeley	Oulton Park	11 April
1	500cc	Seeley	Oulton Park	11 April
Retired	250cc	Cotton	Imola	17 April
6	350cc	Seeley	Imola	17 April
2	500cc	Gilera	Imola	17 April
Retired (big-end)	250cc	Cotton	Cesenatico	24 April
4	350cc	Seeley	Cesenatico	24 April
Retired (magneto)	500cc	Gilera	Cesenatico	24 April
1	250cc (heat)	Cotton	Castle Combe	30 April
Retired (seized engine)	250cc (final)	Cotton	Castle Combe	30 April
2	350cc (heat)	Seeley	Castle Combe	30 April
2	350cc (final)	Seeley	Castle Combe	30 April
1	500cc (heat)	Seeley	Castle Combe	30 April
6	500cc (final)	Seeley	Castle Combe	30 April

Position	Class	Machine	Circuit	Date
6	350cc	Seeley	Brands Hatch	1 May
2	500cc	Seeley	Brands Hatch	1 May
2	1000cc	Seeley 496cc	Brands Hatch	1 May
8	350cc West German GP	Seeley	Hockenheim	22 May
Retired (leaking fuel tank)	500cc West German GP	Seeley	Hockenheim	22 May
1	250cc	Cotton	Snetterton	29 May FL
Retired (flat rear tyre)	350cc (final)	Seeley	Snetterton	29 May
Retired (broken primary chain)	500cc (heat)	Seeley	Snetterton	29 May
4	250cc	Cotton	Brands Hatch	30 May
4	350cc	Seeley	Brands Hatch	30 May
5	1000cc	Seeley	Brands Hatch	30 May
Retired (crash)	250cc (heat)	Cotton	Mallory Park	19 June
Retired (crash)	250cc	Cotton	Castle Combe	9 July FL
1	350cc	Norton	Castle Combe	9 July FL
2	500cc	Seeley	Castle Combe	9 July
2	350cc	Norton	Brands Hatch	14 August
Retired (effects of 250cc crash)	500cc	Norton	Brands Hatch	14 August

1967

Position	Class	Machine	Circuit	Date
Retired (carburation)	350cc (heat)	Norton	Mallory Park	8 March
1	500cc (heat)	Norton	Mallory Park	8 March
3	500cc (final)	Norton	Mallory Park	8 March
6	350cc (final)	Norton	Snetterton	15 March
6	500cc (final)	Norton	Snetterton	15 March
8	500cc	Norton	Modena	22 March
3	350cc	Norton	Brands Hatch	27 March
Retired	500cc	Norton	Brands Hatch	27 March
Retired	1000cc	Norton 499cc	Brands Hatch	27 March
2	350cc	Norton	Oulton Park	29 March
1	500cc	Norton	Oulton Park	29 March FL
9	500cc	Norton	Riccione	5 April
	500cc	Norton	Cervia	12 April
6	350cc		Cesenatico	19 April
5	500cc	Norton	Cesenatico	19 April
12 (pushed in with dead engine)	350cc	Norton	Imola	25 April
4	500cc	Norton	Imola	25 April
12	350cc	Norton	Rimini	17 May

Position	Class	Machine	Circuit	Date
5	500cc	Norton	Rimini	17 May
12	500cc	Norton	Mallory Park	1 May
8	500cc	Norton	Brands Hatch	1 June
6	1000cc	Norton 499cc	Brands Hatch	1 June
16	350cc	Norton	Mallory Park	14 June
15	350cc Dutch TT	Norton	Assen	27 June
6	500cc Dutch TT	Norton	Assen	27 June
6	500cc Belgian GP	Norton	Spa Francorchamps	5 July
1	500cc	Norton	Snetterton	30 July
6	1000cc	Norton	Snetterton	30 July
2	350cc	Norton	Oulton Park	28 August
2	500cc Les Graham Trophy	Norton	Oulton Park	28 August
4	350cc	Norton	Brands Hatch	3 September
1	500cc Redex Trophy	Norton	Brands Hatch	3 September FL
11	Race of the Year	Norton 499cc	Mallory Park	17 September
4	350cc	Norton	Brands Hatch	1 October
2	500cc	Norton	Brands Hatch	1 October
3	Race of the South	Norton 499cc	Brands Hatch	1 October
4	350cc	Norton	Snetterton	15 October
1	500cc (heat)	Norton	Snetterton	15 October RL
1	500cc (final)	Norton	Snetterton	15 October FL
12	1000cc	Curtis 647cc Domiracer	Snetterton	15 October
1	350cc	Norton	Brands Hatch	22 October
2	500cc	Norton	Brands Hatch	22 October
1	1000cc	Curtis 647cc Domiracer	Brands Hatch	22 October

1968

Position	Class	Machine	Circuit	Date
4 in class	500-mile Production (with Reg Everett)	Ducati 340cc	Brands Hatch	14 May

Index